Letters to "Home at Heart"

"Not until I've read your tales in our Harrisburg *Patriot* do I have enough strength to face a new week. It's comforting to know there are others with the same type of home."

—Mrs. Wade A. Barber, State College, Pennsylvania, 1963

"Keep the amusing columns coming. They help us to laugh at the everyday things that occur in raising a family and realize that all parents are going though the same things with us."

—Mrs. Allan L. (Marguerite) Martin, Clearfield, Pennsylvania, 1963

"We feel that we know you as another member of a harassed household."

—Philip H. Feather, Lebanon, Pennsylvania, 1964

"Thank you for the wonderful, consoling column you write each week—consoling to me because our families seem to be duplicates, and our households have the same problems."

—Mrs. Katherine T. Davis, Hughesville, Pennsylvania, 1966

"You have that rare gift of making something monumental from the commonplace."

—Earl F. McGill, Bedford, Pennsylvania, 1968

"Each week I pass your article around our school building for teachers to read. You should hear our comments and be able to know the enjoyment we all receive from it."

—Jean E. Unger, Tower City, Pennsylvania, 1970

"I enjoy your columns so very much.... You have a great gift for discernment and understanding, and a most entertaining talent for writing."

—Mildred Porter, Camp Hill, Pennsylvania, date unknown

Home at Heart

Home at Heart

✦

Raising the Baby Boom:
Dispatches from an American
Mom, 1957–1972

Dottie Lebo

Edited by Diane Lebo Wallace

iUniverse, Inc.
New York Lincoln Shanghai

Home at Heart
Raising the Baby Boom: Dispatches from an American Mom, 1957–1972

iUniverse books may be ordered through booksellers or by contacting:

iUniverse
2021 Pine Lake Road, Suite 100
Lincoln, NE 68512
www.iuniverse.com
1-800-Authors (1-800-288-4677)

Because of the dynamic nature of the Internet, any Web addresses or links contained in this book may have changed since publication and may no longer be valid.

ISBN: 978-0-595-44552-3 (pbk)
ISBN: 978-0-595-68797-8 (cloth)
ISBN: 978-0-595-88879-5 (ebk)

Printed in the United States of America

This selection of "Home at Heart" columns is published with permission of *The Patriot-News*, Harrisburg, Pennsylvania.

Dedicated to Donald E. Lebo
(1932–2002)

Contents

PART II   HOW TO HANDLE 'IT' INQUIRY FAVORITE OF MOST PARENTS
1962–1967

PART III   HAVING TEEN-AGE CHILDREN IS WHAT CAUSES MIDDLE AGE

1968–1972

Acknowledgments

This five-year endeavor was completed over countless weekends and early mornings, through energetic spurts and methodical steps. A number of individuals were instrumental to its successful completion: David Newhouse, executive editor of *The Patriot-News,* for his friendly letter granting permission to reprint these columns; the Paterno Library and its helpful staff at Pennsylvania State University, State College, Pennsylvania; Jean Morey for speedily and cheerfully spending numerous hours accurately retyping hundreds of yellowed and torn newspaper clippings; my daughter, Katie Wallace, for her sharp editing, good questions, and enthusiastic encouragement; my husband, John Wallace, for believing in the value of this project, assisting me at the Paterno Library, and applying his design and digital skills for all graphic elements; and, of course, my mother, Dottie Lebo, for turning in all of my "homework" requests related to this project, and for her bountiful good humor, wisdom and love.

Diane Lebo Wallace

Introduction

For 15 years, my mother, Dottie Lebo, wrote a weekly humor column for the Harrisburg *Sunday Patriot News* confessing the chaos and charms of family life. She wrote with uninhibited mirth and a wry eye toward culture. Her column won her the affection of legions of local fans as she recounted her hilarious misadventures with unruly children, pets and her household.

She chronicled her domestic travails after being quarantined with a houseful of children with chicken pox or enduring slumber parties, and grappled with the parade of plumbers, mailmen, upholsterers and milkmen who unwittingly stepped into our rambunctious territory. The latest pronouncements of "the Baron"—her playful name for our patriarch—provided counterpoint, as he good-naturedly set out to become a "mod" father or herd the family on summer vacations, while holding steadfast to his monthly poker game. Perhaps former Chief of Police Earl F. McGill, of Bedford, Pennsylvania, said it best in the late sixties when he wrote to her and said, "You have that rare gift of making something monumental from the commonplace."

Even so, she also reflected on historic events of the day, including the Apollo moonwalk, the assassination of President Kennedy and the British invasion led by the Beatles. She ruefully contrasted her own daily life with that of celebrities like actress Elizabeth Taylor and occasionally held forth on sports stars like Joe Namath. She pondered a rapidly changing culture as it came home to roost in the form of long hair, basement bands and pop psychology.

Eagerly read by her Harrisburg area following, "Home at Heart" was sometimes compared to "At Wit's End," Erma Bombeck's weekly column that started in 1964 and was syndicated in 1965. Yet while the editors of the Newhouse-owned *Patriot* encouraged her toward syndication in the early sixties, she did not pursue the possibility.

She began writing her column, which she named "Home at Heart," in 1957 at the age of 25 when she was looking to earn money while writing. She had worked as a reporter for the *Patriot News* from the age of 18 and gradually turned toward feature writing because its flexible schedule gave her more time for marriage and children. By 1957, she and my father, Donald, had three children: David, Donna, and myself. She continued writing throughout the sixties and early seventies, each week shutting herself away in her bedroom for a few hours when she was on deadline.

There, next to her usually unmade bed and an ironing board stacked with clean, but wrinkled clothing, she chronicled the everyday life of our family, turning up the volume on its hilarity. We always knew when she was on deadline. She typed behind the closed doors on a 1940s black Underwood, vintage even in those days, and gave us strict orders not to interrupt. Donna remembers her rapid-fire tapping as well as the sibling fights that erupted during this weekly occasion.

We loved reading her columns, though they occasionally astonished us. If we were innocently eating morning cereal and happened upon scissored newsprint mailed to us from grandmothers in Harrisburg, one of us screeched, "But that's not what I said!" or "Is that really supposed to be me?" The Baron, without looking up from the Baltimore *Sun*, would calmly note, "You know how your mother exaggerates." Donna says, "There was always something that wasn't quite right, but then there was always something that was. I liked feeling that I was a little bit famous."

It took many years for us to realize not only that most mothers didn't write for newspapers, but that our Mom's sharp wit and satiric eye made her unique. She is among the generation of mothers who raised the nation's baby boomers: a fifties Mom, but one who could not and would not conform to the era's rigid standards for housewives. Those were days when a new hat could give a gal a pick-me-up and housewives darned socks. Financial planning meant managing charge accounts, layaway plans and collecting S&H green stamps. Young families were learning to love barbeque grills and TV sets. "Home at Heart" ran in a section labeled the women's pages, appearing alongside news of society weddings, club events, recipes and department store fashion ads.

But Dottie didn't try to fit in with well-meaning organizations like the Junior League or the PTA, and she was more like the TV comedian Carol Burnett half-heartedly trying to follow in the footsteps of June Cleaver, the picture-perfect mother on TV's "Leave it to Beaver". In some ways, Mom was a suburban misfit who would nearly always choose a good book over a clean house; cooking was simply a chore. She read *The New York Times* and the works of poets, philosophers and psychologists whether already renowned or on the rise. She put records on the stereo to play music intended for teenagers. While other mothers on the block stayed home with their children, she started working part-time at Johns Hopkins University in the midsixties—a liberal, progressive community that appealed to her appetite for new knowledge and ideas.

As the years piled one on top of the other, so did all of the demands of raising a family. Throughout this time her columns were stashed hastily and at random into a cardboard box. In 1972, Dottie Lebo ended her column without fanfare as she became absorbed by her responsibilities at Johns Hopkins, especially after she was appointed assistant dean of students shortly after the university became coeducational in 1970. She joined the administrative staff of the Oncology Center at the Johns Hopkins Hospital in the late seventies, and retired from her position as human resources manager in 1997.

In 2002, a few months before my father was diagnosed with pancreatic cancer, I recovered most of the columns in a box labeled, "Dottie's junk." In 2006 my husband, John Wallace, and I made a pilgrimage to the Paterno Library at Pennsylvania State University, where we scrolled through ribbons of microfiche and uncovered the last batch of columns from 1972.

Reading this selection of "Home at Heart" columns through the years, one traces the pathway of a woman finding her own voice, and her own identity as well. For our family, these columns are the treasures of a lifetime documenting our childhood, recalling a raft of memories and providing a window to interesting times in American history and culture. My father, who passed away in April 2002, was thrilled that the columns would be archived for the enjoyment of former fans, boomers and generations of new parents.

Diane Lebo Wallace
Ithaca, New York

PART I
Being a Mother Turns out to Be Permanent Post

1957–1961

The Pox Pays off—So Do Measles, Assorted Viruses

May 19, 1957

The question is, "Is chicken pox more worthwhile than measles and what are the mumps getting nowadays?"

With springtime's onslaught of the viruses, suddenly the kiddies have discovered a discreet kind of blackmail known as, "What will you get me if I stay inside while I have the measles?"

After being cooped up with the little menaces in blue denim for three days, parents are almost willing to go out and buy a whole amusement park just to keep them quiet.

The fun begins when your youngster comes home begging for the chicken pox, measles or mumps to come to him soon so he can cash in on the situation, too!

Television, meanwhile, is familiarizing the youngsters with germs and tooth decay demons in the personages of green-eyed monsters creeping out of the screens ready to attack.

It may be Madison Ave.'s million-dollar idea on how to sell more toothpaste and mouthwash, but the kids are insisting they sleep with closed windows at night so the germs can't get in and they're loading their cap pistols ready to shoot down tooth decay. Ever try to explain a microscope to a three-year old?

◆   ◆   ◆

It's really quite a precarious situation in many families lately.

You see, the one and only male heir has reached a point of no return. He's old enough to bargain for a nickel before he rakes the yard and not old enough to be a Cub Scout, so you can't get away with this good deed business.

If the Washington lobbyists really want some excellent field training they ought to listen to their own youngsters' backyard bargaining powers!

One day the housewives of America will band together to erect a statue to the originator of the backyard barbecue. What better way to "pay off" all the social debts accumulating all winter long, and what better way is there to convince father backyard cooking is the vogue?

You'll discover muscles you never knew you owned after going through traffic with three training-pants hoodlums swinging chocolate ice cream cones hither and yon around the upholstery, you, the steering wheel and, of course, each other! For this Barnum and Bailey would pay big money, you say?

◆   ◆   ◆

There is no experience as soul shattering as living day-to-day with a teen-age daughter.

One day she chides you about being "too motherly" because your hair is in a bun. The next day she's hysterical because you wore shorts to mow the grass and it just isn't "motherly."

The salesclerk's best friends—

"Thank you but I'm just looking! (You don't fool her a bit. She knows that charge-a-plate in your purse makes you practically defenseless!)

"Well, I really should wear an 18, but since you don't have my size maybe …" Listen, by the time you leave, she'll have you convinced you make Monroe look like a chairwoman in the same dress!)

"Someday I'd like to have two or three of these but right now we're cutting corners you see." (Layaway, dearie, Layaway, complete with free instructions on how to break the news gently to hubby.)

It's such a thrill when your two-year-old darling points to a picture of a glamorous movie star in a magazine and trills, "Mommy." Two seconds later you're ready for tranquilizers as she turns the page and trills "Mommy" at a picture of a female wrestler with corkscrew curls.

◆　　　◆　　　◆

Why is it radio announcers always address housewives with a plaintive "ladies," engendering a picture of a poor heartbroken gal crying over a scrub bucket in a dark corner of the kitchen? What a blow when he ever finds out she's happily engaged in sunning herself while she weeds petunias or she's remaking a new hat for a wedding she's going to tomorrow!

How can you preach to little boys about keeping their shirt tails tucked in when they point out to you that you don't bother, not knowing, of course, that maternity jackets aren't exactly the kind one tucks in?

Meanwhile, back at the clubhouse …

That caddy must need glasses. Why my ball wasn't anywhere near that creek!"

"Every time I line up a shot she starts on that last operation bit and it just ruins my game!"

"I could have played so much better if Joe had just let me buy that darling little two-piece outfit."

"They say it's good for the figure. Ha! From now on I play only pinochle and Scrabble."

◆   ◆   ◆

There are two times in a woman's life when even the photographer is not quick enough to catch the quicksilver beauty of the light in her eyes. Once, when she walks down the aisle and meets the eyes of her husband-to-be and twice, when she sees her first-born's funny new face.

"We weren't too worried about rock and roll, explains the mother of a teen-age son. "A guitar and sideburns weren't so expensive, and then when calypso came along we were delighted. After all, bare feet and two old oil drums were no expense. All we're hoping for is that no one starts a calliope or organ craze. Just look what happened when the goldfish-eating spree hit the country back when we were young.

Let's All Sign up for a B-i-g Picnic at Mosquito Manor

June 9, 1957

Could it possibly be the big American myth—1957 style?

What we mean is this mass rush to the suburbs and the garden, ah, yes, the garden. Monday morning offices are filled with sunburned suburbanites painfully moving their ruddy necks inside of starched collars, scratching at unseen mosquito and chigger bites and comparing notes on insecticides, radishes and power mowers.

After eight backbreaking hours on our knees hunting for grass among the weeds and learning to identify any kind of plant lice you can name, who could help but wonder? Can life in the city, in a nice quiet apartment with one small window box, be so really awful?

While Pop no doubt spends Saturday browsing in the garden shoppes along with several dozen other self-conscious Bermuda shorts-clad cronies, Mom is busy getting ready for that other great summer myth—the picnic.

"Say, Mom," blandly suggests Dad, "What 'say we give you a little rest tomorrow? We'll just pack a few sandwiches and take off for a little picnic in the country tomorrow."

("Ha, ha," says her conscience. "Sandwiches says he.")

Next afternoon Pop blissfully snoozes after baked beans (eight hours to prepare), potato salad (one hour), one chocolate fudge cake (two trips to the store and half-hour to fix), deviled eggs (half-hour and two phone calls later) and lemonade.

That lemonade almost made Mom feel guilty—it came out of a can.

Sighs Dad, "Now there, wasn't that easier than fussing with dinner all day?"

◆   ◆   ◆

He may be able to take apart any motor in town and have it running smoothly within an hour, but have you ever seen a man who could decide whether the buttons on his toddler daughter's dress belong in the front or in the back?

Men may joke over women's wiles, but what would happen if their own wives suddenly decided to tell the truth, the absolute truth? Can't you see it now?

"Why, Marge, we'd like to play bridge with you and Harry, but frankly Joe just can't stand your ham sandwiches."

"No, Mr. Blooper, Joe won't be able to make it today. He watched the late show last night and he's catching up on his sleep."

"Frankly, dear, I hate to disappoint you, but that pretty blonde wasn't eyeing you at all. She was winking at that sailor behind you.

"Joe, you've been telling that same joke for 12 years now, and, frankly, it bores me stiff!"

It might pay everyone to promise himself to attend at least one high school graduation ceremony a year. Just watching those proud young faces with fresh hopes, fresh dreams and untarnished images is enough to help everyone pick up his own tired dreams by the bootstraps and make a bigger try this year.

◆   ◆   ◆

It's what is known as a "polite filibuster."

By the time little Georgie has reached the "Bless Mommie and Bless Daddy" stage of his nightly prayers, his instinctive filibustering techniques go to work and, while he manages to bless every member of every family (including dogs, cats and bicycles) you know in addition to all and sundry relatives, you are wondering if it would be impolite or sacrilegious to interject a quick "A-men!"

◆　　◆　　◆

Daily routine has lost its tedium and taken on all the vivid aspects of a carnival since one 14-year-old has discovered Hollywood.

One morning she drifts into breakfast languorously trailing her sweater on the floor and gushes, "Mawning, dahlings."

Next morning she's Shelley Winters. "Whatta' day, whatta' day," she chirps, batting her eyelashes and hunching her shoulders.

◆　　◆　　◆

Definition of a genius: a man who can tell instinctively when his wife has just about washed the last diaper, dried the last dish and painted the last cut knee with mercurochrome that she can stand and take her to a quiet movie before the storm breaks.

Every almanac and dictionary has a list of anniversaries and their appropriate gifts, but who's kidding us with all that stuff?

If they printed what really got passed out on anniversaries (including black eyes) the list would go something like this.

First: one dozen red roses for her, silk pajamas for him.

Second: drugstore cologne for her, carton of cigarettes for him.

Tenth: one week's silence for him; two weeks later, a new coat for her.

Fifteenth: one month's silence for him, (he really forgot that time) and a cruise to South America for them both.

Fill in the rest with your own nerve-racking memories.

◆   ◆   ◆

Somebody told our young 16-year-old debutante friend to keep her cologne in the refrigerator in hot weather. There was trouble though. Seems her Dad went for a snack one night and couldn't find the ham salad. What he did find was one angora stole, two leftover white shorts Mom didn't get ironed and three cologne bottles: "Escape," "Escapade" and "Young Love."

Dad raved and ranted for a while, but the deb just reminded him the famous Gabor sisters whom he so admires keep nothing in their refrigerator but orchids and cold cream.

P.S. Junior ate all the ham salad at 8 o'clock anyway.

◆   ◆   ◆

That's a man for you! He uses your nail file to fix the TV, your guest towels to wipe the dust off his shoes and your best lace handkerchief to stop little Georgie's nosebleed, but heaven help you if you snitch one of his worn-out T-shirts for dust rags!

'Lady in Waiting' Finds Hospital No Rest Haven

July 14, 1957

(Everything you will read is intentional, coincidental, and if you happen to be the mother of one, two or three, or just expecting, we hope this will sound familiar as "Home at Heart" takes a week's vacation in the hospital with her newest subject close by her side.)

Just when it's getting to that place where you have to empty the trash or hang up wash for fear you'll throw something at the next person who says, "You still here?" it happens!

You are going to the hospital to have a baby, but suddenly to husband, children, nurses, doctors, you are practically unimportant.

Husband is worried about getting gas, the kids are worried about getting their allowances, and suddenly you wish people would stop buzzing around you like some exotic tropical plant.

You would like a drink of water and maybe a peanut butter jelly sandwich but you're afraid your husband might pass out while he's making it so you sit quietly while everyone has mild hysteria.

Most patients on maternity floors are pretty easy to identify. That one who hops out of bed every morning and paces outside the nursery window, who reads magazines, talks endlessly on the telephone, writes dozens of letters, this is her first trip. She is now the mother of one.

Now the girl in the next room maybe sleeps all morning and then divides her afternoon between the telephone and the nursery window. She's the mother of two.

But take that girl in the third room. What does she do? She sleeps, and then she sleeps some more and when she's done with that she sleeps in between. She is the wise, wise mother of three who's storing up on what she won't get any of at home!

Usually about the third day worries begin to set in. What if little Georgie doesn't get his vitamins and will husband remember that baby Gertrude won't go to sleep without her toy monkey? Georgie always catches cold in a draft and Gertrude is terrified of bugs and does husband know all this? What are they eating besides hot dogs and root beer and did he remember to pay the milkman?

By visiting hours you are convinced that your home is in ruins and your children desolate, so what does husband do? Oh, he blithely convinces you that this housekeeping is nothing when you're efficient and the children are cherubs when they're disciplined. (Get those dirty digs about efficiency and discipline!)

None of this really bowls you over until you tearfully call little Georgie and Gertrude on the telephone and they calmly inform you they are much too busy to talk because they are "giving the supper dishes a nice bath with their bubble bath while Daddy is resting."

You feel a little silly when you get your face washed, and all you do is sit back and order your meals and then shove the dirty dishes away. But when the friendly nurse comes around with all sorts of delightful prize packages of capsules, pills, hypodermics and such, you have a sneaky feeling this "vacation" has got its limitations!

For the first time in five years you have time to do your nails, wear cologne, fix your hair, give yourself a pedicure. In fact, you can do it all several times a day and instead there you are, yearning for the sticky squeeze of your youngest or the raucous shout of your oldest when he hits the front porch after baseball practice. Maybe the doctor will let you go home a day early, you begin to think. (P.S. You're only home two days until you wish you could go back for one good night's sleep.)

By the end of a week you have three new recipes for ground beef, the address of a good piano teacher, a new way to do your hair and the address of a good upholsterer. You have become an amateur expert on medical free advice, and everyone on the floor knows how you and your husband met and what grades your son made last year in the fourth grade. You've managed to find out the family status of all the interns, nurses and maids. And distressingly enough you discover all the last minute you're still not a size 14!

Suddenly the bustle of visiting hours is over, the voices quiet, the flowers are taken into the halls for the night, and the hospital takes on its "night face."

You stand there in front of the nursery watching that tiny bundle with peewee fists and a button for a nose and it dawns on you. That little fellow had everyone working as a team efficiently, accurately and speedily to make his arrival in this world safe and secure.

So many Dads, Grammas and Grampas press their noses against that glass each evening that it keeps one person busy just cleaning the glass. Will he ever be president? Will she be beautiful and talented?

For a few precious midnight minutes you can afford to catch that elusive warmth, mystery, the drama of a new life in the palm of your hands.

Tomorrow will be time enough for formulas, colic, teething rings, report cards and band-aids, hugs and kisses, the making of a person!

Time to go home and you can pack up all those magazines you didn't read, the box of stationery you only half used, the high heels you find aren't really comfortable yet, and oh yes, that pink and blue armful who could never in a million light years be called a "L'il stranger."

Dad hasn't a clean shirt to his name, the house is a shambles and, boy, are we tired of spaghetti! "Welcome home, Mom."

They Both Speak English—But She Uses More Words

January 5, 1958

It has become accepted that men and women speak two different languages.

(Just look at all the husbands raising their eyebrows and saying, "This is new?")

Men never will understand how two women can discuss "whoosit" who apparently sat at someone's luncheon table with a "whachamacallit" on her hat. Not only that, but did you see the "thingamabob" around her wrist!

Now the whole thing may be done in code, but the ladies have conveyed down to the last detail the extraordinary taste of one of their friends. On the other hand men appear to hate with all their heart the presence of details.

"Saw Bill in town today. Had an operation." He imparts this bit of information to his wife between the mashed potatoes and green beans.

Immediately his wife picks up the thread with all the avid interest of a hound pursuing the rabbit.

"You did? Where was Marge? Are they still living at the same house? What was his operation for? Did he lose any of that weight? (Well, whose weight did she think he would be losing!) How does he look? His face, was it pale? Do they have hospitalization? How old are the children?"

Prying all these bits of information from husband who is much more fond of Swiss steak than gossip is like opening a refrigerator door which has been stuck fast with chocolate syrup.

By the time the dishes are done, wife will have pinpointed the whole casual meeting down to the diner at which her husband and Bill met, the overcoat Bill was wearing and even the pork barbecue he ordered. (Washington could use her!)

At this point husband will reconsider rapidly and decide just to omit the fact he also ran into her high school history teacher on the way back to the office.

(Remember, she was the one who always wore a "wachmajigger" on her fur coat?)

◆   ◆   ◆

We are really getting concerned that our children have imaginary rabbits and dogs and such.

All the books we read eventually have a chapter about an imaginary companion the author kept with him until he packed to leave for Princeton.

Maybe our youngsters are sadly lacking in imagination or perhaps the house is just too noisy for fictitious dogs and boys.

But just how do you approach a child on this delicate matter.

Surely you just don't walk up and say, "Timmy dear, let's make up a new little playmate for you, a little imaginary blue dog we'll call "Cornstarch!"

No doubt Timmy will eye you with the speculative interest of someone viewing impending disaster. He will decide you are probably reading too much Dr. Spock and this is the day he will ask for chocolate ice cream for lunch.

The one and only time we got bold enough to bring up the idea of importing a dear imaginary playmate, our 5-year-old became so immersed in the idea of getting bunk beds and two Roy Rogers gun-and-holster sets that we quietly withdrew.

Sad though, isn't it? If any of the children ever become famous and write their memoirs, they'll never be able to write about a little blue dog named "Cornstarch."

We really should not give up this precious bit of information, but it is actually too good to keep.

There was the day when we felt as out of place in a record shop as we would in a Turkish bath.

Weaving our way between the crew cuts, white bucks and thumping beat of Danny and the Juniors, we felt almost ashamed to ask for the counter where they keep standard dance tunes.

The looks given to us were comparable to those a man receives in a very high class restaurant when he orders a hot dog with relish.

Knowing that only the high school set can afford the very newest and the latest batch of records, we have discovered the old unsellables are really quite pleasant for listening.

Of course all this is really quite rash.

This will produce a rush and all the unsellable "sale" records will go back on the racks with the standards. Oh, well, at least we'll have a few years mild enjoyment until we have to start to wear the same winter coat for five years while our own children stampede the record shops.

It's a sign of the times, the hurried Sputnik era.

The day after Christmas not one, but two people called to see which weeks this summer we were taking our vacation. If poinsettias can look surprised, ours did when we started dragging our bathing suits.

Great words I wish I had never spoken:

"I'll put the children to bed, dear."

"But in six months we'll have it paid off."

"Three clubs."

"Well, if you insist, but I've never worn purple before."

"Three clubs."

"There's nothing to it. Just takes an hour to bake."

"Three clubs."

We are developing a new involved science called "wearyology." This is for weary mothers who dearly yearn to catch forty extra winks in the morning but who do not want their children wandering over vast stretches of scrambled eggs and peanut butter toast without them.

The primary theory of this new science is that one must close one's ears to ALL.

Lying in bed you will undoubtedly hear such fascinating odds and ends of conversation: "Gimme half." "Mommy keeps them in the potato bin." "Wash them in the bathtub."

Now you must relax and stop lying there with every muscle tensed and every fiber of your brain crying out, "Gimme what? What do I keep in the potato bin? Wash what?

However, we do not have the daring of experimental scientists and we have not tested our theories on "wearyology." Oh, once we did, that was the morning they greased the picture window with spry. Now we consider our theories while dozing over the ironing board.

The Real Lowdown about Our Willie: He's a Real Boy!

March 30, 1958

What mother can resist sending a note to school the first day?

Dear teacher:

Here is Willie, our first, born in the cradle of happiness, reared in confusion, equipped for action.

He has had: chicken pox, two dog bites, one tooth filled, measles, a broken ankle, innumerable visiting viruses.

He has not had: mumps, a fractured collarbone, or a quiet minute since the age of eight months.

He likes: ice cream, marbles, mud, cap pistols, Dad, television, the movies, comic books, dogs, bikes, peanut butter, hammers, chocolate cake and any kind of noise.

He does not like: water, brussel sprouts, short pants, freckles, poached eggs, bed, his sister, soap, girls in general, hairbrushes and kissing.

He has: two turtles, a Zorro hat, assorted grandparents, about 50 marbles, a dog who boards in the country because he likes to eat suede shoes, a closet full of cardboard "garages" and a mother and father.

He does not have (although he has expressed the fervent desire that he might have): 12 more boxes of his favorite cereal, a parachute (to go with the plane he will get with 15,093 box tops), a real space helmet, a pony, a brother, soap that tastes like chocolate.

He adores being read to especially if the hero flies to the moon or is devoured by 40 sea monsters on the first page.

He laughs easily and often, needs frequent airings and is not easily confined to one area for more than ten minutes at a time.

When he was born I was only twenty, but now that he is five, and I am 95, I think I know him better. Thank you and may heaven protect you!

Sincerely,
Willie's Mother.

P.S. There is a handkerchief in his shirt pocket.

If I could do my country only one great service, I would compile a list of defenses for the sneaky telephone sales approach.

For instance, when the cool and cultured voice comes over the phone with, "We have a free gift for you," snap her up in the middle of the sentence … "wonderful, wonderful! Unfortunately I won't be home but just leave it behind the storm door and thanks loads." (This is sure fire since most free gifts designed as door openers fit conveniently behind the storm door anyway.)

Then there is the "Congratulations, you have just won" bit, which you also jump in the middle with, "Oh, how disappointing. My tax lawyers have just informed me I'm in the 90 percent bracket and I can't accept another thing."

Of course, there is the guy who pulls on your parental sense of obligation with, "Knowing what a fine parent you are we are sure you will want to provide your child with the finest …"

Catch him quick! "You're darn right I do. That's why the missus and I send him cookies every week at reform school. Last time he was there we always sent him homemade blackberry jam."

After I finish this great documentary I'm going to start on another fascinating study that will include what to do if the local lending library calls up to say your book is two weeks' overdue.

(Just break in with a deep voice: "Sorry this is an FBI classified number. Please hang up immediately.")

◆   ◆   ◆

If shoe stores were smart they would provide handy wall silhouettes of the male from 5 to 7 feet. Then the lady shopper can try on her new heels and stand beside the silhouette to compare her new height with that of her escort.

This would eliminate that old social bugaboo of rushing back upstairs to change shoes when the gal discovers her heels make her a half-inch taller than that old beau's new crew-cut.

A Poor, Poor Mom Has a Tough Job; Resign? Never!!

May 11, 1958

An open letter to my boss:

Dear Boss:

For years the unofficial spokesman of the unofficial union to which the members of my profession haphazardly belong has been screaming for shorter hours, more pay and every laurel wreath of victory not claimed since Caesar.

Since the union is not really a union, I'll risk expulsion by saying thanks, but no thanks!

Shorter hours might be nice in some respects but I and the other members of our union find we are unable to turn out quality products under conditions involving shorter work weeks.

More recognition is a goal to be sought in almost any field, but at this point we would like to point out the high cost of mistakes in my field.

Suppose you pay me $50 a week.

Well, I figure that counting the cakes that fell, the pans that were scorched and the sweaters that were shrunk and the paint that was chipped, I will owe you about $300 by the time I "retire."

As for the time study you suggested, how can you put into hours and minutes the time it takes to soothe a broken heart, bake a perfect cake or rear a happy child?

It's true I have to be housekeeper, secretary, nurse, teacher, gardener and, on occasion, veterinarian without benefit of degree.

It's also true that I can't balance a budget, that I always lose my temper at least twice a day.

I always leave the hedge clippers out in the rain and fall asleep in the middle of the best television programs.

I forget to bring in the milk and let out the dog.

I forget to sew on buttons and let down hems.

Sometimes I even forget and burn the bacon, or I just might forget entirely to defrost the meat.

One thing, though, I have never forgotten your birthdays, nor your heartaches, nor your precious bubbles of happiness.

About fifty percent of the time I work in a jungle of cries, yells and screams surrounded by a sea of peanut butter smudges that would make Central Africa seem as tame as an English lawn party.

The other fifty percent of the time I rule with a gentle hand the buttons on all my electrical helpmates which on fifty days of the year manage to work together at the same time without blowing a fuse or setting the house on fire.

In other words, half the time I am in a state of hypertension similar to the boiled custard that gets watery and the other half of the time I am as ecstatic as a lemon sponge pie.

There are days when I feel a robot or a complete idiot could handle my ministrations just as well: sweeping up broken glass, answering the 14 phone calls feeding the turtles.

Then there are the other days.

I need a mechanic's certificate to get the mixer to mix and the washer to wash.

I need a degree from the best language school in the country to decipher what my 2 year-old wants for lunch.

I need a doctor's diploma to take care of all the spots, bruises and cuts and a psychiatrist's degree to handle their neuroses.

Most of all I need a facial, a manicure and about two good weeks of reducing.

Unfortunately, the union funds now are tied up in more important projects such as new handlebars, Girl Scout cookies, rose bushes, vitamins and grass seed.

Most of the time I am convinced I should have stayed in bed or, better yet, never have been born.

These are the days you and your cronies conspire so tirelessly that even Khrushchev would cringe should he come for dinner.

You can't understand why I sob hysterically when you upset an ashtray.

And you wryly shake your head as I smile benignly when the ironing board crashes down upon the puppy dog.

But then the other most of the time I am so happy to know that no matter how often I rant and rave you always bring the very first bouquet of spring violets just to me.

'Alvin' Moves in, Takes over Spot Left by Rudolph

December 21, 1958

"Alvin" the chipmunk has come to stay at our house.

Last year it was Rudolph the red-nosed reindeer, whom we could accept with some good grace since he was in Santa's fold.

But just how "Alvin" got into the melee we're not too sure; nevertheless, "Alvin" is here at breakfast, and lunch, and dinner. We have our first steaming cup of coffee in the morning while listening to tales of dreaming about devils, and much worse things. Now we share this one-time pleasant ten minutes with the chipmunks while the children squeal ecstatically every time "Alvin's" name is shouted.

"Now why couldn't I think up something like that?" murmurs husband.

What will it be next year to join "Alvin," Frosty the Snowman, Rudolph. Maybe Jing-a-Ling, the elf with the blanched almond ears, or Yule, the Mule?

These last minute substitutions are beginning to get Santa down.

For six weeks No. 1 son talked fire engine, night and day, with fervor and genuine yearning.

Now he has calmly announced that fire engines are for the birds and what he is really flipping for is a dump truck.

His sister has stuck to her guns though, but six weeks has not made it any easier to decipher just what a "brideldoop" might be. From her descriptions it seems to be a combination doll-power mower that makes a noise like a kitty and is cuddly to hold.

Looking back to her first Christmas, when she ignored all the bright new toys for a lovely old battered box of paper handkerchiefs, maybe a "brideldoop" is something simple like an old sauerkraut can or a 1946 election button.

◆   ◆   ◆

For those busy wives who haven't the time or the funds for a new Christmas Eve dress: Sprinkle eyes well with stardust, tuck a holly sprig into the hair, tiny gold bells at your ears, and splash liberally with favorite cologne. Add to recipes for making husbands happy.

You wish there would be just one special way to say thank you and to make their holidays happy because your heart is warm in their year-round thoughtfulness: The doctor whose patient care keeps your family whole and happy and the counterman who serves your coffee with a smile and a friendly comment; the paper boy who remembers to shield your Sunday comics from the weather; the courteous milkman; the always-friendly postman; the baby-sitter who stays that extra ten minutes with a smile—and all the other dozens of moments of warmth from those who take time to make yours a happy year.

When you were young and gay and had time for a weekly manicure you probably took your husband of a few months aside and tenderly described to him the joys of making family traditions.

Now as you sit in the middle of paper chains, popcorn balls, felt mittens, walnuts, coconut and evergreen boughs, do you get the feeling your own traditions are choking you to death?

The dog has eaten the Christmas decorations from the bedroom windows for lunch.

First grader Tim has informed you that your tree cookies are crooked and you have the feeling he thinks you have committed the No. 1 sin—even worse than making him brush his teeth before he goes to bed.

Baby is eating the pills that make the engine smoke and she is almost hitting .400 with her Christmas tree ball swinging average.

Sister was put to bed in yon big bed for a nap and spent the hour fastening carolers, bells and Santas and a million other seals on the headboard of your bed.

Those maddening little beasts! How will you ever endure three more days of this Christmas cyclone? Traditions, hah! You would gladly trade all the popcorn balls and date and nut balls in the house for a good hot bath and manicure.

You have forgotten to mail Uncle Teddy his annual box of cigars.

First grader is howling because you won't let him take your best bottle of perfume to his teacher. Now he is slyly wrapping up the silver ashtray off the coffee table. Good grief, you think next he'll be taking her his old coffee can in which he keeps his treasures.

Baby is cheerfully beating puppy on the head with a candy cane and then thoughtfully munching on the pieces as they drop off. (Candy canes, not puppy!)

Sister has eaten eight of the 12 cookies you have taken from the oven and already is eyeing the icing dish.

"Mother! Aren't we ever going to eat supper?

Supper? It can't be time for supper. I haven't even had my second cup of coffee.

Did anyone think to pay the egg man?

"I don't care if you are going to give those macaroons to your best friend. You are not to hide them in the pockets of your Daddy's best suit."

Traditions, you mutter. Traditions are something that look good in magazines, that sound pretty when you don't have two baskets of ironing, one basket of mending and 10,000 other things to do.

But the magic that is by children blessed spins its mystic spell and by Christmas Eve no one has a sniffly nose, the train is running like a charm and even the crooked tree cookies look lovely in the candle-light.

Baby seems blissfully content to hold the sleeping puppy in her arms and stare sleepy-eyed into the soft tree lights.

Bathtime took on wider horizons this week when we pretended the tub was a rocket launched into outer space and the soap was our secret electronic equipment to record satellite tracks across our own skin.

The only trouble was one junior space cadet decided to fire off the shower handle and this aeronautical engineer got drenched. Next time we better wear our special plastic space helmets.

Now we know why schoolroom ceilings are so high. Our first grade Picasso has plastered the four walls of his bedroom already with his first prints and either he will have to switch rooms or else revise his art collection, replacing Farmer Jones' red barn for his newest Mighty Mouse etching.

First grader Tim admits you make the best fudge of anyone he knows with the possible exception of Popeye. You take this as a real compliment.

Sister presents you with the gift she has wrapped herself with all the seals, ribbons, stars, paste and cellophane tape she could get around the handkerchief.

Clear little voices sing the manger song and sudden unexpected tears rise sharply in your throat. Christmas is truly in the hearts of children. God bless them. God bless the traditions. Truly, truly, a merry birthday for the fairest child of them all.

It's Spring Again: Birds on the Wing, Kids Sick in Bed

March 29, 1959

Anniversary roses are exciting, birthday chocolates enticing, but nothing is quite so dear, nor quite so refreshing as a new Easter bonnet.

And as one sage observer put it this morning, "There's twice as many posies on the ladies' heads as there are in the garden right now."

Lillies of the valley give us hope, red roses make us feel chic, daisies romantic, and with a peppermint straw, how can anyone help but feel enchanted?

Just imagine all the money spent on vitamins and "pep" pills laid end to end around the hat boxes of the world. Just think of all the gorgeous hats we would be wearing for Easters to come.

What is more, there's no finer gauge of womanhood. When your darling daughter stops throwing her Easter bonnet on the floor or feeding it to the baby peeps for lunch, then you know she has become a lady—in love with her hat!

While almost every husband at some time has to be dragged into "assisting" with the Christmas decorations, all his artistic instincts rise to the surface during the Easter season and he considers his work on the colored eggs almost as great as the chicken's original triumph.

He will decorate every egg in the refrigerator cheerfully, including those meant for the cake you intended to bake—even those that haven't been hard cooked.

What a blissful sight he is there in his new worsted, the spanking white shirt and the pink, blue, yellow, green and—yes—purple painted fingers: the Picasso of the Peter Cottontail set.

The arrival of spring and the Easter Bunny all at once was almost usurped in this household by the arrival of the measles.

While measles popped out between the freckles, our patient was delighted to show off his latest acquisition to his sisters, friends and all who showed the least bit of interest.

Somewhere along the line he acquired the somewhat dubious bit of medical information that one always had one's tonsils removed during a siege of the measles. Once this parcel of information was rectified, he was quite content to lie and bask in his newfound glory.

Not to be outdone, his sister has abandoned the search for the first crocus in the yard and has settled down to wait for the first measle.

As any mother of a child forced to stay in bed all day can tell you, it is quite possible that she could deliver mail to 13 city blocks with the steps she puts in between bedroom and kitchen.

"Mommy, Mommy, come quick!"

What can it be? A nose that is bleeding? A dizzy spell?

Up the steps, down the hall, into the bedroom.

"Mommy, did you know that the Lone Ranger's horse is white?"

Count slowly to thirty, "Yes, dear. Now read your book."

Back down to the kitchen and the breakfast dishes.

"Mommy, Mommy! Oh hurry, Mommy."

Up the stairs et cetera. Oh, how your feet are killing you.

"Mommy, where do measles go at night?"

And so while the dishes pile up, the dust has kittens and the cakes go unbaked, we have seminars on cowboy boots, the price of kites, swimming lessons, snake bites, chocolate covered peanuts, all those intricate little things which make up the day of a bedridden boy lost in a sea of comic books.

When a wife asks her husband if this is the day he goes to the barber shop, he's insulted.

When a husband asks a wife if this isn't the week she's due to get "something" done to her hair, she holds out her hand for a check.

It is a commonly accepted fact that children hate to sleep alone. We have been used to them sharing their beds with books, balls, doll babies, crayons and even catcher's mitts.

But picture the jolt we got as we tiptoed in to the bedroom to cover our 3-year-old and found her sound asleep wearing red-framed dark glasses and pearl earrings and clutching her best purse in one hand!

Spring is that delicious season, replete with sunshine and warmth, which brings by a neighbor and golf clubs just as husband is fixing to change the storm windows and screens.

It delivers a lovely young thing of 15 with straw-colored hair and tennis racquet just as your senior son volunteers to beat the rugs.

It sends across town a dozen Scouts with knapsacks, bound for the meadows just as your 12-year-old offers to wash the car.

And it sets a lovely butterfly skimming across the lawn. Your first-grader speeds off to follow—leaving her rake and broom behind.

Last of all, it sent a robin to sit on the fence post just as you were about to hand out the wash.

Now who in this world can just go and hang up wash with that lovely robin sitting right there and all this glorious sunshine?

Who has spring fever? Me? Are you crazy, or something? I always go bare-footed the first day of spring and comb the cocker's fur with my best pearl packed brush.

Isn't the air simply intoxicating?

We have withstood the thump-thump of balls thrown against the walls, the rattling of baby's pull toy, even the whine and whir of toy anti-aircraft guns. But somehow the monotonous click-clack, click-clack that baby daughters make while dragging around in cast-off high-heeled pumps strains the limit of endurance.

Time was we thought it the height of orderliness and caution when our friends kept their better shoes carefully packed away in boxes.

Now we consider it our regular line of defense when the call goes out, "Let's play dress-up!"

Oh, Little People, take my veils, my jewels, my petticoats if you must, but spare me those clickety-clackety heels on wooden floors!

As we see it "décor" is just a fancier way to say "decoration."

In other words, if your drapes and slipcovers match, you are improving the décor of your room, but if you got your slipcovers on sale and dyed your drapes to match the old sheets, you are decorating the room.

Interior decorating is that fine art of making cousin Sarah's old couch and your new Danish modern armchairs look as though they are kin to the rug you bought second-hand at the auction last month.

Think of all the hard work and years that go into authentically "aging" a good piece of furniture—when our kids can accomplish it without effort in two short weeks.

After you have succeeded in potty-training your little ones you will find a much harder task awaits for you: chair-training.

It is practically impossible for a child from one to 16 to sit in a chair. He can perch like a crane, sprawl like a fat brown bear, jiggle, scoot and skid, but he cannot sit.

He eats dinner riding an imaginary scooter and bouncing on one hip at the same time giving you the nervous impression he is about to snatch up your tossed salad and make a clean getaway.

He watches television sprawled upside down with his elbows on the floor and his feet across one arm. There are endless variations and some children become quite adept at never "sitting" in a chair.

Puppy doesn't mind at all. She loves our chairs!

Closet Treasures to be "Reburied," It's Cleanup Time

March 26, 1960

I'm almost certain I don't really have claustrophobia, having spent so much time on elevators going from one clearance sale to the next!

But every time I open the door to one of the children's closets I get the severest symptoms of claustrophobia!

That is, IF I get the door open.

For weeks our 4-year-old kept a little red suitcase packed for some nebulous trip or safari she was planning. In fact, each time she wanted to brush her teeth, she would rush to the closet and unpack the suitcase for her toothbrush. It was that serious.

But each time I opened her closet door out tumbled the suitcase and its important contents—the top to a mayonnaise jar, a ball of string, doll dress, some peanuts, a pair of dirty socks, old chewing gum wrappers and, of course, the toothbrush.

Naturally we don't have this sort of problem with our son.

Suitcases are completely unnecessary when he can carry a can of oil, 64 baseball cards, a chocolate bar, Boy Scout knife and compass in the pocket of his jeans.

But when I notice there are very few if any of his clothes in the wash, a trip to his closet is almost inevitable.

Certain dangers are inevitable thereafter.

His door is invariably booby-trapped with rubber bands that snap off your fingertips or piles of books that crash down on your head from the shelf above. For days I went around smelling like airplane glue following the last booby-trap episode.

We remind ourselves to point out the location of the clothes hamper to him as we pick up this week's mound of dirty shirts from the floor of the closet.

Actually we are priding ourselves on the remarkable calm with which the entire incident is being met. Secretly we know that this calm comes from the simple satisfaction in knowing that Casper, the caterpillar, is no longer with us, nor Willie, the earthworm, nor Torrence, the turtle.

(I can never be certain, of course, but I'm sure that first white hair came the day I reached for the mound of shirts on the closet floor and came up with a wiggling Willie!)

When the children were younger, they always wanted their closet doors shut tightly at night "so the goblins won't come out."

Now they just want the doors shut so all the extraneous material wealth of childhood doesn't tumble, drip, fall and otherwise eject themselves from the depths.

The last time we counted, they had Christmas cards from the 1956 season and marbles from the year one.

Sharing a closet with a daughter has always seemed to me to be one of the more inspiring things about raising a family. I pictured the pleasant little gossip sessions while I hung my dresses beside her tiny garments.

Never did I picture myself fighting through an onslaught of old teddy bears, paper doilies and plastic teapots.

Is it a question of survival or habit when I check the toes of all my shoes for marbles, jacks or paper clips before donning them?

In early apartment days when one closet held all our earthly possessions, walk-in closets seemed the height of good living.

Now I am not so sure.

Fascinated by the mere act of walking in one side of a closet and out the other, the girls conducted tours for days, stopping to play house in the midst of the hatboxes. Every time I opened the closet door I almost expected to see an entire den pack step out.

What is there about kids that make it impossible for them to find anything interesting to do in a quarter-of-an-acre, but possible to find two thousand interesting things to do in a three-foot square closet?

Fortunately, spring cleaning days are upon us, and for one beautiful week the closet doors will swing open wide, shoes will stand in orderly rows, and clothes will find their way to the clothes hamper.

But is the satisfaction really worth it? How does it look when one's daughter keeps her red suitcase in the front hallway and Daddy finds Torrence, the turtle in his hat in the downstairs closet?

So we make a house rule. Anything that can be turned over to the zoo, traded for more baseball cards or fit through the front door, hinges on, may not be stored in bedroom closets.

It will take the children at least three weeks to find a loophole in that while I finish the rest of the spring-cleaning!

The nicest thing about children ... when the bills are the highest ... and the headaches the longest ... is that they never let us forget ... or leave behind ... the magical little boy and little girl world of make-believe where all things are still possible.

And where laughter picks you up faster than a nap and where the story time hour is the salve that soothes a hundred little aches of the day.

Being a Mother Turns out to Be Permanent Post

May 8, 1960

When one of the neighborhood 4-year-olds demurely remarks that she wants to be a Mommie when she grows up, the rest of the children gaze upon her with that special look reserved for girls, idiots, mothers and asparagus.

And most of the time, I am inclined to go along with them. Especially when someone turns the refrigerator dial up to freeze and there is nothing but icy pickled eggs for lunch.

But then, there are other times …

Somehow all the while I am tying shoes, mopping noses, loading the washing machine, feeding puppies, reading aloud, ironing white shirts, I keep thinking of that college professor who implored us semester after semester to prepare for that time when the "little ones will fly from the nest."

I keep wanting to write to her and tell her to please stop worrying. When they fly, I'll be catching up on my sleep for at least five years.

I suppose it is a very good thing that motherhood is a pretty permanent position.

It's certain no bookkeeper alive would dare to take the chance with her double entries that I've taken with trial recipes, fallen cakes and scorched shirts!

Someone, obviously someone who never had a baby with colic, originated the well-worn phrase, "But children keep you so young."

I have been trying now for years to keep feeling young through chicken pox, broken windows and upset tummies. I never really feel my age as much as I do the morning after I pitch ball with the kids in the back yard. My friends with teen-agers have convinced me that there is little hope since they find the shag and double chocolate malt-eds are not terribly rejuvenating.

Then just what is it that makes me want to sit back in bed on Mother's Day morning and take my burnt toast and cold egg like a veteran? I suppose it's the peaceful times before and after the storms, the silver linings that are at the bottom of every bowl of cereal dumped on the kitchen floor.

If it's true that our eyes are the windows of our souls, then our kids have the best-washed souls on Main Street. Tears over lost pencils, tears over bloody noses and tears over broken dolls.

Surprisingly, one day, tears over a beautiful piece of music. Can the little rascal in dirty denim be sprouting a seed of warmth and appreciation beneath his upstart exterior!

Monotony becomes a tedious refrain—pick up the pajamas, don't forget the dentist appointment, something for dessert, polish the shoes and press, press, press.

A splinter of knowledge just awakened shreds the monotony into a thousand delightful pieces, and we don't stop to pick them up as we spend the afternoon watching a caterpillar, the first tulip or reading a new book together.

So while we fill the drawer with milk carton pencil holders, pot holders and hankies with purple daisies as the Mother's Days fly by, we forget for a blissful day the snail who lived for a time in the refrigerator and the great day of the war with whipping cream in the water pistols.

You see, they are being so divinely "correct," that I haven't the heart to wonder what the neighbor's prize rose is doing on my break-fast tray.

As I said, the job is permanent, and there's lots of time tomorrow to ask them.

Jam Sandwiches Gone, So Family Ends Woods Trip

June 12, 1960

Ever since some nitwit wrote the word "togetherness" and left out the hyphen there has been a big thing going for family trips.

These trips are supposed to weld together family relationships and make it possible for parents to understand their children better.

There are times, when staggering home from these trips hot, sticky and tired, loaded down with five pounds of things we didn't need, I think, "So who wants to understand them?"

But this is really an act of treason.

Let us consider the last trip to the woods.

Forsaking his golf game, father announced with a great deal of suppressed excitement that tomorrow we would take an all-day trip to the woods.

"Gee whiz, I'll miss all the cartoons on TV," was the first ecstatic response he got.

"Can we take pickles and olives and ice cream and things to eat?" worried this week's Great Wrecker of the Food Bill.

"Jam," chimed in an interested 2-year-old who thinks the streets of heaven are paved with strawberry jam.

"Yes," soothes Daddy, "we're going to see trees, and birds, and all the beautiful trees in the woods."

"Gee whiz," grumbled keeper of cartoon channels. "I bet they don't have any dinosaurs or man-eating lilies."

"Don't be silly, Freddy," gobbled his sister. "Mrs. Castle has a whole garden full of dinosaurs, and she let Mary Ann and me taste one with sugar and salt on."

(Remind me to walk over to Mrs. Castle's garden right after dinner is finished).

Naturally it rained. I believe it rained when anything of importance has happened in this world—like the time Marie Antionette was beheaded or our new hardware store opened.

(I mentioned this to hubby and asked him, did he ever think of all the soggy potato chips consumed in the past 5,000 years? He gave me the funniest look and offered to help with the dishes when I hadn't even hinted).

Nevertheless we had our little trip to the woods. The children climbed trees without TV antennas, threw rocks in the lake, did all those carefree things children did before chain-link fencing and plastic pools were invented.

The eldest discovered a dead fish, which he discussed at great length during the picnic. After all, a dead fish is almost—not quite—but almost as newsworthy as a dinosaur.

But pretty soon the jam sandwiches were all gone. Time to go back to civilization.

I really wasn't discouraged because the next day I went to a P-TA meeting where a wonderful speaker encouraged parents to take their children on as many trips as possible to "broaden their horizons."

I wish I knew what he meant specifically by "broadening their horizons."

In the past month the children have toured a gigantic naval destroyer, visited the White House, toured a library and zipped through the zoo two or three times.

Know what they're talking about?

One: Does the president of the United States have to eat vegetables?

Two: Can they have a turtle race on my coffee table?

Three: Next time we go to the zoo can they buy a flag, balloon, whistle, windmill, peanuts funny book, et cetera, et cetera, et cetera?

Not that I would ever discourage any parent from a trip. As they say, different age groups.

The Washington Monument was dedicated to the spirit of the first president. Our eldest grasped this immediately but couldn't understand why they couldn't have a soft-drink machine in the lobby.

The medium size one was a little hazy and missed the meaning completely as she grew impatient "waitin' here for that ole' Mr. Washington to come down on the elevator."

Our neighbor made the mistake of talking her husband into attending that P-TA meeting about "broadening horizons."

Born and reared in the city, he is now broadening his horizons to the tune of a hundred dollars worth of pup tents, sleeping bags and other extraneous camping gear.

We are giving them a gala send-off party this evening with one giant-sized bottle of insect repellent, packed into one large family-sized carton—for togetherness—of course.

I only got to chapter five in Dr. Spock when I had to put the book down suddenly and dash off to the hospital for my second child.

Seems as though I got pretty busy after that and just this week I picked up and started in again. Now I discover to my dismay that all three of them have gone through thumb sucking, nail biting and hair pulling and are already on knuckle cracking without my knowing a thing about it.

Now I am thinking quite seriously about enrolling the 3-year old in a local branch of nail biting anonymous. Then every time she gets the urge to gnaw on a nail she can call a friend over for a low-calorie lollipop and they can see the thing through together.

Pediatricians have agreed that all these little habits that children pick up are signs of tension, and the best solution is lots of love and activity.

They are getting enough activity, lots of love—and now I am tense!

Little Girl's Party Is Made of Iced Chaos, Puppy's Ear

June 26, 1960

What are little girls' parties made of?

I'm sure you've seen dozens of pamphlets telling how to give a successful children's party.

I am sure they were devised and written by people in fallout shelters protected by cinder block and stamina from children's parties!

In the first place who says children's parties need planning?

Children are the greatest planners in the world.

The night before the big day we informed our 4-year-old she was about to be 5. A 5-year-old planner, that is.

"Well, now let me see. We'll have to have cake, lots of ice cream and a pin-the-tail-on-the-donkey game, and I'll ask Kimmy, Pat, Karen, Kathy, Louise …

She was happily droning on as we turned out the light and covered her up.

The next morning bright and early we awoke to find a 5-year-old planner perched on our pillow with sunglasses, water pistol and four rings on her fingers.

… Harry, Tommy, Eddie, Leslie, Doris, Elmer, Henry and I think maybe we ought to have pink lemonade to drink. Did you bake the cake yet?

See what I mean.

At 10 a.m. they had visited two square blocks to bring glad tidings of the festivities to come.

By noon I was compelled to ask just how many had been asked thus far. Believe me, a Gallup poll couldn't have done better.

"Half the fun of parties is allowing your children to participate in the preparations," it says in the books.

Participate? Well, did they participate!

We iced two layer cakes, three dozen cupcakes, one kitchen chair and a puppy ear.

We made four quarts of pink lemonade and drank three.

We blew up 25 balloons and rubbed them on our hair and then stuck them fast to the ceilings, walls, telephone and, naturally, puppy's ear.

When the first little guests arrived I was busy brushing pale green icing out of the pale blonde ponytail belonging to the "hostest with the mostest." (Mostest cupcakes?)

Then I was too busy greeting those at the front door to keep track of those arriving at the back door.

Soon I met them all in the dining room, however, where a balloon-breaking contest was in full swing.

Everyone had ample time to count the candles on the cake. Then we lit them 17 times so each one of the guests could have a chance to blow out the lights and make sure her wish would "really and truly come true."

Things got underway fast. We discovered one small entrepreneur of 3 situated in a kitchen corner trading five peanuts for every lollipop.

Another young business executive was working up a raffle for the more tempting of the gifts.

At the height of the melee it was necessary to send out for reinforcements—two more super-sized bags of peanuts.

A great peanut hunt in the garden followed. We found a baseball that had been missing for weeks, several paper dolls, a sand shovel and, of course, dozens and dozens of peanuts.

At dinner hour, there still was a small trickle of visitors through the backyard, sure there might still be one or two peanuts beneath the rose bushes.

As I swept the two or three pounds of peanut shells into the dust pan, puppy dog sat idly by carefully licking the remaining pale green icing from the screen door.

Looking fondly at the children plopped all over the garden intently counting their candies and favors, I thought, "Now what could be nicer?"

"Two hundred and ninety-eight, two hundred and ninety-nine, gee whiz! One more and I'll have 300 popsicle sticks for my bureau. Three hundred!"

Now I ask you what could be more gloriously satisfying, when you are 5, than to possess 300 popsicle sticks?

"Mom, birthdays are so grand, we decided to have another tomorrow and ice the cakes with pink icing this time."

Friends, loyal members of the P-TA, and mothers, call your children home, but do come again, when we are 6.

It's Really Easy to Give up
TV—For Four Days

August 14, 1960

I guess it was really the seventeenth reading of "A Day at the Zoo" that did it!

When the TV set went out on an unauthorized strike, we accepted the news calmly and with a certain amount of anticipation.

We had read the exciting stories of those who had "taken the cure," turned off their TV for an entire year and memorized the entire "A-Ala" volume of the encyclopedia.

Many of our friends had sworn off TV for as long as a month at a time and emerged smiling and clear-eyed from so much sleep.

I was always there when a P-TA committee was formed to demand better TV programs. (Of course I cheerfully let the kids become demoralized with Popeye every day at 5 while I browned the meat and mashed potatoes.)

And we always were sure to let it drop at the Tuesday night bridge games that we had seen Omnibus[1] on Sunday (even if we had been making fudge in the kitchen after the second commercial.)

Our friends came forth to help us in our self-improvement program.

They loaned us their encyclopedia, anagram and Scrabble, and Parcheesi. Then they went home. There was a spectacular on at 8 that night that they didn't want to miss.

The first day it was really rather easy. We read four full pages on Aztec jewelry and got nine good hours sleep.

The second night everything went very well until someone pulled the Scrabble game out and the eldest goofball insisted that "glunk" was a perfectly acceptable word.

After we had separated him and his sister and put a band-aid on each of their noses, the spirit of togetherness waned a bit.

At this point Dad had the audacity to suggest he might slip next door to watch Peter Gunn on the neighbor's TV. (And he said TV like a naughty word.)

It was as though he had quietly suggested slipping down to the corner of Hollywood and Vine and pouring ketchup on Fabian's pompadour.

It was amazing how noisy our silence became. I had almost forgotten that the youngest one grates her teeth when annoyed. Her brother began making sounds like a naval destroyer under enemy fire as he threw popcorn morsels into his mouth.

Almost immediately my nail file and the sounds it was making caused a United Nations type crisis and I retired in a huff to read three more pages on Aztec jewelry.

It wasn't too long though until I gave up on that and pulled out Arlene Francis'[2] new charm book. You see it is very necessary to read something reliable to charm the repairman from his den of condensers and resistors.

I have a special Arlene Francis voice which I reserve especially for him and the week of the Girl Scout cookie sale.

The TV repairman was not in a mood to play "What's My Line." He had a toothache. (And, I'll just bet the dentist's SX-649 had gone bad too!)

At this point I decided to get the children caught up with their reading and we began with "A Day at the Zoo." Two hours later we were still not up to the lion's cage. An hour later we had passed the lion's cage and started over for the seventeenth time. That did it.

We loaded the one-eyed monster into the car and sped to the neighborhood TV center where, with just the right hint of a sob in our throat, we pled our case.

Happily the man on duty was fond of chocolate cake and money. He fixed the poor monster's ailing innards for a sizeable chunk of my chocolate cake and a loan from Ft. Knox.

We raced home to find our reformed neighbors waiting on the front porch, craving a game of anagrams. Dragging them along inside we all settled down blissfully to watch our first Indian massacre in four days. My, but it was refreshing!

◆   ◆   ◆

Next time we are at a party and I can get some free advice from our psychiatrist friend I must ask him what it means to be "almost but not quite" all the time.

I have been meaning to write a book about the delights of daughters ever since we bought our first ruffled pinafore. One day we went into the bookstore to buy some carbon paper and discovered that thirty other mothers of delightful daughters had already written books.

It was just as well though, because that was the day they shampooed their hair in the toothpaste and the delight was nil for a while.

Chic young wives down at the playground talk about tossing in a few chickens and shrimps for a cheese casserole supper.

We go home and toss in a casserole and immediately Pop threatens to call the city about its garbage collections.

It took us almost six months to work up courage to wear the sack. That was the day the new line came out with kimono sleeves and bloused waistline.

I am always catching the wrong bus and walking home. Walking is great for the legs but it sure knock the heck out of the shoe repair bills.

I would love to take up golf yet this summer but sure as I do they'll turn the golf course into a racetrack and horses bore me stiff!

Delightful Peal of School Bells

August 28, 1960

Pardon my dry eyes.

The summer tans are splotchy.

Swimsuits have splits in the seats. Sneakers are in the final state of decay.

The hole in the front screen door is now large enough to admit an army of grasshoppers.

AND it's almost time for that first day of school!

Excuse our candid enthusiasm, but the mothers on our block agree that first day of school is second to none, even Mother's Day!

Whoever conjured up the picture of mother with weeping, red eyes sending her brood down to the school bus must have had her August memories diluted through the years.

At this point I am able, with the greatest of happiness, to surrender my offspring to their teachers while I collapse in the nearest chair without a broken spring or cracked baseball bat.

I long to put the peanut butter jar away and eat a nice respectable ham sandwich.

I long to quit playing "Simon Says" and watch a completely demoralizing daytime soap opera for a full uninterrupted 15 minutes.

I long to stop playing second base and give myself a really decent manicure.

Most of all I suppose I long to take a solitary bath without the presence of a three-masted sailing schooner and tin teapot in the bath water.

Next I believe I shall pack away the charcoal grill, and we will have a sit-down meal in the dining room because I am almost certain that beneath all those seashells, catcher's mitts and inner tubes there is still a dining room table!

The kitchen will become a kitchen once more and not a processing plant for highly expensive and highly-watered lemonade.

The basement will once again become a storage place for three-masted sailing schooners and tin teapots and not a clubhouse for 15 first graders with exceptionally large stomachs and over-active voice boxes.

(If we may, a moment of silent prayer for all sweet young first grade teachers who must contain all those outdoor backyard voices into restrained "indoor" voices.)

Forgive us for being so callous but it's practically impossible to be sentimental when one no longer has a refrigerator she can call her own.

Ah, but soon, the chocolate pudding will stay on the shelf for longer than 15 minutes, bottle caps will stay on bottles and not in the mashed potatoes. Ice cube trays will once more produce normal ice cubes instead of purple monster variations.

Whilst the wee ones learn fractions, the peal of the telephone will no longer strike terror into the simple housewife's heart.

It can no longer be Jeremy Beetle calling to inquire if he may cool his pet black snake in our deep freeze. Jeremy is safely absorbed in Miss Willet's fourth grade.

When the doorbell rings I feel safe. It can only be the cleaner, the milkman or some polite salesman of toothbrushes—no frightening 9-year-old selling homemade glue or a bevy of pig-tailed misses who have been twice dared to kiss the male heir of this household.

The screeching of brakes outside can no longer mean the youngest has pitched her tree-ripened peach through the window of a passing car. It must be some poor mother rushing home to clear her clothes-basket of roller skates.

Veterans of the summer "withers" assure me it is still possible to remember Goren's bridge rules after eleven weeks of "Old Maids." A quiet remedy they suggest, replace the stack of nursery rhyme records with some real cornball music, violins and all.

We can see nothing ahead but pleasurable surprises for husbands, too.

Once again he will come home and find us engaged in some motherly task such as mashing potatoes or polishing candle sticks—no more playing second base, patching inner tubes, roller skating on the patio and other pursuits.

The thought of all this weakens me so that I may just volunteer to sell tickets for the next P-TA turkey raffle.

Excuse me, please. "What do you mean we're out of sugar?" You made seven quarts of lemonade yesterday and there was enough sugar then!"

Ring school bells, Ring!

Baby Sitter Hard to Find—And Harder to Keep

September 25, 1960

What is the biggest problem in a new community?

Getting a good piano tuner? Plumber? Tutor?

No, it's getting a good baby-sitter!

Half an hour after a family has moved into a new neighborhood, the children have canvassed the place and already know how many dogs, turtles and kiddies are in the block, and who has the biggest wading pool and the most toys in the back yard.

The next day they branch out and can even tell you where is the best spot to buy fresh doughnuts or have your shoes half-soled.

But it remains for Mom to discover the baby-sitters. She has to get to know someone who knows someone who has a 15-year-old sister.

You can imagine our stunned surprise though when a 15-year-old popped in on the family to announce her baby-sitting services. She was all poise and charm, spouting nursery rhymes at the children, and inquiring as to our tastes in records.

When I told her I really couldn't put myself on record as to whether Johnny Mathis[3] or Frankie Avalon[4] was the most, she gave me a mildly disturbed look. Five minutes later, when she discovered we had nothing but an old-fashioned record player with only one speaker, she left.

Now, we're looking for baby-sitters who are more of the peanut butter fudge type and not so much "stereo type." Everyone in the bridge circuit says it's next to impossible to get a really good baby-sitter without a "mean teen record collection." They even admit their children are almost getting to like the lyrics about a girl with a strawberry curls on the way to her first drag race.

Of course, parents with tiny babies don't have quite the same difficulty. The smaller the baby the older the baby-sitter must be so they look for some nice middle-aged lady who still remembers how to make formula. Trouble is, the only middle-aged lady on our block does the meanest cha-cha in town and I'm afraid, would be severely insulted if a baby-sitting job were offered her.

The older the children get, the younger the baby-sitters get. If possible cultivate many friends at women's clubs with growing girls who are out to win all the badges in the Girl Scout manual.

That year, when a Girl Scout takes over, is sheer bliss. She bathes, feeds and disciplines the children with such fire of devotion that it leaves one stunned.

Before you come out of this numbed state, however, she gets all her badges, grows up another year and discovers a very disconcerting thing.

She finds that by tying her hair back in a pony tail and keeping her glasses in her pocketbook she looks just like Tuesday Weld[5]. (If you don't know who Tuesday is, you haven't had a young baby-sitter in years!) What's more, the boys notice it, too.

Where before she was ready to sacrifice her all so you might get to the dance an hour early, she is now ready to sacrifice your all so she might have a date with the junior quarterback.

She will borrow your hair curlers, your eye shadow and your Christmas cologne and then return it in time to tell you she can't baby-sit because the junior quarterback winked at her in the hall today and he just might call tonight!

It is now time, friends, to look for the 16-year-old and the 17-year-old bookworms.

It is unnerving at first, but you get used to it.

She gives you a half-disdainful, half-Bette Davis[6] look because you will be cavorting around at a P-TA budget meeting while she studies her theorems and theories.

The children are very tolerant. They let her quote Shakespeare while they fill their water pistols, and as long as she leaves on the TV, they're happy.

I just refused to buckle under like the next-door neighbor who always went out and bought a copy of the *New Yorker* to put on the coffee table every time her baby-sitter was coming. We just wiped the dust off the World Atlas and put the Mickey Spillane[7] paperbacks underneath the towels in the upstairs linen closet.

It was probably good for the children. They always talked about Newton and the law of gravity at breakfast the next morning instead of reading the cereal boxes out loud to me.

But this fall, I was due for a shock. Blithely calling three of the "old reliables" I discovered they're all off to the university to study life and the world. It figured.

But this morning I saw the nicest girl go down the street with a little Scout beret perched on her curls. She was just starting to help the middle-aged cha-cha champion across the street when I stopped her.

Then I discovered the most delightful thing! The dear girl has four sisters, all younger. Talk about lifetime insurance!

I must hurry now and cook up a batch of peanut butter fudge. Things are looking up!

Examples Show Most Husbands Are Mysterious

March 5, 1961

Husbands are the most mysterious creatures.

Take phone calls for instance. When a woman hangs up the receiver she makes a nice, sensible statement: "Marge wants us for bridge and dinner next Thursday." When a man hangs up the receiver he lights a cigarette and opens the newspaper.

The conversation on the telephone might have sounded to his wife like this: Yeah? Three thousand you say? But in Jamaica? Well, if you say so. The right front wheel? Mmnn, I thought maybe from the sound it was the carburetor. Yep, she's a good-looker all right."

By this time his wife isn't sure if he's talking about his good looking secretary going to Jamaica or their car going to the repair shop.

But husbands, unfortunately, believe in the Chinese torture method. They let us ask. "Somebody important?"

"No, just Al Wilkens."

"Oh. Al at the gas station."

"No the Al with the green Jaguar."

Now she doesn't know anyone with a sports car, green or red. So where did he meet Al?

If you think the telephone mysteries are bad, wait until he gets to the library.

She takes his arm and shows him the new best seller and the gardening book she's chosen. He shifts his book to the other arm.

"New mystery?" she asks sweetly.

"Nope. Tired of mysteries." "What then, what is it?"

"It's a study on mining methods used in South America. Al told me about it. Very up-to-date on emeralds." Al again!

The following week he takes home a long, gray treatise on sheep grazing habits in Tibet. The next week it's the cultural patterns of a remote Indian tribe in the Arctic.

If she wasn't sure he was top man in the bowling league right now, she could swear he was getting the wanderlust! And at his age!

Husbands are always bringing home mysterious packages. When a wife brings home a package she immediately tears off the paper and proclaims to the world, "Lamb chops on sale for two days only!"

When a man brings a package home he lays it on the hall table and continues to ignore it all through dinner, tucking in the children, and late coffee.

"Some new golf balls darling?" she asks.

"Mummmn? No, no, much too early for golf."

About this time she is sure Al is a foreign agent and has maneuvered her husband into some shady scheme, and in that package is some lethal weapon or secret ink, something like that!

"Can you be ready by 8?" he mumbles.

"Ready for what?"

"Al is picking us up."

She hasn't time to take a tranquilizer but she zips into a dress worthy of a green sports car and gives her husband the closest scrutiny he's had since army days.

Al looks as if his suit was hand woven in Hong Kong, but he's a man and he's mysterious.

"My, Mr. Wilkens, what a simply gorgeous fabric. Did your wife select it for you?" (A woman would come right out with it: "Do you really like it? It was reduced for a song and the fabric is really only cotton but it feels like silk.")

But Mr. Wilkens only smiles enigmatically and you get the feeling he has a tailor in some select little shop who does nothing but wait for Mr. Wilkens to call. You know how men are!

"Did you bring the package?" he asks your husband.

"Yep, and she's a beauty!"

Well!

At this time any woman has a right to know what is going on. So he tells her!

"Didn't I tell you? Al's our new scoutmaster and he's going to show slides his uncle took on a world tour so we can show them to the kids tonight. I picked up the new projector for him on my lunch hour."

As I said, husbands are really quite easy to understand—once you get to know them.

Itinerary Retraced by Mail in Hunt for Camp Ring

July 23, 1961

Dear "Stay Awhile" Motel:

We seem to be missing a pair of red sneakers after spending a weekend at one of your units this month. The manager—I think it was Mr. Kettle or Mr. Skettle—will be certain to remember us since it was our dog who chewed up the Venetian blind.

We would appreciate receiving the red sneakers. Please just disregard the turtle marked "Mamie" in red nail polish. If you should by chance run across a letter postmarked Cleveland or a blue and white striped pair of shorts you could send them along.

And if it wouldn't be too much trouble, the next time your people drain the pool would they keep an eye open for a gold signet ring with Smokey the Bear's picture on it?

Dear Cottage Blue-Skies:

Thank you for your considerate letter. My husband's ankle is healing nicely and the doctor says by early fall he will be spry as an eel. I suppose the rain just couldn't be helped and your organized games after the third day were quite welcome. It certainly was not your fault he could no longer vault the ping-pong table.

I believe if you check you will find the cord to an electric razor in the third floor bathroom. Would you just send it along with the tennis racquets next time you go into town.

Oh yes, when you drain the pool next time would you keep an eye open for a Smokey the Bear gold signet ring?

As for our reservation next year, I believe we will think things over and let you know sometime later.

Dear Commissioner, New Jersey Turnpike:

Enclosed please find coins to cover our recent trip on your highway. Through an oversight we neglected to pay the proper amount. Our baby threw her bottle at the toll-collector and in the ensuing confusion the subject of fares was completely overlooked.

Dear Handy Little Diner:

I am enclosing two teaspoons with your diner's name on the handles. We stopped for breakfast one morning last week and by some odd coincidence these spoons turned up later in the children's tote bag. I suppose not every family brings along their own cereal and perhaps things got mixed up that way.

Dear Ethel:

How exciting to hear you're heading east again. My but it must be nice to see all the new shows in New York and do it up big. We certainly would be happy to have you use our place for headquarters while you look up the old gang, but things are rather uncertain around here and perhaps conditions would not be just what you expect.

I know how Bob loves those chicken dinners but I just have not found much time this month with getting the children ready for camp and taking care of George.

Poor dear. He was being his usual madcap athletic self and broke his ankle.

We haven't seen the Murdocks since your trip last year. I understand she filed a counter-suit and it's still going through the courts.

Do drop us a card from the big city and let us know how you are.

Dear Camp Laughing-Waters:

The children will be arriving on the Saturday a.m. train as per usual. Their trunks will arrive by Monday with or without nametags. I am very sorry but I simply did not have time to buy them butterfly nets or telescopes. As for the riding breeches it appears to me one can fall off a horse just as well in chinos, is it not so? (I hope you have done away with "Fireball" as Terry's right arm never has knit together as well as we would like.)

The camp rings are a lovely idea but right now I shall have to veto the suggestion. While the thought is touching I am afraid I am still emotionally involved with finding their Smokey the Bear gold signet rings. Don't you think $7.95 a bit out of line considering they are only 6-year-olds?

With much remorse we shall have to forego plans for this year's parent weekend. George is recovering from a broken ankle but we will be thinking of you all playing musical chairs in the big lodge. Have they fixed the chimney yet, or does it still get smoky in the night air?

It's all in a Midsummer's Nightmare!

Dear Teachers: It's up to You From Here on in

September 3, 1961

Forgive my yodeling.

But don't all mother yodel these last few days before school opens?

Find empty cigar boxes and lengthen hems. Throw away tennis shoes and jump for joy!

Dear teachers, may you return to the schoolrooms refreshed and ready.

Because we're beat!

I can pick up no more popsicle sticks.

Not one more blade of crab grass can I fight.

Not one more picnic basket can I pack. Deliver me safely from hard-boiled eggs and chocolate cupcakes!

The time is here when I can no longer face another inner tube patch or a wading pool to be blown to enormous size. I have lost my zest for flying kites and pitching ball. The bathing suits are almost all a-tattered.

This week I dropped a goldfish on the floor and ironed a Japanese beetle quite unintentionally. It's all part of the end-of-the-summer collapse.

Their shirts and skirts are starched. New shoes squeak and shine. The budget is really shot!

Oh, the experiences they have to share with you! How are you at receiving a one-hour monologue devoted to zoos and parks, cows that moo and the perils of becoming a 7-year-old skin-diver?

I send them off to you tanned and healthy, operating steadily on the premise that energy creates more energy.

Too bad their own mother no longer operates on that simple premise. She gets kinks in her back when she has to crawl on her hands and knees under the neighbor's shrubs to hunt for roller skates. She moans when she has to unpack picnic baskets while everyone else collapses in front of the TV set.

She is a dear old Mom, but if they ask her once more for another cupcake she is going to ruin her vocal cords for life.

She sends the children back to you, dear teacher, with horizons broadened. Just as you suggested. They've been exposed to the whimsy of Milne, saturated in Mickey Mouse.

Don't be too shocked if they sing you their own robust rendition of a Princeton drinking song.

They've adventured into far lands, (the summer playground) and come home to speak of bullfights in Spain and hidden treasure in the Mediterranean.

They are experts now on bees, watermelons, the dead man's float and how to open a locked screen door from the outside. Too bad they haven't learned how to shut same door without slamming it.

Some have learned to whistle. Some lost a few teeth, by way of Mother Nature or the bratty kid down the block.

A few have fallen in love with the ice cream vendor, more with Mickey Mantle[8]. Almost all have become experts in tree climbing and refrigerator-raiding.

They have listened to the north wind and tasted the salt of the sea. They have learned to ride bicycles with no hands. But of this you can be sure.

Now they awake like silly little sparrows with the dawn. Come the first morning of school, they shall all be victims of such sleeping sickness as this world has ever seen!

Breakfast is now consumed in the length of time it takes to hop into a bathing suit and skin into a pair of tennis shoes. We now go into that period of eating toast while running for the school bus or "What do you mean, you left your math book on the kitchen table!"

As for me, I just plan to take a nice solitary bath without three plastic sail boats and a few empty plastic soap bottles.

Then I'll just slam the screen door a few times now and then so I don't get homesick!

Lecturer Makes Mother Realize She Has Savages

September 24, 1961

About once a year our P-TA engages a traveling lecturer who bedazzles us all with her plea to expose our children to culture.

I usually come home so keyed up and enthused I want to yank the sleeping children out of their warm beds to listen to Beethoven's Fifth.

This is nothing so exciting as you might think, because I happen to be the kind of person who gets enthused about any idea that might help to distinguish this household from Madison Square Garden.

Seldom do I cherish the thought, however, that we will all form a string quartet and rise an hour earlier each morning to practice together. The only thing that would get this family up an hour early would be chocolate pie for breakfast. And that isn't culture!

I remember reading in a freshman psychology course that once a child has been read to aloud from the classics he retains much of what he has heard far beyond infancy. The same is supposed to be true for playing classical music.

The book neglected to mention that most parents of young infants are too impoverished from buying vitamins and baby food to invest in a music library.

At a very tender age our children began to adore one of those amateur radio shows where everyone sings just one half note off-key.

Occasionally they even rejected Brahms's time-honored lullaby in favor of a jingle extolling the virtues of canned soup!

Greek mythology left them disinterested but polite. They simply wandered off to the kitchen and built houses out of pie tins until we got around to the really good stories like "The Little Engine That Could."

Gradually exposing them to culture got filed away with other "grand ideas" while we went on with the booster shots, reading readiness tests, nail biting, pie-baking and other activities connected with the care and feeding of small ones.

Then the visiting lecturer comes to town, and I know that when I get home I will discover I have a house full of little savages.

Dear things, eating their breakfast and troubling their fragile little minds over cereal box tops and Captain Kangaroo.[9] Here I was about to open the world of Picasso and Rembrandt, Mozart and Chopin. "Mom, Mom, would you please stop day-dreaming and open this oatmeal box!"

We began with the Smithsonian Institution. Hubby and I became so absorbed in the marvelous exhibits we almost lost track of the youngsters who were having a perfectly lovely time showing their yoyos to a yawning guard.

We also amassed the following vital information: There are no chewing gum machines in the building but there is a grand lounge in the Indian exhibits where tired 2-year-olds can doze. It is also quite easy to get lost upon leaving Washington, despite what they say. When this happens it has a very damaging effect upon husband to mention that your good suede gloves are back in the lounge of the Indian exhibit.

Next on the culture schedule seems to be a symphony. At first the kids were a bit miffed when they found out they might even have to miss the latest horror movie playing at the neighborhood theater. The oldest one found it even more difficult to understand why he could not possibly learn to play the organ and the bass drum at once because they were his favorite instruments.

While almost all children learn one or two childhood songs in another language they consider it completely mad to try to ask for something in a foreign language when they know English so well.

We still have the Museum of Modern Art saved up for a rainy fall afternoon. We just might make contact here because our 3-year-old seems to dig Picasso, but I haven't delved into her interest too far, because I am afraid she thinks there is some connection between this revered gentleman and pizza pie, which is her favorite food.

I hope the next visiting lecturer picks a nice safe subject like the birdcalls of South American jungle birds.

'Mommy, Can't I Be Everybody?'

October 29, 1961

If Halloween doesn't soon get here I am going to collapse in front of the nearest counter full of masks.

I am so familiar with the Halloween stock of the nearest three stores that I am thinking of applying for a job as Halloween inventory clerk.

Our children have the "I-don't-know" jitters. This affliction arrives a week before the great tricks or treat celebration and does not abate until the very night itself.

"How would you like to be a nice spooky skeleton?" I chirp, trying to make it sound as exciting as brownies for breakfast.

"I don't know."

"Well then," I grin, grinding my potato masher into the green beans, "how about Snow White?"

"I don't know."

But we get to the store along with 50 other mothers and assorted children. Then they know. They want to be a spooky skeleton and Snow White, Casper the ghost, an old-fashioned lady, Little Red Riding Hood, Batman and a few other famous people. All at once.

It doesn't matter that we have a gray phantom and a clown costume at home from last year. This year has to be fantastic, the best Halloween ever!

A day before Halloween one of the girls comes home in tears because someone in her class is going to be a bride and wear real diamonds. Seems that this girl's mother made her costume and she is even going to be allowed to wear real pink lipstick.

If it isn't spooks, it's crises!

I consider it a genuine tribute to children's unconscious good sense that no one has yet considered going as Eliot Ness[10]!

In my short career with Halloweenitis, Scouts and kindergarten pageants, I've made an Indian costume and a shepherd boy's tunic, but a skindiver's suit? Who ya kidding?

I would love to go to our neighborhood party as Mata Hari[11] with a bejeweled cigarette holder but some quiet voice is telling me I'd better settle for something easy like Mrs. Flintstone[12] in original burlap.

The male member of this household is also one of the last-minute "I-don't-knows." Up until fifteen minutes before the party he doesn't really know if he'll go. Then suddenly he wonders if I couldn't just throw together a costume, say Napoleon Bonaparte or Julius Caesar.

Know what I'm going to do? I'm going to throw this sewing box in the drawer and sit down and pick out some nice trick or treat candy. No one will argue about that!

When the fall air has a special fragrance ... and when the firethorn bush breaks into color ... when bedtime prayers are serious but not stern ... and the day has been full and gay ... my heart is as wide as the sky.

Children's Needs Give Fine Arts an Added Twist

December 3, 1961

I'm certainly not the first nor shall I be the last to discover it.

Each day now I keep thinking of all those courses in medieval literature I was taking when I should have been learning how to bake brownies for first grade dinners.

Those reams and reams of college papers we wrote on merrie England and Mr. Shakespeare, and never once did I learn how to make angel wings out of clothes hangers!

Somehow I find my education lacking in the wee a.m. when all the household is sleeping and I am fringing an old pair of slacks for the November pageant or the Columbus Day program.

Funny that the children never volunteer for something easy like the chorus (white shirts) or the stagehands. They have to get the Marco Polo and Magellan parts.

All my gold dangling earrings are on pirates sailing their cardboard ships around the school auditorium.

My oatmeal is resting in ice cube trays, cheese trays and everything else available while I wrap yards and yards of silver foil around cardboard crowns.

The other oatmeal boxes are painted with Indian symbols and will make the tom-tom chorus.

The children take such a casual approach to their life with the fine arts. About five minutes before bedtime one of them will announce that the rehearsal for the flower festival is tomorrow and they are each supposed to bring five yards of red crepe paper.

I have interrupted the closing of the corner store so many times to buy a few yards of crepe paper or another box of silver foil that I'm sure they all are saying by now, "Oh no, not her again!"

This I can take.

It's the early morning shocks that tend to unnerve me. I am trying to explain exclamatory sentences to our fourth grader and tie together a completely disintegrated pair of shoelaces for the baby. Cocoa is boiling merrily over the side of the pan and our 4-year-old is making toast by the dozens.

"Oh, Mom! We're supposed to bring some old pieces of sheets and an army hat. I'm in the foreign legion in the Thursday afternoon assembly!"

Or they present me with a mimeographed poem five stanzas long. "Will you teach me this in a hurry? You know how I hate poems!"

The poster paint has washed off the "Indian" faces and their fringes have fringed themselves to death. Columbus set sail in glory and pilgrims marched from the house in starched white caps and foil buckles. (If anyone finds a spare buckle it belongs to my good black suede pumps and I'd like to wear them to the New Year's Eve dance!)

And just around the next corner comes Christmas.

Now that I've got the knack of twisting wire coat hangers into angel's wings it's for certain they won't be angels again. There's a wilted shepherd boy tunic in the attic and an old yarn beard for good King Wencelas. But I would be almost willing to bet they'll be reindeer and I'll be making antlers out of coat hangers in another week.

This complete absorption in the arts just comes right home with them. Last night for dinner we had as our guests Sleeping Beauty, Papa Bear and Beauty and the Beast. They were a pretty good bunch though. It turned out they all love baked beans and hot dogs despite their dignified place in the theater!

Can you blame me that I am more than suspicious when one of the teachers approaches me with 25 yards of green felt and chintz. "You do have a sewing machine, don't you, my dear?"

My dear Helen Hayes[13], wherever you are, don't blame me, but my heart just ain't in it anymore!

Welcome the month of December so glorious it can't be contained in a mere calendar … the hush and expectancy of the first Advent candle … bright gift catalogs … the ageless music … the hint of sugar and cinnamon baking is just beginning … and as it is every year the days are scarcely long enough to contain the work, the errands, the lists and oh, yes, the warm inner comfort of the holiday season.

PART II
How to Handle 'It'
Inquiry Favorite of
Most Parents

1962–1967

Mother's Work Is Never Done, But It's Surely a Labor of Love

May 13, 1962

Our 4-year-old daughter recently asked me with great emotion, "Mommy, when I am a mother, will I really be able to blow bubbles?"

She has trouble with bubble gum and in her mind achieving motherhood would somehow solve this messy problem.

It was one of her sweetest compliments, and I polished it up for Mother's Day.

When she was but 3 and was having similar complications regarding roller skating, she signed in envy, "Golly, just think, Mothers can roller skate!"

A mother rarely equals this pinnacle of perfection again. When they are 3 they think she is a storehouse of valuable knowledge. She can roller skate. She can draw rabbits. She can blow up balloons.

When they are thirteen they are more likely to lament, "Mother, you aren't going to the store with your hair looking like that?"

Ten years ago it was fashionable and correct to take a marriage course at college, to read Dr. Spock[14] and to learn how to set up a budget.

You learned where to spend your honeymoon and how much to spend for your linens.

You learned how to be a good hostess and how to make friends with your butcher.

You learned how to toss off words like "super-ego" and "neuroses" in casual conversation.

But no one ever really told you what it's like to be a mother.

All your married friends gave you mysterious looks and wailed about their children saying, "You'll understand once you're a mother!"

And you thought the understanding would come in a small light-weight package along with the bill from the obstetrician and the bassinet delivered for baby.

Once in a while you thought you almost caught hold of understanding by the tail during one of the pre-dawn sessions with colic, then tummy aches, then heart aches.

You never knew it meant playing checkers on rainy days until you could scream.

Did you dream it meant escorting thirty wiry energetic boys on a mountain hike or learning to play football?

Did you stop counting the furniture you're painted or the knees you've patched? Or the budgets you've cried over?

Do you know it is possible to save twenty minutes out of every day just by learning how to tie shoes so tightly they can't ever come untied?

A mother is well on her way to learning when she can listen to three different conversations at once and at the same time plan the evening's dinner.

When they are 3 they sigh in delight, "Oh boy, spaghetti again!"

When they are 13, they are apt to wail, "Don't you know how to make anything besides this stuff?"

A mother has to be able to remember that the 3-year-old and 13-year-old are still the same child. She may have to swallow horror at green eye shadow and bouffant hair-dos. She will have to think back to the days of mud pies in the bathtub when a simple bath cured the day's troubles.

A mother has to like animals. This includes snakes and toads. In the desk. In the kitchen sink.

She will have to develop a taste for all the various medicines throughout life that she will taste and then proclaim. "It's good! Now you take it."

She will develop a knack of calling her doctor at 2 a.m. and convincing him that she is not some fluttering mother worried over three million spots on her children's bare tummies.

She will learn to bake cupcakes, thousands of them. She will become an expert on removing crayon marks form walls and chewing gum form ponytails.

In her time she will share enthusiasm for Mickey Mantle, the adoration of Rock Hudson[15], the excitement of romance.

Whey they are 3 she will quiet their tears with lollipops and hugs.

When they are 13 she will comfort the tears with the loan of sheer nylons or the promise of a real party with boys!

She will learn the art of applying makeup in the car because the bathroom is never empty.

She will learn when to stop kissing her son or hugging him in public. She will learn even to take time to coach plays, sell tickets, paint furniture and share a never-ending stream of enthusiasms with equal tact.

After the very first Mother's Day in her distinguished, we hope, "career," she will stop caring terribly about the boxes of flowers or candy that arrive in gleaming packages.

But she will treasure the sudden unasked-for hugs and impulsive kisses.

And she will cherish the wisdom that comes shining through their youthful faces year by year.

And she will zealously guard the vein of joy and its crop of laughter that lightens the tragic moments that accompany every day of growing up.

I suppose, finally, she will become an excellent checker player on rainy days!

Happy Summer Days Near End, Shop Windows Remind Cruelly

August 19, 1962

Can it be the middle of August already with the hint of September in the shop windows so full of wonderful dark plaids and plastic paste pots, school bags and lunch boxes?

Evening drops upon us more suddenly. With the instinct of ages, the children are playing tag football and roller-skating through the swift twilight.

There is something marvelous about the beach at the end of summer, almost as entrancing as playing hooky. You know that schedules and school buses are just around the corner, but the hot summer sun and monotonous surf lull you back into a summer mood with soothing sameness.

College girls are wearing tiny madras headscarves and bulky sweaters. Gone are the hot pinks and vibrant oranges of spring, and back are the mellow tans and smart blacks. Tiki charms are all the rage and the twist is going sophisticated.

Boardwalk haunts bounce to Dixieland, and a bespectacled short order cook browses through Proust. "Authentic" colonial reproductions are becoming the rage in everything from hand-dipped candles to old-fashioned lavender sachets.

There is time for musings and reflections, perhaps for resolutions and regulations. Time to shift gears and gather momentum for the fall rush. Time to see and to hear and to feel the steady miraculous growth of children in all directions. Time to talk of ships and sails and faraway places.

With so few wildernesses left to conquer more families are answering the lure of the sea or the open road and investing all their spare time and money in beautiful little ships or camping wagons.

Sea gulls swoop over the marinas at morning and the waves make tiny slip-slaps against the piers. There is that tiny suspicion that life in the real is just around the next bend of marsh grass in the bay.

We resolve to build a model clipper ship for the mantel, and when winter surrounds us we will look at the ship and smile.

Where did that terrible axiom come from, the one that says, "It's a nice place to visit but I'd hate to live there"?

Stroll through a strange town Sunday morning and savor its newness.

Fifth Avenue on an early Sunday morning is a vast empty cavern full of sleepy sounds and the undefined mystic attraction of the big city.

Washington on an early Sunday morning is bustling with tourists: A Midwestern camping family, Lebanese students, beautiful Indian women in traditional dress.

Sunday mornings in new places make one feel like sipping orange juice from champagne goblets in the surf—or eating pastrami sandwiches in Central Park. (The most wonderful breakfast I've ever had was apple pie and vanilla ice cream.)

Summer is the time to vary your reading menu as well. Spice the bestseller list with a few old favorites and a few "thinking" books and your brain will reel with new ideas. Philosophy discussions and the sprouting of enthusiasm need not be packed away with the college books and pennants.

Our small 1-year-old friend has a disparaging view of the demands of civilization. Twice in one morning she discarded her new shoes, once in the trash can and once in a bucket of sudsy water.

How to Handle 'It' Inquiry Favorite of Most Parents

1962

Just because a person has an egg for breakfast he does not go out and write a pamphlet on French omelets.

Neither does the fellow who has completed his first jet plane trip go home to deliver a series of lecturers on aerodynamics.

But there is something special about the problems of family life.

It releases a flow of advice that never dwindles from that day forth. Mention "gas turbine" at a neighborhood social and you get no reaction. Mention "three-month-old colic" and you have 14 avid and interested participants in giving free advice.

The one thing no red-blooded American parent can resist asking another parent is the "How do you handle it?" question.

This applies mostly to discipline problems such as the child's biting the dog, throwing his wet oatmeal at the neighbors' kids and other every day "crises."

There is something so soothing about a backyard barbecue that after the second or third hot dog you really let down your hair and ask your neighbor of three houses away what he does when his kid crayons his name in the hallway.

This gives him a good chance to have a chuckle or two over your kids' latest mad escapade. Then he can give you his ideas on discipline. These are a mixture of Dr. Spock, common sense and his Irish temper!

I, myself, carefully read both Dr. Spock and Dr. Gessell[16] on the problem of discipline among pre-schoolers. But when I trip over the footstool my natural inclination is to kick the offending footstool; and you can easily see what happened when the kids left their plastic blocks on the stairway and they knocked me down the steps three at a time. Of course I didn't really kick the kids because that isn't "good sport." After 14 verses of an old Cherokee hunting song I would hop up and down the room without screaming, but there is something about the sight of those big bags of plastic blocks in toy stores that starts my adrenalin juices bubbling even to this day.

Early discipline problems are largely physical. ("No, we never bite the postman." "No, we don't throw our spoon at the nice waitress." "No, we mustn't grab hats in the elevator or we can't take the nice ride!")

Next come legal complications of ownership. ("But darling the giraffe belongs in the zoo." "But lovey, where did you find the lovely big red azalea bush?" "But sweetie, the wagon is not yours and you must give it back to Charlie." "No, No, don't shove it down the hill at poor Charlie.")

Having graduated with honors in potty training and high chair gymnastics the youngster goes on to bigger things and the parent goes on a pack-and-a-half of cigarettes a day.

Back to the physical problems.

("No, dear, an umbrella will not work the same as a parachute no matter what Charlie says." "What do you mean you've locked the plumber in the basement?" "Untie your father this instant, boys!"

As school begins we progress into the world of logic, having one's seat changed because of talking, and aspirin by the one hundred-fold. (Two a day with homework sessions, four on report card and exam days.)

"I still don't understand. If you were copying the homework how could you have time to catch the rotten apple that Charlie threw across the room?"

"I can't think of another five words let alone fifty on why you should not pinch girls in study hall!"

By the time you have congratulated yourself on licking the problem of spilled oatmeal and hurled spoons, the youngster has all of a sudden turned into a six-footer whose greatest problem in life is keeping his stomach filled constantly.

Much too rapidly after that his problems fill the romantic vein—whom should he marry, how can he tell when it's love and when can they get married?

After this you can come into your finer glory because before too many years fly by you will be a grandparent and start catching the spoons your grandchildren hurl at you!

Two Field Trips in Week
Deflate Mother

1963

The "time of the field trip" is upon us.

Sounds almost poetic, doesn't it, like the season of seven moons or the valley of hidden happiness?

Field trips are designed to expose children of school age to the arts, culture, history and Mother Nature.

The first trip took us to an art museum, where a 5-year-old baritone explained a Picasso etching to me and where a piece of modern art featuring a crumpled orange juice can was selling for $750.

The second field trip took forty wildly enthusiastic kindergarten youngsters and fifteen brave mothers to the zoo, where the animals viewed us in varying degreed of scorn, astonishment and dismay.

An authentic Egyptian mummy was star attraction at the art museum. The children were blasé with respect to modern art, bored silly with 18th century landscapes and mostly interested in the primitive sculptures of oceanic tribes.

Properly mellowed by an afternoon's saturation of the greats in the artistic world, we inquisitively asked one sturdy 5-year-old: "What do you remember best, Stuart?" (How his mind labored over the machinery of culture! Would it be the Degas or the Egyptian stone carving?)

Stuart smiled gently. "Well, mostly I remember the floors. They were so slippery and shiny, sort of like bowling alleys!"

Stuart was definitely impressed at the zoo by the antics of the sea lions cavorting in their spacious tank.

In a burst of enthusiasm the excited child tossed in his lunch bag, which the sea lion viewed disinterestedly.

Accepting the commiseration of his comrades, Stuart's only comment was: "S'alright. It was bologna sandwiches anyway, and I hate bologna!"

On the zoo excursion each child had a lunch bag and a bag with bits of stale bread and peanuts to feed the animals. I couldn't help but notice several elegant tigers dining later that same morning on peanut butter crackers and chocolate brownies.

Three black bear sisters named affectionately, "Faith, Hope and Charity," fought vehemently over the possession of a stale piece of bread.

Pulling out a fresh pair of shoes and a vacuum of hot coffee, a mother sympathized, "You should have been here the year the monkeys grabbed all the balloons and ran. That was some year!"

I tried to look experienced and cracked another peanut shell. Absently mindedly, I ate the shell and handed the peanut to the nearest child.

Later that evening hubby suggested we go downstairs and see what friend hamster was doing. "I can't watch anything more in a cage," I screamed. He was startled. "Well, if that's the way you feel about it all right. But I thought you didn't want him running around loose upstairs.

I think that is where I began to cry. Next week I am going on another field trip, this one to a hat shop, then to a beauty salon and then to a good sad movie!

Hideaway Room Always Desired, But Never Required

May 26, 1963

A newly married couple is likely to start housekeeping with a glittering assortment of 37 sterling silver candy dishes, an electric blanket and a card table.

Their first worry is: "How are we going to fill up all this space?" (Two rooms and a bath.)

Ten years and several children later, when all the candy dishes have been packed away or exchanged for tea towels, this couple will be sighing: "If only we had another room" (For the bunk beds and bassinette, the tricycles and trunks, kitties and kites.)

The family has innocently moved into a three-room apartment, then a four-bedroom home, then a five-bedroom home, all the while praying the house will somehow absorb their possessions which are bubbling out of the house like rice out of a too-small kettle.

Somehow "One more room" seems like the answer to all their problems. The objects continue to swell to fill the expanding quarters.

The once pristine beauty of a guest bedroom with its four-poster is now submerged in tennis racquets, winter coats, overgrown high chairs, skis and books.

A car is parked in the driveway because the garage is at the moment overflowing with lawn furniture, snow shovels, abandoned hobbies and turtle boarding there in a box temporarily.

Twice a year, at spring cleaning and fall cleaning time, mother tries to thin out the clutter.

Children form early, passionate attachments to objects. "You're not going to throw out that doll with no head? Someday I might find a doll with no body!" they say.

Husbands are tireless protectors of old raincoats they never wear, glass jars full of rusty nails they never intend to use, college algebra notebooks, broken grass rakes and a million other things.

Now take that artful arrangement of gold candlesticks and white pottery base on the mantel. It took you two days to get that group attractively spaced to ease the eye.

Take a good look. It will probably be the last time you see it so esthetically pleasing.

Tomorrow, lounging beside the candlesticks will be an apple core and an arithmetic book.

Next day added to the treasure pole will be a tennis sock with a hole in the tow and a few dead dandelions.

The artful arrangement of asters you labored so lovingly over for the dining room table will harbor a stick of chewing gum and a tennis ball before the week is finished!

Considering this state of affairs, it is no wonder a woman looks back in astonishment at that short innocent year with the 37 candy dishes and two rooms and bath.

Of course she hopes to save for herself an island of serenity in this house of burgeoning possessions: a dressing table, a bureau top, perhaps her own desk.

The bureau top turns into a haven for heelless socks needing attention.

The dressing table top becomes a catchall for husband's shoe shining equipment and her son's model airplane parts. The desktop is a shrieking potpourri of vegetable, animal and mineral running the gamut from sick turtles to over-ripe bananas!

Now that the days of the sand box are upon us, no one dares to tread the bedroom floors in bare feet. A sneakerful in every drawer in every place in every way is our cheerful pre-schooler's unassuming aim in life!

(An educated palate is her latest acquisition as she praised me for my "college cheese.")

If we only had one more room we would have a place for all those records we no longer play, the books we've read again and again and the thirteen kids who come in to play on rainy days!

If we only had one more room we could set up the painting easel, wash and block the sweaters, have the neighbors in for tea!

If we only had one more room we could put in a ping-pong table, a card table, a sewing machine and lathe, some teen-agers and poodle dog needing baths!

If we only had one more room I could lock myself inside and look at all that beautiful empty space for just one hour!

Who, for heaven's sake, put that pair of size thirteen fishing boots on my beautiful mantel?

Husband's Lack of Memory Miffs Mate

August 18, 1963

Isn't it amazing the way a man can casually glance one day at a sagging door frame and three weeks later stroll into a hardware store, buying the correct hinges down to the last eighth of an inch?

Here is a man who can't remember if he left his raincoat in Detroit or Singapore. Here is a man who can't recall if he tried the sweet potato casserole so he takes three helpings to be sure.

Husbands have that maddening characteristic of saying the most obtuse thing in the world right at the moment when one needs something very definite.

Per example: You come downstairs, dressed and groomed to the teeth after trying on three different necklaces with your best sheath.

"What do you think, darling," you purr in your best Suzy Parker[17] voice.

"I think our lawn mover needs sharpening from the way that lawn looks," he murmurs.

The dress, the necklace, me," you hiss through clenched teeth.

"Fine, you look just fine," he admits, and you wonder why that should bother you until fifteen minutes later you happen to think that is the same expression he uses when he inspects the clean-up job the youngsters did in the basement.

The worst thing in the world is to be invited to a party arranged by husbands. If a woman calls, you can be sure within five minutes whether to wear pink crepe or blue denim. When hubby comes home to announce, "We're invited to the Carlsons Saturday at one," you never can be sure if it is a swimming party or a formal dinner.

"Could be a swimming party at that," admits the perplexed head of house, "Henry did put in a pool couple of years back." Then several days later while you are wondering how to approach him on the subject of $20 for a bathing suit, he beams: "That thing Saturday—it's a brunch in honor of some cousins from Cleveland." Great, just great, and what are cousins from Cleveland wearing this season?

Then there is this business of telephone messages. About thirty seconds before I am ready to drop off to sleep hubby announces sleepily, "Oh yeah, a Mrs. Spleen or Miss Green or something called while you were putting the kids to bed."

"She did, she really did?" I shriek. "Did she say anything about getting Janie into Brownies? We've been on a waiting list for months!"

"Nuh," he yawns, "nuh, I think it was something about an antique show." She'll call back. Nice voice." Yawn.

Days later, it was a Miss Green wanting to know if I would like to buy five pounds of peanut brittle!

This is the darling who can remember Joe DiMaggio's[18] batting average for every year he played. This is the guy who can recall percentages, percentiles, dividends, premiums and postal zone numbers, not to mention dog tag numbers and golf scores from ten years ago.

Please, please whatever you do, don't ask him how many weeks since he's had a haircut.

Ask a man what he's had for lunch, and he's likely to say: "Beef, I think."

What he was treated to was beef stroganoff or maybe it was a simple hamburger. You'll never really know for sure. Men are pretty vague about food and dates. Unless, of course, it happens to pertain to their own refrigerators.

In which case, I'll have a sandwich from that meatloaf leftover last night and a bowl of salad and give me a couple of those cookies you made Saturday! He's a walking inventory.

Now when he invites "a couple of" friends in for Saturday supper I prepare for twenty, and then I don't look too surprised when 23 show up. Sent for a pound of butter he is apt to bring home a pound of salami. Asked to mail a letter he is apt to drop his hat off at the cleaners.

Someday I suppose some dear husband will phone his wife and ask, "Where are you, sweetie? The house is empty." "What do you mean I didn't tell you we were moving yesterday?"

It can't be or won't ever be that bad. But I suppose that is why it is so hard to keep that dazzle out of my eyes when the head of the house walks in with a big bouquet of red roses.

"Darling, you remembered. You really did!" (It's Lincoln's birthday but I haven't the heart to tell him.)

Women Weary of 'Women' Books

November 10, 1963

Each time we pass the village bookshop we see another spanking new book on the shelf extolling women, admonishing women, explaining women, interpreting the role of women.

It's appalling.

Now that so many have explored the infinite varieties of womanly foibles in the world can't we have some noble written works of art on how to discourage your husband from starting more than six do-it-yourself projects at once?

Or something practical such as what to give the mailman and the milkman on holidays?

Or how to get along with the boss' wife and how to be a den mother two years running without losing one's sensibilities?

We grow weary of hearing again and again how downtrodden we women are, how limited are our horizons for intellectual capacities, how limited our scope of the world.

After one short evening of discussing the world crisis with a sixth grader, dividing fractions and past participles with other grade schoolers, our national economy with hubby, we feel like doing something dreadfully unstimulating and unproductive and unprovocative—like our nails!

If anyone dares to mention to me how things were done in the old days once more he shall get a good swat with my best chipped coffee cup.

We're all for home-baked bread, hand-made mittens and start-from-scratch cookies.

Thank you, we're already got half a basement filled with unfinished furniture.

Having decided staunchly not to pay for factory-made Halloween costumes, we resolutely went about making our own. Ingenuity does not always come cheaply as we discovered after investing in material, gold paper, patterns, piano wire, yarn for wigs and so forth.

Beds went unmade and dinners became hasty affairs the last two days before the big holiday as we worked feverishly over our designs. The resultant glow in their eyes when they viewed the finished products was well worth every effort and when hubby tallied the results, he found we had spent approximately three times as much as if we had run down to the local drug store and bought them off the shelf.

◆   ◆   ◆

Have you heard?

A renowned psychologist and research director admits we have for too long ignored a much-neglected mental process—the hunch. Or that peculiar form of mental shortcut so familiar and dear to the female gender: intuition!

That dear man shall have cream in his coffee and a rose in his lapel all the rest of his days.

How many days have you wakened with that feeling of foreboding, disregarded it and ended up with a cake and a sunken middle or a car with a bent muffler? Or that funny little tickle when you look in the mirror in the morning and put off doing your hair? Isn't that always the evening hubby comes home and suggests dinner out and then a movie?

All hail the return of mythical institution, mover of moods.

Perhaps some of the myth has been dissolved much to the chagrin of many a husband on this old earth who has heard more than once these words: "I just have the oddest f-e-e-l-i-n-g." Then the appointment may be canceled, the trip moved up to another day, the black suit changed for another, the pearls worn instead of the gold, the chocolate pie substituted for lemon meringue, a hasty letter written to an old sorority sister, a phone call answered only after the fourth ring. Care to add to the list?

Gratitude for Intangibles, Material Blessings

November 24, 1963

Ere we carve the turkey this week, we thank Thee for the last brilliant burst of chrysanthemums, for frosty mornings, for stars and man made stars, for the beam in a husband's eyes ...

For the courage of one's convictions, for friendly librarians, for church bells, for apple pie with whipped cream, for college scholarships we give thanks, too.

We thank Thee for the smell of bayberry candles, expensive perfume, little girls' hair, freshly ironed clothes, pipe smoke, fall leaves, and spring dogwood blossoms.

Before we forget we thank Thee for girlish giggles, for boys who wear out the knees of dungarees before they wear out their mothers, for kites in the spring, for dolls that talk almost as much as their owners, for 900-calorie food and dentists with a sense of humor.

For letters from old friends, witty sayings, marble monuments, pancake mix, husbands who blush, football helmets, stretch socks, and the rabbit who comes so bravely to munch at our back steps on blustery mornings, we thank Thee ...

And for the blue jay's outrageously cheerful call, for stereo and those who love it, for acoustical ceilings, sticky apples, TV programs that put us to sleep, and TV commercials that don't take themselves too seriously.

We thank Thee for patient teachers and exciting books, for the times we have to be alone, and for the times the walls shake with children's laughter, and for wisdom, and for daily strength to use the wisdom.

This Thanksgiving Day we give thanks for grandmothers who sew, for sons big enough to swim and play tennis, and toss a basketball the way their fathers used to, and for daughters with light and lilting laughter and their belief in all the good things yet to come ...

For checkbook stubs that are numbered, name tags, mittens that match, frugality (and whatever happened to that word after 1900?), doctors who come in the middle of the night, garage mechanics with the patience of saints, pretty shop girls, and school bus drivers, the cheerful "hello" on gray mornings.

Before the pumpkin pie has disappeared completely we thank Thee for scrapbooks, baby shoes so scuffed and worn, old matchbook covers, college football programs, yellow roses pressed in a book, and for the constant tick-tock that keeps us looking ahead instead of comfortably back.

For Texas' great cattle for California's fragrant fruit groves, for Iowa's fat corn fields and New York's celery fields, for Maryland's crabs, for the seven sweets and seven sours of Pennsylvania, we thank Thee, too, and for the supermarket that serves them up to us daily wrapped in cellophane ...

And for the goodness of children shining through the mud, for detergents that scrub, and the right to choose, for history books that make learning fun, for election without duress, for strong leaders, and our enjoyment of the right to gripe.

"Ere we discover who has the wishbone we thank Thee for starch in spray cans, paint that glows in the dark, hems that "grow," candlelight, the sassy wink of a passer-by, the lovely whoosh of a passing sports car, for gas in the tank on rainy mornings, for stockings without runners, for P-TA meetings that never bore.

For nurses who guard the sick against the night, for the policeman at the corner who loves our children much as we do, for ships that ply through storms, for the friendly zoom of an airplane overhead, for lounge chairs and mohair sweaters, for museums that cost us nothing to gape and gaze, and for march music that puts a lump in our throat and a tap to our toes—we give thanks.

We thank Thee for those who can make marvelous coffee, and for instant coffee for those who cannot, for doorbell chimes, for the heritage of men like Washington and Jefferson, for baseball and football heroes, men who climb mountains and men who build ideas.

For church steeples, for loyal pets for city planners, for suspension bridges, for the stimulus of new ideas, and for transistor radios, we give thanks too.

And for a million other blessings, yet undiscovered, we thank Thee.

Housewife's Chores Take Time Needed for Beauty Care

January 5, 1964

Now that we've had four good days in which to break our first fifty New Year resolutions, we've decided to have a long hard look at all the free advice handed out by beauty editors.

It is their continuing hope that by the end of 1964 we will all be slim, chic, svelte, charming and new!

It is also our continuing hope, but somehow things like chicken pox, scraped knees, chocolate cake, children, dogs and husbands have a way of interrupting.

Presumably all this free-flowing advice is written by long and lean beauty editors who wear Chanel suits, lunch at "21" and wouldn't know a can of modeling clay if it were monogrammed at Tiffany's.

Item one: "A ten minute facial before going out for the evening does wonders for tired facial muscles and sagging spirits."

In that precious ten minutes before we go out for the evening I will have to (1) sew a middle button on my husband's gray suit, (2) get the supper casserole dish really clean, (3) read a chapter of "Peter Rabbit" aloud, (4) and hunt for my pearls in the girls' bedroom. If I am lucky I will have the bathroom mirror to myself for two full minutes.

Item two: "A languid bath with a drop or two of one's favorite bath oil ensures that really fresh start."

Have you ever tried taking a languid bath at 4:30 in the afternoon with the television blaring and nine or ten little ones sprawled around, and the casserole that looked so beautiful in picture form now turned a ghastly shade of green in the oven?

What this country really needs is more college scholarships and stronger locks on bathroom doors!

Item three: "Treat yourself to a really brisk ten minute walk daily and watch the pounds disappear."

O.K.! So who wouldn't lose weight dressing three youngsters in boots and snow regalia for a ten-minute trot around the block with several sleds and assorted neighborhood dogs, all of whom seem to be subsisting this winter on mittens and snow boots?

Item four: "Thorough brushing ensures well-groomed hair when you want to look your best."

"What do you mean the dog got wet in the snow and you only wanted to brush her dry?

Item five: "Steady exercise keeps hands supple and young looking."

"I don't know how anyone could possibly get a whole tube of airplane glue wedged in the sugar bowl but if I ever get this mess off my fingers the first thing I am going to do ..."

"I know it says to insert Tab B in Slot B darling but Mommy's fingers won't fit in that tiny spot and crying just isn't going to get your doll house put together!"

Item six: "Sameness is dullness. Try something new daily to boost you out of the doldrums."

"No. I am not sick! It's gold eye shadow and it cost $1.49!"

"This dress is not called a bag. It's a shift."

"But a wig wouldn't cost any more than a leaf gatherer or a power mower and you know what a boost they gave you!"

"The girl in the beauty shop said it will wash out in three or four weeks and we're not going anywhere for a month, so what's the fuss all about?"

Mother Weighs Life's Best 'Gift'—A Child's Love

May 10, 1964

If mothers were to write to their children everywhere today, they might say something like this:

"One sunny afternoon there were three little girls sitting beneath the window playing jacks and talking solemnly about their future.

"I'm going to Egypt and study pyramids," declared the serious one in braids who always remembers to say "Yes, please," and "No, thank you."

"I'm going to Hollywood and eat ice cream three times a day," said the frivolous one who never knows what has become of her tennis shoes.

"And, I'm going to be a mother!" glowed the third one and I hugged the thought to my secret self happily, thinking perhaps this one should have another cookie. She continued, "Then I shall drink coffee and eat doughnuts and read and read," and I reserved judgment on the added cookie!

Today is Mother's Day and for a week you have been dutifully and sometimes painfully (considering your financial status) thinking of gifts.

The picture of the orange sailboat skimming over bright blue waves was especially dear because you know how we love the sea and the promise of excitement beyond.

The huge bouquet of peach blossoms and their heady fragrance has left me weak and are you quite certain the lady said you might pick them? (Do you remember the giant tulips last year from the churchyard and the painful apology to the rector?)

The potholders wrapped in a beautiful box with all my aluminum foil and every speck of ribbon in the house are exactly what I need. Out of the thirty or forty pot holders you've made for me, not one is like another, and I shall remember forever the fiercely concentrated head bent over deft little fingers hour after hour.

But you have given me so much more, and forgive me, that being a mother, I shall continue to take.

You have given me laughter.

In this time when pressure and progress cloak our days in solemnity and scientific idioms, you have given back the precious gift of seeing us as we are.

When mashed potatoes fly through the air and land with a particularly zestful plop on a black spaniel's perplexed nose, who can help but join in the shouting laughter?

When your skirt button breaks and we have to stop in the middle of a parade to sew you back together, we have added a box of giggles to our store of treasure.

You have given the gift of surprise.

Motherhood itself, in fact, usually arrives in an aura of surprise, despite the solemn calculations of medical men and mothers. It comes during blizzards and when the washing isn't done, when husbands are painting the house and when the car is almost out of gasoline.

And from that day forward you have taken tedium from the morning and added brightness. You have taken weariness from the evening and replaced it with discovery. Imagination is your faithful navigator.

You have given love.

There have been countless stray animals, innumerable lonely friends who needed a cookie and some talk, and there have been expensive exuberant hugs and capricious kisses when the realities of life have tended to weigh down these grownups out of proportion to their worth.

You have given back simplicity.

In a time when dolls have the elaborate wardrobes of queens and when television brings outer space into our living room, you above all have learned the art of sorting out what is really important to the nurturing of one's soul.

You never fail to draw my attention to the rich smell of grass after a heavy summer rain.

You find pieces of stone that look like silver. You ask difficult questions which I yearn to answer in complicated dialectics and which require, in the end, only simple answers, as all truths and beauty in life are very simple.

You have given me music (which I hereby admit will surely someday drive me completely mad).

You have given me art (which lines the walls of every room).

You have given me literature. ("Dear Mom, I am plaguing dools at Missesus Kane's back yard. You got a call, but I ferget who, Dadd, mebbe.")

You have given me Santa Claus, the tooth fairy, Dr. Seuss and Dr. Spock, countless sleepless nights and a big shiny key to tomorrow's hundred exciting doors.

What need I of hyacinths to feed my soul when I have you?

Housework Given Rightful Place, Like Homework

May 24, 1964

Question: Do you think children should help around the house?

Answer: I do, but don't ask them what they think!

Q. At what age should a child start to care for his own room?

A. As soon as he begins collecting living things that require trivia such as bowls, nests, cages, feed and occasional pre-natal care.

Q. What method do you employ to get the children to help with household chores?

A. I feel a pleasant manner, a great deal of psychology and an appeal to their higher natures is vital. Right now I intend to use this approach on some 11-year-olds who are watching the fourth rerun of an old movie in the basement, which comes close to being a national disaster area.

Q. Does it work?

A. No, but then I yell.

Q. Don't you feel that offering extra privileges or increased allowance to accomplish work is a form of bribery?

A. You call it what you want. I'll call it what I want. (At our house we call it "friendly persuasion.")

Q. At what age did your children begin to make their own beds?

A. My dear, our children have been "making their own beds" since the Year 1. All they do is gaze intently at the heap of covers, throw a bedspread over the humps and lumps and sit a pink bunny on top.

Q. What do you do when the children quarrel over the distribution of chores?

A. Well, first of all I sit down with them and discuss it democratically. Then I cry.

Q. How do you feel about boys dusting and girls cutting the grass?

A. Marvelous!

Q. Do you feel caring for family pets should be part of the children's job?

A. We-l-l, yes, but feeding the dog the last piece of lemon meringue pie?

Q. How do you handle excuses, heavy homework, headaches, previous engagements and so forth?

A. I just turn up the radio a little louder and smile.

Q. Do you think girls or boys are the greater help around the house?

A. It depends whether you are talking about sweeping the dust under the beds or sweeping the grass clippings onto the neighbor's lawn.

Q. Do you find most children enjoy "heavier" work such as simply carpentry or painting?

A. Are you kidding? Doesn't everyone with children have pink back porches?

Q. Would you say an automatic dish washing machine might be the kids' favorite laborsaving device?

A. No, not really, our kids are wild about aerosol cans. Now if they could just read the directions we could all relax. Last week they starched the dog, cleaned the mirrors with dessert topping and sprayed the wash with the dog's flea and tick preparation.

Q. What do you think about the condition of teen-agers' bedrooms?

A. Please, I have enough trouble getting baby sitters Saturday nights. Aren't all teen-agers neat, tidy quiet, kind and generous?

Q. Do you feel housework should be a form of punishment?

A. You mean all those dishes I've been doing for 15 years are a reward!

Q. How do you account for the fact that children work readily for other mothers and that other children work agreeably for you?

A. My dear, I really couldn't say right now. All I know is that my kids are next door stacking a cord of wood and smiling! And I've got to go because the kids from next door are coming over to scrub the screens for me. They love peanut butter cookies.

'It's Wonderful!' Mother Exclaims at Class Reunion

September 6, 1964

Broadway was in its summer slump, Barry Goldwater[19] was trying to explain himself and it was only a week until we were going back to a class reunion.

I was on the floor pretending to do a strenuous set of sit-ups and push-ups. Being a natural coward, I collapsed with my nose in the newest Superman comic book. "I'll never make it, I'm a hundred years old if I'm a day."

"What I can't understand," commented our 11-year-old from the depths of his father's chair, "is why anybody would want to go back to school once you're done, for cryin' out loud!"

"Gosh, Mama, did you really go to school?" asked our youngest in awe. She considers my bathtub-scouring and cookie-baking beyond the realm of academic preparation.

"You could buy a wig," offered the second daughter eyeing my end-of-the-summer hair.

"The very least you could do," commented hubby from behind the sports pages, "is to wear tennis sneakers that match."

Guiltily I hid one green-clad foot behind the other one in tan.

"You want your dress-ups back?" inquired the oldest girl in a very defensive tone.

"No, darling," I replied icily, "I am borrowing your brother's Batman costume and your father is buying me purple felt sneakers!"

President Johnson had a hundred people over for supper, our refrigerator died an untimely death, I found four white hairs just over my right eyebrow and now it was five days until reunion.

I had just tried curling my eyelashes and nearly removed one eye. Hubby was muttering blackly, "You look like Theda Bara[20] with all that coloring book stuff on your eyes."

"Mama, did they have electric lights when you went to school?" inquired our youngest brightly.

"Boy, oh boy," emphatically declared number one son, "If I ever get out of school I'm getting on a boat and sail around the world and never, never go back to school!"

The World's Fair had a peak day, Castro made a four-hour speech, my sunburn began to peel in great layers and there were only two days left.

I was on my hands and knees in the attic searching for the yearbook. "I'll be glad when we can go back to normal around here and have something to eat besides tapioca pudding," pronounced hubby.

Memories began tumbling over one another. I committed the cardinal parental error of reminiscence. "Gosh, you sound like 'This Was the Week That Was' or '20th Century' on TV" moaned the children.

Remember when little boys wore knickers, remember when World War II ended, remember "sloppy joe" sweaters, spring prom, detention hall—"Ah, Mother," they cried, "Cut it out!"

R-Day, "I've never been so old in all my life," I muttered darkly. "And aren't you glad that eyelash curler didn't give you a black eye?" asked hubby.

Suddenly there was a room full of the most attractive people I have ever seen, all of them vaguely familiar.

They danced to every dance as though six o'clock bottles and dental bills were a million miles away.

Talk shifted from the great universities to the great cities of the world and skipped gracefully over things like broken water heaters, low-calorie diets and mortgages.

Shy young boys who once threw spitballs had turned into distinguished executives, and the girls they threw spitballs at had turned into poised and chic mothers and career women.

"It's wonderful!" I gasped and handed my ice cream to hubby. "Now can we have something besides tapioca pudding?" he glowed happily.

The orchid corsage door prize rested in the refrigerator next to the sliced tomatoes. "Can't we fly to Hong Kong for the weekend?" I sighed. "Such a shame to just let a beautiful flower like that stay in the refrigerator."

"Can't go to Hong Kong. Good show on TV tonight."

So who was it that said we are all a little mad most of the time? Most people wouldn't look twice at an ordinary housewife Monday morning hanging out the wash attired in her usual tan shorts, oxford shirt, old tennis sneakers and a large orchid corsage!

Never, never have I felt younger.

Pilgrims' Dream Is in Us; We Should Be Thankful

November 22, 1964

We shall remember the first bleak chill morning when Thanksgiving came to be.

We shall remember because we must.

These were men and women and children who had come through the narrow channel between life and death and had paused in grateful oneness for the very sweetness that is now.

We too must walk the narrow channel between today and never, fearing the worst, steadfastly believing in the ever.

And so, we, too pause to give thanks.

For candles that light the way along the dark corridors of ignorance and intolerance.

And for those who carry the candles, always refusing to turn back or to admit discouragement.

We shall remember how it was that first Thanksgiving morning three hundred years ago when men gave up the green pastures of home for the strange unknown new world, knowing full well that freedom was the only green pastures where man would find true happiness.

We shall remember because we must.

For beacons that light our way along the twisting paths of injustice and corruption we give thanks.

For men like George Washington, Thomas Jefferson, Abraham Lincoln and John Fitzgerald Kennedy, who was made to suffer the final injustice of all and whose belief in his country breathes in all of us now.

Before the day is finished and all the precious memories laid to rest, we give thanks for misty morning light and starry night.

For navigators who plot the flight of aircraft and statesmen who plot the fate of nations.

God grant them wisdom.

For children, black and white, red and brown, who are tomorrow all wrapped up in pigtails and scuffed toes, bright eyes and hearts full of joy and life.

They are our hope.

We give thanks for teachers who must fire their imagination and challenge their ever-questing minds and for parents who must mold them into adults with grace.

God grant them wisdom.

It was cold that morning long ago on New England's wind-swept rocky coast and the Pilgrims could feel the chill through their threadbare garments. Their tools were primitive and their fears many.

But courage was the golden coin that would buy them freedom.

This, too, we remember, because we must.

For there are those of us who would be tempted by the hatemongers and doubters.

May God grant us all strength.

When November's swift twilight settled on that first Thanksgiving Day, we cannot be sure just what the Pilgrims were thinking of, but we know their dreams.

For we are living their dream.

And their dream is in us.

America sings out in every heart throughout the land from simple farmer to business tycoon, from immigrant laborer to college president, across the mountain peaks and desert land from heart to heart.

For 20th century Pilgrims we give grateful thanks.

For hope which makes it all worthwhile.
For love which makes hope possible.
We, too, give thanks.

Mother Admits She's a Coward—Can't Say 'No' When Bright-Eyed Kids Invite Her to Rink

January 10, 1965

Temporary amnesia is that affliction which strikes parents between school vacations.

While school is in session and the house is still and quiet, parents tend to forget how noisy, how active and how busy children actually are.

During vacations they remember.

This profound thought occurred to me as I was hanging onto the railing of an ice-skating rink and resting my right foot, which felt as if it were about to drop off with frostbite, pain or strangulation.

I smiled gaily at the children gliding by on their new Christmas skates and wondered why in the world I wasn't sitting in some comfortable armchair reading.

First of all, I suppose, because I, too, was carried away by the children's enthusiasm and zest for planning this vacation like an old mountain climber whose heart beats faster at the mere mention of Mt. Everest.

Secondly, because I hadn't been skating in so long I had forgotten what physical torture could be. (All right, scoffers, YOU go out there for two hours on two blades, then report right back!)

Third, I'm a coward. I can't say "No" when they look at you with that shiny look in their bright eyes.

After we had laced and re-laced our skates to the right degree of perfection on that thin line between ankle strangulation and ankle collapse, we walked for miles and miles on those ridiculously thin blades to the rink.

I wondered if our hospitalization would cover a housekeeper if I broke my leg. I wondered how many bones were in the human foot. I felt positively brittle. The children zoomed onto the ice with the natural grace of ducklings meeting water.

I crashed into the uniformed rink attendant who asked for our tickets. He picked me up and assured me I would live through the afternoon. Then he regaled me with the winter's history of broken bones and bruises, obviously a fireside surgeon.

I discovered that by hanging over the side of the railing I could allow the blood to drain back into my aching toes and watch the clock which hardly moved all during the next two hours.

The next afternoon we returned to the rink. The sun and fresh air were glorious and the children came home ravenous. You would think no one had ever seen a middle-aged woman sitting in the back of the family car doing the week's darning at an ice skating rink for heaven's sake.

The youngsters were convinced the new sleds went at least 25 mph. They went 100 if they went a mile! Believe me, as a grown adult, it is not easy to explain a situation when you have just run over a neighbor with your sled and that neighbor was carrying home a weekend's supply of eggs and milk.

When they build a sled with automatic gearshift and power steering let me know and I'll give a thought to trying again, but not before.

I wonder, how does one placate a neighbor, after he has been mowed down by an adult on a skateboard in October and again by the same adult on a sled in December? (Thank heavens, it wasn't his dahlia bed the dog dug up a few years by or an Australian sheep ranch.)

While I was sitting with the heating pad and a cup of cocoa the children took pity and suggested Monopoly. I went bankrupt inside of an hour.

Next came Scrabble. Lost by forty points.

I'd rather not even mention Pick-up Sticks or Old Maids if you don't mind.

I held the record in ping-pong—32 straight losses.

And with this, the children, full of candor, suggested I go out to the kitchen and whip up a cake while Daddy took them skating by moonlight.

I accepted as gracefully as possible and watched them leave. I'll have the heating pad, rubbing alcohol and hot cocoa ready when he gets back. I wonder how he'll do at Monopoly.

Car Pools Raise Harassed Mom's Blood Pressure

January 17, 1965

A car pool is a 20th century device designed to hasten the flow of transportation and conserve human resources.

Strangely enough, it sometimes has the opposite effect. Car pools can make grown men weep and grown women kick the whitewall tires. Well, almost.

Like budgets, car pools look innocently simple on black and white paper.

Transferred to human elements, they take on a different light. Tom will drive Monday and Tuesday, Jerry on Wednesday and Harry on Thursday and Friday. Simple, so far?

Well, Tom's wife will need the car on alternate Tuesdays, which means he will switch off with Harry until Harry's mother-in-law arrives for her annual three-week stay. Then Jerry will pull full shift unless his kids have the measles in which case his wife will need the car to take them to the doctor. All this, of course, hinges on whether Tom's car holds out through the winter weather and Harry gets snow tires for his aging vehicle with delusions of grandeur. Try to get that on paper!

I have been in bowling pools, kindergarten pools, Brownie pools, Scout pools, Sunday School pools and swimming pools (swimming pool car pools, that is!) and, I must say that up until now I have been a simple girl, fond of early morning bird song and homemade vegetable soup.

Lately when anyone mentions car pool to me, I break out in a cold sweat, look hastily for the nearest exit and run for that door talking quietly to myself to forestall any weakening on my part which would mean getting hooked up to a 16-week alternating shift car pool in order to get to the supermarket in time for the Wednesday pork chop specials.

Thursday is choir car pool day. The phone rings about the time we sit down to dinner. Mary Lou will not be going—mumps this time. Second call is to say Johnnie is going but would I please pick him up at his grandmother's and would I take Sally back home after choir.

Someone calls and asks just who the heck is the guy supposed to drive this week. They lost the schedule.

Another call. This one is miffed because she has exchanged turns twice with another and her turn is coming up again and her husband needs the car for bowling. Now I can't remember if I ate the mashed potatoes. Hubby mentions the spark plugs are acting foolishly again, and if I run out of gas there is a brand new can in the trunk. Fun and games for everyone tonight!

Meanwhile, our children have decided they don't want to go to choir tonight and are faking great piles of homework, assorted headaches and fevers. I take everyone's temperature, run out and check the gas gauge and lay down orders: Everyone goes to choir tonight. No exceptions granted.

Lucy's mother calls to say please don't let Lucy come home from choir without her green mittens, which she left at church two weeks ago. And did I find a blue umbrella in the back seat of the car after the Halloween parade?

Johnny's mother calls back to say that Johnny is now back at home and to disregard the previous request to pick him up at his grandmother's.

It is at their particular exciting moment of the drama when I discover I have no car keys. The family is extremely well oriented to disaster. The girls look in all the coat pockets while number one son does the desk, mantel and kitchen windowsill. Hubby sits about looking calm and detached. I hate him momentarily, and rashly promise a 15-cent reward for the finder.

I keep thinking of small South Pacific islands where surely one can walk to choir practice, bowling and kindergarten! Or does one form a canoe pool?

The keys are found in the refrigerator with the empty milk jug (brilliant deduction on the part of friend husband).

There is a horn honking out front. I part the draperies. It is Jane Ridgely with a station wagon full of small faces. "It's my turn for choir pool. Did you forget? Are they ready?"

And I must confess, in all candor, I wept. Don't anyone mention CAR POOL to me!

January Spells out Scrabble for Mother

Monday, January 1965

In January the doldrums set in.

This time of the year we usually decide what we all need is an exciting new hobby, a grand passion.

Last winter we plunged heart and soul into the Royal Canadian Air Force's physical fitness program. After several nights of panting and puffing, we decided the RCAF would lose its brilliant reputation if we continued.

Hilary and Jim Webb were taking jujitsu lessons at the Y. The Browns were deep in Great Books discussions. Our next-door neighbors were wild about roller-skating. Maisie and Biff Conklin were taking up cake decorating. We were just looking for the "right" thing.

Himself was all for buying a pool table and I was hankering for a classical guitar. By the time we got through arguing winter was over and baseball cured the doldrums.

January is back and the Scrabble board is in the center of the living room. A truce is in session.

"I don't care what you say "Q-u-a-k" is illegal and I never ever heard of "V-r-u-m.""

"Where is the Monopoly game?"

The children won't tell.

"Every time Daddy plays he buys up all the railroads and I go b-r-o-k-e," wails our financially scarred first grader.

"Sky-diving anyone?" inquires Himself.

"My parachute's at the cleaner's," I glare.

"Ha, ha, very funny," he snorted. "Let's go sledding."

So we rented our youngest's sled that Santa Claus had brought her. She yelled after us, "It's time and a half after the first hour, and don't scratch the runners."

She shouldn't have worried. One nerve-shattering, screaming slide down the schoolyard hill cured me for life. "Heh, heh, pretty much fun," chuckled hubby.

"What do you mean?" I screamed. "You almost hit that oak tree and we're only two inches from the lake?"

"Let's face it sweetie," he said soothingly, "You're just not Olympic material." I was beginning to think his pool table wasn't such a bad idea after all. I limped home and paid the rental on the sled and ate three chocolate brownies in a row out of sheer love of life!

Next came bowling. The only thing was I let the ball go in the wrong direction and everyone laughed outrageously when Himself explained he had that slight limp because his wife plunked him accidentally with a bowling ball. My heart just wasn't in the right lane when it came to bowling.

His toenail turned blue and then black. The children kept waiting for the entire toe to fall off. Then we took up ice-skating.

He hadn't forgotten a thing about skating. How can such a big man who falls over one little crayon on the living room rug at least once a week be so agile on skates?

"Gee, Daddy, where did you learn to skate so fast?" The children were absolutely awed.

"Go pick up your mother, children," he commanded.

"I'm all right," I yelled as three children skated over my left ankle.

There was a skating instructress with silver-blonde hair and the grace of a gazelle. "Hey, I think skating is really going to be fun this winter," cheerfully commented Himself as he whizzed by the third time.

"C'mon, kids, it's time to go home. I can hear the roast burning," I said.

"But Mom, how can you HEAR a roast burning?"

"Be quiet, darling, and see if Mommy's left foot is still in her skate. I think it just fell off," I muttered.

The next day hubby said, "What about skiing?"

So off to the nearest hillside we went to reconnoiter. He paled a bit when he priced skis ($119.50) and Austrian-made boots ($55).

Just then the fire department ambulance pulled up to the front door of the ski lodge and two men in white coats jumped out with a stretcher. He paled once more.

"What did you do with the Scrabble board?"

You know something? "V-r-u-m" is the sound a skier makes just as he gains speed and smacks into the first oak tree midway down the slope.

Columbus Smart, He Didn't Bring Family on Voyage

July 25, 1965

Why is it that a perfectly happy couple that has not weathered the storms of unbalanced check books and measle-prone children always seem to notice each other's faults when it comes time to pack the car trunk for vacation?

"I thought you said we were going to take less this year," he says glumly eyeing the tower of possessions lining the driveway.

"We are!" she answers indignantly. "Why, we didn't take the little brown suitcase of the fishbowl or the grill ..."

"What's that?" he interrupts.

"My hairdryer, darling," she coos handing him the can of potato chips and the dog's blanket.

About this time the children arrive bearing fins for the water, a guitar, 14 table games and assorted friends.

"No, no, no," he begins to sob, really coming apart at the seams now, "Maybe we could move the whole house down, transport the whole confounded thing!" he shouts casting his arms heavenward.

"Oh Daddy, could we?" sighs the youngest ecstatically, shifting the weight of her teddy bear, Barbie doll and domino box to the other hip.

It's enough to make a person wonder about vacations, you know. There you have been ironing and baking for two days, writing notes to the paperboy and milkman and trying to remember if you paid the water bill. Then there you are at 6 a.m. on the curb between a golf bag and tennis racquet while all your neighbors are placidly sleeping in their own tidy bedrooms.

"Do we have to take five blankets?" he mutters.

"Remember the year the temperature dropped 20 degrees and we all caught cold."

"All right! Blankets, yes. Hairdryer, no!"

A chorus of protest. "What about the golf clubs? They take an AWFUL lot of room!"

Truce.

"It is simply a matter of managed space and efficient time control," he pronounces as he shoves the two-gallon thermos into a hatbox. "And that's another thing! Whose idea was it to get such a gigantic thermos? What are we, a bunch of giraffes?"

He is reminded as kindly as possible: "It was YOUR idea, remember? You said the price of soft drinks was highway robbery on trips like this?"

One of the children is bearing a mysterious shopworn paper bag.

"What's that?"

"My seashell collection."

He is counting: "One … two … three … good grief, child, we are going where there are hundreds, no, thousands of seashells, more than you can imagine!"

He sits down on the ice chest, pushing aside a carton of beach toys and a plastic bag of hair rollers.

She sits down on the trunk and offers him a cigarette: "What are you thinking about, dear?"

"I am thinking about Columbus and how smart he was not to take his family on his voyages on account of the ships would have sunk with all that weight!"

The children are growing restless except for the one reading comics placidly in the back seat of the car. They begin to rummage in the cardboard carton of food supplies, digging out cereal boxes and little snacks.

The neighbors are beginning to get up. Somewhere a dog barks. Dog. "Where's the dog?" someone shouts.

She gets up, trots in the house and calls endearments. There is a puzzled bark. She goes into the bedroom and there is man's best friend, the frisky all-American pup curled up napping in the open suitcase between her best lace slip and three of his white shirts.

The dog raises a nose quizzically and knocks a pile of handkerchiefs to the floor. Suddenly it is all too much and too funny. She sits on the floor and howls. Dog gets up, insulted and marches off down hallway dragging necktie with her.

"Hey, it's all in," he shouts triumphantly charging up the stairway. Then he sees the suitcase. He sits on the floor and they both howl.

"What's the matter with Mommy and Daddy?" ask one of the children.

"Who knows?" answers the one in the back seat reading comic books. "They always get a little nutty when it's time to pack the car for vacation."

Children's Party Hint Book Useless When Kids Arrive

August 15, 1965

Our village library boasts almost as many volumes on children's parties as it does books about psychology. Happily, they are located on the same aisle.

Our local supermarket boasts a long expanse of stacks and stacks of goodies to be played with, eaten, thrown, blown up or wound up at the children's birthday parties.

Happily it is located right next to a display of headache remedies. These parallels do not occur to us until the annual party panic is upon us.

As a scarred but accomplished giver of children's parties, we might say that it is perfectly easy to give an imaginative and original children's party.

It is impossible to predict the children's reactions.

They may all be allergic to strawberry ice cream. They may develop mumps in the middle of the afternoon.

They may forget to laugh in the right places.

They may fight over prizes. But it is marvelous practice if your husband ever goes into the diplomatic corps and you have to give extensive parties.

Our most recent birthday miss began relentless planning for her big day a full two weeks prior to the big day. For a child who is usually planning no further ahead than the next 30 seconds, this in itself was quite an accomplishment.

At the end of a week she had pared her guest list down to 25. Two days before B-Day her mother had pared it down to twelve! (Which just conveniently happens to be the number of chairs we can squeeze around the dining room table.)

Since she could not import the Beatles or Ed Sullivan's Italian mouse[21], she began to plan with precision all the games they would play. At this point it is best to abandon the book's advice since the authors have obviously never witnessed twelve children playing leap-frog in a 10-by-12 room. Or else they require so many ill-assorted objects like twenty empty oatmeal boxes and a hundred pipe cleaners that it is hopeless to begin.

It is then best to go back to those old reliables: pin-the-tail-on-the-donkey and dropping clothespins in an empty milk bottle.

The games do not matter so much as the prizes. Rule No. 1 is that every child must go home with a prize.

Children are addicted to this practice and it is best to provide thoroughly else you see the little guests departing with your new frying pan and some records tucked under their arms!

The table was set, the prizes wrapped with pretty pink ribbons, and the guests began to arrive, all starched and pretty in pastels and ruffled petticoats. They were subdued but underneath their polished exteriors I recognized the robust souls who haunt my cookie jar the other 364 days of the year.

Suddenly shy in their best attire, they achieved their natural enthusiasm when the games began. There were a dozen chiefs and no Indians, a dozen generals and no privates, a dozen admirals and no sailors. We declared it a state of siege and made ourselves commanders-in-chief for the duration. The games ran smoothly thereupon!

The books will tell you how to make a "perfectly lovely" fruit punch. They forget to warn you to put it far back from the aim of elbows and whistles. The books will tell you how to make a "marvelous" lemon supreme cake. They neglect to tell you what to do when the small guests surreptitiously feed it all to the innocent canine sitting strategically under the dining room table.

Bless their hearts, they even tell you to set specific hours for the party, but what do you do to get them to go home?

And what do you do with the kid who says to you as the last guest leaves: "Oh, Mommy, I have the best ideas for next year's party!"

If You Can't Go to South Seas, Go Roller Skating, Mom Told

September 12, 1965

Why is it the college alumni magazine always arrives on a day when the children are monsters, the dining room ceiling is falling and you can't remember what makes your husband so charming?

Like postcards from friends on Mediterranean cruises, it never comes in sunny weather when you've just had your hair done, the children have all passed modern math and your husband has remembered to hang up his towel.

The fall issue came with the grape crop. Since the girls were playing Parcheesi all over the table and the counters were filled with grapes and dishes, I sat on the kitchen floor to read the up-to-the-minute alumni news.

Friend husband wandered in, stepping carefully over my legs, the dog and the neighbor's toddler, "Have you seen my jar of paint brushes?" he asked in his most pleasant and patient, "I-Shall-Not-Scream-Yet" voice.

"Do you know what Maggie and Dan Ogglethum are doing? They've rented a yacht and they're taking a six-month cruise through the South Pacific!"

He opened the refrigerator door, known mostly as "Seward's Real Folly" and gazed blankly at an emaciated ham bone. "I hope they have enough paint brushes on the yacht."

"Did you look on my dressing table?" I asked. "There's sharp cheese behind the ham bone. Oh, my heavens, Chirpie Maxwell is going to marry that Broadway actor. She must be five years older than he is!"

No. 1 son arrived in his ghastly sneakers, falling over my outstretched feet and throwing his football into the breadbox. "Hi Mom," he smiled (and I thought of the dentist's bill), "Any apple pie left?" The neighborhood mutt came in on his heels and settled down on the floor with the rest of us.

"Why don't you do something around here besides EAT?" I snapped.

"What's the matter?" he asked all solicitous and humble. Then he saw the alumni magazine. "Oh."

On page four I read that Marthie Capp Boonton, the one who wore boots long before they were chic, has designed and sewn an entire matching fall wardrobe for herself and three daughters. "When not sewing." the article continues, "our inimitable Marthie is learning to play classical guitar and accompanying her husband on business trips to Portugal and the south of France."

"I didn't find the paint brushes, but I found the hedge clippers!" gloated the man in my life. He sat on the floor companionably and offered me one of his crackers.

"What's new with the mafia?" he said, pointing to the magazine.

"Why don't you ever take me exciting places like the south of France?" I wailed.

"Mostly," he answered calmly, "because we're too busy going to P-TA meetings and paying things like the mortgage and the dentist bill. What are you moaning about anyway? Didn't we go to the A&P last night and didn't we get six bags of doughnuts on sale?" I swatted him with the cracker box.

Hubby stood with a flourish and I remembered guiltily I had promised to sew the buttons on that shirt for more than two weeks. "Take charge here," he gestured to the dogs, "Madame and I are leaving immediately for the south backyard where we shall paint the fence and we shall require lemonade to be served at once!"

The girls giggled. Their brother grinned. "What you need, Mom," he directed, "is to get out of this kitchen and do something like pass football or go roller skating or something!"

'Little Girl' Look Good for Girls—But Not Mom

September 26, 1965

I was sitting there perfectly happy in my comfortable five-year-old shorts, my twelve-year-old pullover and contemplating my two-year-old loafers (which still hurt) when I decided it was time to do something drastic.

Like going to town to buy a dress.

After all, summer was officially over and there were several big occasions coming up, such as meeting my third grader's new teacher for the first time and returning all my overdue summer books to the village library. Besides, I felt like being fashionable and svelte and swinging and getting away from the oatmeal cookie and leaky refrigerator routine.

I felt like black velvet and pearls and lunch in a quietly elegant bistro!

So I put on my wrap-around skirt, my wrap-around blouse and my wrap-around shoes and carefully walked all around the family car before getting in and saying the usual prayer regarding the contents of the gas gauge.

Have you ever gone back to an old neighborhood only to find the familiar landmarks razed and a streamlined new office building in their place? This is what happened to fashion whilst we were asleep on the beach drying out skin and hair and gaining avoirdupois.

The designers were all hard at work in their air-conditioned cubbyholes, eating yogurt and wheat germ and going quietly but absolutely mad!

"I would like something special." I smiled at a petite saleswoman whose false eyelashes were as long as her spiked heels were high.

I got the impression she didn't like the wrap-around skirts. I followed her through a jungle of ankle-length broadloom and decided nastily that she probably hated mongrel dogs and cookouts too.

She brought out a nifty little number with suspender straps and a charming sailor hat to match. "No, you don't understand," I pled. "It's not for my little girl. It's for me."

She flicked her eyelashes and gave it to me deadpan, so help me. "This is for you. It's the latest thing, the Little Girl Look."

All I needed was an all-day lollipop and roller skates and I could go down to the supermarket and skate on the big wide sidewalks. The only trouble is there aren't many other 30-year-old kids playing down there.

It is no longer just chic to be back to a size 12. One has to starve down to a 10, or better still an 8.

There was always some hope of getting back to that 12 one day—but size 8? A person could die of starvation before the first P-TA meeting.

There also were "little girl" type shoes to go with this ensemble, reminiscent of the "Mary Jane" sandals my own children have been wearing and rejoice to leave behind for tennis shoes and loafers.

"Have you got something—something more mature?" I ventured.

Again, the sweep of the eyelashes and the hike through the broadloom. This time it was a two-piece silk in pop art prints. The top was black-and-white checks of one size.

The skirt had graduated sizes of black and white checks. I looked like a checkerboard caught in the drip dry cycle, a billboard gone mad, the kitchen linoleum on a foggy morning.

"Pop art prints," informed my guide.

"Have you got something in a nice red and green Norman Rockwell type print for fall?"

No sense of humor. I thought so.

The next dress was a British thing that I felt would only look suitable with nose-length bangs. The waistline came up to my armpits and it had a great ungraceful neckline with a bow big enough to rope a steer.

This was to be worn with white boots—calf length. It had long stockings with some wild color combination that would have made the man in the paint store take something for an upset stomach.

Then there were the bell-bottom trousers and matching top in a clinging jersey material. If they bring out a turban, I'll scream, I thought.

So I could look like a refugee from Liverpool, and overgrown kid or a tall sailor. "Look, haven't you got a nice simple wool sheath—something I could wear to church with my family?

Long eyelashes focused for a moment. "Oh, that would be downstairs in Everyday Dresses.

But somehow the lure of something special had lost its flavor. I no longer felt like black velvet and pearls and good perfume. So I put on my wrap-around skirt and my wrap-around blouse and my wrap-around shoes and went to the nice normal local drug store where I had an egg sandwich and a Coke and, for free, read something from the newsstand all about "What's Wrong with Suburbia?"

It was, considering all things, a very inexpensive afternoon.

Comparing Moms Is Child's Game for Two to Play

1965

Included among games children play well is "Comparing Mommies." Devious are the unwritten rules and devastating are the effects on parents.

"I can keep up with the Joneses, the mythical ones, that is," sighed a friend. "It's all the other mothers I can't keep up with—the ones who bake better cookies and build better block houses."

I know what she means.

Our sometimes solemn 8-year-old daughter had just returned from a weekend visit with a former school chum. She was perched on the kitchen counter munching on raisins. I was on my hands and knees trying to mop up what appeared to be part of the mud from the backyard.

"Samantha's mother makes all their rugs."

"Makes their rugs?" I groaned.

"Yep, she has a big frame and weaves them up and puts them on the floors. They're very pretty."

I was politely impressed. "Marvelous," I commented, pushing a frolicsome dog out of my way.

"She paints pictures too. She painted a picture of Samantha and her little brother and hung it over their fireplace."

"Samantha's mother," I admitted, must be a very talented person."
I pictured a short sturdy woman with long braids bending over her
looms and brushes late into the night.

That night at dinner Samantha's mother began to be a problem.
When the bread was passed our daughter commented idly, "Samantha's mother makes her own."

"Baskets too?" I squeaked.

"No, bread."

Several days later we ran into Samantha and her mother and her
little brothers, carrot tops all, a confusing assemblage of arms and legs
and grins surrounding a Saint Bernard dog in the back of a station
wagon.

Samantha's mother reminded me vaguely of someone familiar.
Her stunning hair was worn high off her forehead, and she was calm
and radiant in the midst of impending chaos behind the driver's seat.

I felt clumsy and oddly out of sorts. I complimented her on her
dress.

"Oh, do you really like it?" she smiled. "I made it last evening for
the lack of something exciting to do. It used to be the draperies in the
den."

(Shades of Scarlett. How much can the soul of a mother endure,
held up to such comparisons?)

Later I remembered whom she reminded me of. It was the model
on the cover of Vogue. By this time I had noticed fifteen new white
hairs, a vague gloomy feeling of a cold coming on and a definite sense
of sinking.

"How much do you think it would cost to make a rug?" I asked
my husband.

"Whatever happened to the sweater you started for me two years
ago? How would that look on the living room floor?"

"I can't stand people who make snide remarks," I sniffed. "Just
remember how you felt when you discovered Jamie Parkinson's father
could hit a fly ball into left field twice as far as you ever could."

He looked remorseful. "Yes, and remember when I was the first father to quit playing Capture the Flag in the rain even after Corkie Schnepper's Dad had sprained his ankle. It took me months to get over that blow."

We consoled one another.

I bought a small set of watercolors and practiced quietly in odd moments during the day. I eyed the draperies in the den, but frankly they wouldn't have made a good bedspread for the dog's basket-bed.

Eventually Samantha's mother faded from our conversation. Then Samantha's daughter came to spend the weekend with us, a reciprocal trade agreement, or some such thing.

We had pancakes for Saturday morning breakfast, and the pancakes were made in the shapes of turtles and pussycats. (I feel most quixotic on Saturday mornings. I suppose it is the relief of not having to pack all those lunches and find all those missing homework papers.)

"Boy," rhapsodized Samantha's daughter. "They sure are great pancakes. My mother makes lousy pancakes."

I raised my eyebrows. Then in the best tradition of the diplomatic corps of comparison mommies, I lowered my eyes demurely and said, "Why thank you, my dear, but I'm sure your mother has many, many other talents."

Then I added eagerly, for heady are the delights of flattery: "Have another pancake."

Mother of Three Loses Identity in Dream World

1965

Occasionally I lose myself. Quite often really.

I don't lose myself in a book or a play or a piece of stirring music, which is nice to do also. I simply have trouble finding out who I am, which is pretty bad, especially when all nice backyard amateur psychologist friends say it is normal to go through an "identity crisis" at age 19. But at 35, with three budding children, a neurotic parakeet and ironing which has been accumulating steadily since the end of World War II?

Ah well, I suppose it all began with the story of Elizabeth Taylor[22] and the twelve pearl buttons on her pink velvet gown which was to be worn that evening to a premier or a party. Elizabeth began to brood about those pearl buttons and Tiziana, the Rome couture house, instantly sent over "Mr. Richard" and a small swatch of pink velvet. Mr. Richard spent the better part of three hours re-covering Elizabeth's tacky pearl buttons and, although we're not told, we must assume that the party or premier was a smashing success. The following day Elizabeth gave away the dress.

While my heart leaned toward Elizabeth, my sympathy went out to Mr. Richard since I seem to spend most of my late night hours with glamorous guests on the television set—and the sewing box, taking up hems, sewing on buttons, all of which must be finished by 7 a.m.

Have you ever tried wrapping a newly hemmed Scout uniform around a sleeping child in the half-light of a bedroom at 2 a.m., yawning, and trying to remember whether it was an inch or an inch-and-a-half?

Of course you have! This is when I dip into my Walter Mitty[23] bag. I want the genie to appear and take all the safety pins out of my closet (at which time everything would probably collapse). It would be so interesting to do something else, I keep thinking.

For a time I fancy A-line skirts and matching cardigans and good leather loafers. The night school courses are intriguing and we toss around phrases like "self-concepts" and "repertoire of learned responses" and go home exhilarated and swollen with learning. Then one night we discover ourselves sleeping over the textbook and watching the Dean Martin show instead of outlining chapters.

It continues: not too long ago we went to an adult birthday party. This was such a treat! I couldn't imagine a birthday party without pin-the-tail and peanut races! I forgot to think about couture and went to the party in my standard PTA-church-party dress. It was a disaster. Everyone was wearing vinyl mini-skirts, fishnet hose and wigs. I felt like someone's Aunt Letitia from Milwaukee.

The following weekend we went out to dinner with friends. I wore my op art (not really, more impressionistic) dress with the almost-mini skirt and dangling earrings. The wives of our dinner partners wore their little navy blue wool suits with single strands of pearls. This time I felt like the saloonkeeper's daughter in 1878 Kansas City and longed for Aunt Letitia's return. "Stop leering," I snarled at an amused husband.

I have always admired the gaggle of Kennedy girls with their long artfully coiffed hair and superb bone structure. For four months now I have been trying to cultivate such a mane.

The parakeet is beginning to look at me with new interest. The nesting instinct? The children keep asking me when I am going to brush my hair. Since it is impossible to change bone structure without the dedicated assistance of three Viennese surgeons, I have developed "interesting" circles under my eyes, which is fine if you have an archaeological bent and enjoy antiquities!

My fondest vision is of the youthful suburban mother in her smart slack suit, long mane of hair and elegant little Alfa Romeo tooling along to the local fruit market to shop for avocados for luncheon guests. Naturally the children are attired in smart flannel jumpers with co-coordinated polo shirts.

Then what am I doing in this faded denim wrap around skirt, 1959 sneakers (ah, that was a good year for sneakers), and this motley crew of blue-jean, sweat-shirt clad children singing "Ninety-nine Bottles of Beer" and eating chocolate bars in the back of the family sedan?

But just this morning as I was wondering what the down payment would run on a small sports car my youngest ran into the house with her skateboard and a box of band-aids. "Oh mother," she sighed with noticeable relief. "There you are! Come try out my skateboard. It's really neat!"

She recognized me! She really recognized me, me with the flour in the hair, capped tooth and all! It was a thrilling moment, believe me, and I won't soon forget it once I'm out there in California as I whiz down the last half-mile stretch of the National Skateboard Championship course in my op-art slacks, good pearls and horn-rimmed bifocals!

It's a Big Leap from Typing Pool to the Hectic State of Motherhood

May 8, 1966

It's not as easy as it looks! But it has its moments! (Being a mother, that is.)

It's a pretty big leap from campus proms or the office typing pool to the hectic state of motherhood.

For one thing you've got to compete the rest of your life with Captain Kangaroo, Miss Nancy[24], and beautiful second grade teachers (or fourth, or first, etcetera) who never lost their tempers about goldfish in the clam chowder.

It is true also that the handsome basketball star and the debonair salesman do not fall readily into the patient papa routine, but that's another story.

There is hope for all of us, thanks to Dr. Spock, grandmothers and the elementary school starting gate for 6-year-olds!

There are certain elemental facts about motherhood not to be gleaned from florists' advertisements and sentimental balladeers.

Primarily, it takes a lot of time. There are always unfinished ends like appointments at the dentist, midnight pies and unfinished sweaters. You may even have to put off that trip around the world and the book and the Egyptian "dig" for twenty years or so, which isn't very long when you consider the amount of vanilla pudding you've got to cook in that period of time!

Secondly, most of the information you have accumulated up until now is really pretty useless. That course in music appreciation won't impress cranky 3-year-olds, but of course it might come in handy fifteen years hence to dazzle a daughter's intellectual swain.

The speed at shorthand fails to bemuse a kid whose last bottle of formula you've dropped and broke at 3 a.m.

It is important to know that the Mamas and the Papas[25] is not the local P-TA but an "in" record group.

And that the Watusi[26] is not an anthropological grouping but a tribal dance performed at pizza parties.

And that "camp" is "out."

And that nobody but squares take handkerchiefs to camp. Confusing? We've just begun.

Just when you've begun to get the hand of managing two or three toddlers and keeping them out of the neighbor's perennials, you've got to take on animals. It comes with the deal. What's a family worth its weight without a cat or dog or five or six, assorted goldfish, hamsters, ponies, giraffes and whatever do you have in that basket Johnny darling?

And to think they laughed when I wanted to substitute animal husbandry for 17th century French literature the second semester!

Somewhere along the line you will have come under the false impression that you will spend a great part of your life as a mother imparting choice bits of wisdom about "life" to the tender offshoots. (Philosophy 201). This will take various forms—"What do you mean he was safe on second base? He was out by a mile" (Smile. That umpire is the fifth grade geography teacher!)

"The next guy who tracks mud in this kitchen is going to be smashed!" (Smile. That kid next to your Johnny, in the muddy boots, has a father who is a psychologist!)

Then, "You're not going out with that sloppy saxophone player AGAIN are you?" (Smile. By 1984 he'll be president of General Motors.)

You pack them off to school and camp and college and christenings and proms and baseball games and concerts. Then just when you catch your breath they marry the saxophone player, who is not selling automobiles, buy a little cottage and start a family.

You go off to write that book and paint that picture. And there is a phone call: "Mother, we were wondering if you could keep the baby this weekend. It would give you something to do."

It's a Black Day as Mother Starts to Whip up Dress

May 15, 1966

While being agreeably matter-of-fact about most things, there are times when in a fit of fantasy or some kind of spring madness, I decide to make some dresses.

This generally occurs after having seen a friend who is wearing a stunning dress she just "whipped up" the other evening.

Believe me, no dress is just "whipped up," unless of course you can equate this with "whipping up" the San Francisco Bay Bridge or a pennant for the Mets.

But being gullible and having an inborn fear of elegant sales clerks in black crepe with white pique collars, I rush off to the nearest fabric center and drown in a sea of color and design.

There are three types of patterns and 10,000 patterns or more to choose from. They are designed for Beginners, Easy-to-Sew and Complete Idiots. I choose the latter.

To indicate the degree of my naiveté, I can never bear to make just a dress. It will be a wardrobe, a veritable paradise in suburbia. I can barely stand the excitement of all that broadcloth and denim and chiffon waiting to be cut into.

First will be the sundress, then the tunic, then the bareback, then hip huggers, oh I can hardly wait to get home and begin to sew!

Zippers, thread, pins and needles, hurry, hurry, Dior was never more inspired.

The easy part is finished. We have chosen the pattern, the material, the zipper, paid for them and driven home safely.

Now begins the shattering experience known as "The Black Day Mother Began to Sew."

First the dress must be cut out. Scissors. Has anyone seen the scissors? Pinking shears. The pinking shears were last seen backstage at the kindergarten dress rehearsal of the Christmas pageant three years ago. The scissors are in the desk, sandbox, basement, kitchen drawer, hutch, China?

Three days later the pinking shears arrive by camel's route from a friend of a friend. Now we can cut.

The dining room table has a model in the process, three coloring books, a social studies project and three dubious bananas. Out, out, all of it, out. Mother is shouting, what a demon she is!

Two days later the dining room table is cleared. NOW we can cut.

PIN, PIN, PIN, such excitement there is in cutting the first fold. What do they mean place on fold? I haven't any folds left! Is anybody out there listening in pattern-land? I think I've goofed. Come back here with those pins and unhand those pinking shears. This table is MINE.

"Why is your mother shouting so? Just because she's making a dress? Gee whiz!"

We are eating in the kitchen because Mommy is making a beautiful dress. Don't walk on that! It's the collar interfacing. Has anyone seen the seam binding?

Then comes the judicious coaxing of the resentful sewing machine, the studied relearning of all the parts. Why does it take twenty minutes to thread it and why can't I remember where to set the tension? Children, you are walking on the sleeves of my dress! What a lot of room it takes just to make a dress!

Absurd, a woman who can spot a fresh cantaloupe at 25 yard ought to be able to tell the wrong side from the right side, shouldn't she? Of course I'm not crying, don't be absurd. It's just that I'm so tired of sewing and I haven't sewn more than a yard!

Three days later the side seams are in place and the shoulder seams! The rug is covered with lint and threads but the children are happily making beanbags and doll clothes from the scraps. I walk around happily in the skeleton of my new dress. Isn't it great, I crow?

"Very nice," comments a dubious husband, "but when are you going to finish it?" Such a blow!

One evening for the hem.

At last it is finished, and the lint is vacuumed from the floor and the dining room table is relinquished to social studies projects and homework.

I swear I could not resist it. Time heals all. A friend exclaimed over the pretty print shift. Hiding my needle-scarred thumb, I calmly said, "Oh, it was just a little something I whipped up last week!"

But let me tell you, there is this darling tunic dress, with bell sleeves, and insets, crepe I think should make up beautifully ...

Life of a Square Has Problem for Mid-Aged Lady

August 1966

Being a square is not as easy as you might think.

It helps if you're approaching middle age, even though you only admit it only occasionally.

It helps if you remember the era of big bands, World War II and Spencer Tracy[27].

All this came to mind recently while sitting on the porch with a group of the lively set, their transistors and their guitars. I happened to be putting my hair up in rollers.

"Mother," shrieked a voice, "You aren't going to make your hair curly?" in the same tone used when I serve spinach more than twice a year.

"You've got to iron your hair to make it really straight," chorused another voice coming from behind a silky screen of very long tawny hair.

"But I've already got enough ironing to do." I protested. Thence began My Education as A Hippie. (Any references to current reducing fads is inconsequential.) The fact that this happened to occur on an afternoon when the thermometer soared to 103 degrees was entirely coincidental. I have these streaks of madness in the wintertime also.

To begin with, it is extremely difficult to iron your hair unless it is about eight feet long. And I just don't know if I trust my children well enough to have them iron it for me.

There was the evening Himself called down the basement stairs, "What are you doing? How about some Scrabble?"

"I can't," I shouted. "I'm ironing." "Oh let it go another month or so," was his wry answer.

"I can't. It's my hair!"

I must say he was there in record time. For once I won over Sandy Koufax[28] and Brooks Robinson[29] in gaining his maximum attention.

Dancing was something else again. I had progressed to the twist several years ago and then retired gracefully to become an interested spectator of American Bandstand.

Now began my strenuous indoctrination into the frog, the Watusi, the hokey-mokey and some other dance forms with names like ice cream sodas. Let me tell you something. After doing these dances for a day or two, the Royal Canadian Air Force fitness program begins to look like romper room antics.

I was humming a witty little ditty called "Nineteenth Nervous Breakdown" and doing the Watusi to demonstrate my progress to the chagrin of hubby. "That will never do," sternly reprimanded one of my instructors.

"You look as though you are enjoying yourself. Try looking bored."

Whatever will the ladies in the Gardenville Floral Society think of me?

Just when I was beginning to enjoy everything, the tempo changed and we went all grim, learning and writing protest songs.

It was so difficult thinking of all those words that had to rhyme with "bomb." It would be so much easier to think of "June" and "moon" and "spoon." And nothing rhymes with China!

Then came the evening we strolled into the village music store. While the girls scanned the sheet music racks and hubby disappeared into a stack of stereo records, I began idly fingering a guitar with a very handsome embroidered carrying strap.

In a flash friend husband grabbed me by the back of my loden green poor boy sweater. "No, no, no, it will never do," he protested.

"A tambourine?" I squeaked.

"The dog would howl," he further protested.

"A little harmonica?" I squeaked.

"Would you settle for a Ferrante and Teicher record?" He grinned.

I sold out, had a pixie haircut, took a book of Edna St. Vincent Millay poems out of the library and firmly turned the two or three transistors down ten decibels.

"C'mon, Mom, let's wheel on down to the drive-in for a pizza?"

"You go ahead, we're playing Scrabble," I smiled quite comfortably, adjusting the corners of my square!

Uncertainty Is the Best Part of Halloween

October 30, 1966

"The play's the thing," we're reminded again and again.

Don't you believe it. It's the rehearsal of what is to come that provides us with anxiety, a delicious uncertainty, a unique excitement.

This, too, we know. If the goblins don't soon come, we'll drop from exhaustion with all this rehearsing for Halloween.

The big box from the attic has been opened, and out spill remnants of other Halloweens: A wand, a sword, a witch's wig; Betsy Ross' apron, tattered angel wings, a Pilgrim cap, silver buckles, a cowboy vest and Indian tunic.

The children sit surrounded by all this and mutter worriedly, "What shall I be?"

This is the very best part of the indecision, the wealth of possibilities all to be narrowed down to one.

Batman and Robin are in the hallway giggling.

Lawrence of Arabia is in the hallway tying a white terry cloth turban around his head.

Mary, Queen of Scots, is in the hall closet with my fur muff.

There is a go-go girl in the bathroom applying purple eye shadow and doing the Watusi with all the vigor of a girl's basketball team.

I ask them all, "Have you seen my children?" The dishes are unrinsed, the books where they threw them, where in the world are my children? Shrieking and giggling, they scurry from room to room.

The next night it is more of the same.

Morticia is reading a Scout manual on her father's chair.

A skeleton is playing the piano in the playroom.

Two hobos are trying on their father's best hats, squashing them into proper anonymous shapes.

Superman is eating a popsicle in the den.

And Tarzan is in my sewing basket hunting some black yarn.

"Where in the world are my fine upstanding children?" I ask once more stepping over a sneaker here, a sneaker there. Again, wild shrieks and threats of goblins-will-get-you—if you don't watch out.

I feel bereft wandering about as plain old me. Contemporaries are busy sewing up Charlie Chaplin costumes for the school party that draws adults by the droves in elaborate hilarious costumes.

The Queen of Hearts is in the kitchen making a peanut butter and jelly sandwich.

Dracula is in the den making potholders.

The hobos are in the dining room playing dominoes.

A wicked witch is hiding in the hall closet. My scream and exaggerated fainting spell provide her with a wealth of sensation, which she will talk about for weeks.

Ah, to be 9 and knowing the delicious fright of never knowing for sure that the dark shape behind the oak in the front yard is perhaps—a real witch—and not Mrs. Singleton walking her French poodle.

Ghosts are swinging in the treetops and gypsy girls dance in the dry and brittle leaves.

My son is a doctor, lawyer, Indian chief, beatnik, skeleton, piano player, Zorro, King of the Jungle. Where and who is my son?

The sixth-grade teacher lives down the street with sweet and trusting care. Her pupils pace by her house, giggling like nervous starlets, thinking of trash cans on the roof, soap etchings on her car windows. They spend hours discussing the possibilities, frightening each other half to death. Then they meekly march to her door and parade in costume, hungry for her praise.

Dave Clark and his five yarn-topped moppets are on the back porch scaring the milkman and all the younger children in the neighborhood.

Dad arrives, a stranger from town, so formal in his gray flannel suit and button-down oxford. "How many days till Halloween?" he asks me, never noticing my broom floating about just beneath the kitchen ceiling.

11-Year-Old Girl Often Is Enigma to Weary Mother

1966

"An enigma," says the venerable Mr. Webster, is anything inscrutable, a riddle.

We have at least two of these enigmas and sometimes three, in residence at our house.

Enigma Number One is an 11-year-old daughter (either going on 5 or 25, depending on the wind and other mysterious forces). One day, Mata Hari, another day, Doris Day[30], and still another day, Buffalo Bill.

I am still her over-21-mother (either going on 17 or 97, depending upon the pressures and other no-so-mysterious forces).

Take, for example, the recent holiday during which she received a basketball from her comrade and confidant, Papa. For nigh unto three months basketball has been her grand passion. When not actually playing on the courts or taking part in tournaments, she has been taking up the game with great animation and fervor. In her two long pigtails and cut-off blue jeans she was a great candidate for an athletic scholarship to MIT!

The basketball was a bad guess. She spent the afternoon in tears. "I wish I had a corsage of tiny rosebuds and real perfume," she admitted between great wet tears forever, or so it seems, running down the front of her willow-green suit.

Aghast, her father stared at the basketball lying placidly on the coffee table." What happened to our athlete?" he asked me hastily behind the refrigerator door.

"Have a cookie," I offered in my best laissez-faire policy. "She's growing up, that's all."

That evening she came downstairs in her "granny" nightgown, three pounds of cold cream and smelling of a multitude of cosmetic essences.

The following day she demurely walked about the house in ruffled blouse, ski slacks and far-off expression, listening to the hi-fi, which gave out alternately with "Madame Butterfly" and the Monkees[31], during which time I took three aspirins and resolved to stay neutral at all costs.

One of the neighborhood boys came to the door and asked her to play touch football. She gave him a withering glance and told him she had to "do" her nails. Then she asked me if I had to wear those old scruffy slippers to hang out the clothes. What would the neighbors think?

(I didn't tell her, but I decided they had more serious things to think about, such as figuring out their adolescent children!)

Then came such a rapid change in personality I became alarmed. One lunchtime she did the dishes without being threatened, cajoled or ordered. ("It's good for my nails," she explained.)

She tried trimming her eyebrows with blunt-edged manicure scissors, the effect was startling. She offered to carry a lunch tray to her brother, who had become glued to the television set during spring vacation, and began to call her younger sister, "Little Sister" in ominous Doris Day tones.

The next few days showed no signs of change. Then just as radically she picked off her nail polish made a tent on the clothesline with old bedspreads and spent an afternoon with the tea party and Tiny Tears doll baby circuit.

It was anything but dull. We never knew if she would show up for dinner with a stoved finger from football, long fingernails covered with shiny-white polish or a doll's dress that needed a new snap.

The uncertainty of it was beginning to make us all edgy.

There was her brother, just a normal uncommunicative, guitar-strumming teenager with long bangs, and her "Little Sister" relentlessly plowing her way through the Nancy Drew mystery books and this—this enigma.

Things appear to be leveling off, however, and the identity crisis is almost over. Last evening she challenged her Dad to a game of basketball, clipped her brother on the back and yelled at her sister. I noticed only one hand had fingernail polish on the nails, and she has stopped noticing my dreadful slippers.

Let's hope it lasts a day or two!

Holiday Projects May Test Dad's Christmas Spirit

December 4, 1966

"Why can't we ever enter the festive season sensibly?" lamented the head of the household.

"What exactly do you mean by sensibly?" I asked demurely from beneath a pile of felt remnants and odd fragments of patterns.

"Well, last year it was wreaths and the year before that it was coat hanger trees. Heaven only knows what it will be this year."

I interrupted his soliloquy. "Look, I forgot all about these darling Santas." There were a dozen or so red felt Santa faces in a box marked "Maps and Folders."

We were sitting on the floor in the midst of what in some homes might be called "artful clutter,' in others, "dust collectors" and in our particular abode goes by the name of "Lower Slobovia." It contains all the marking of do-it-yourself projects, many unfinished projects and enough sequins, braid, felt and assorted trivia to decorate Times Square.

"If you ever would get rid of some of this, I'll build you the book-shelves you always are talking about," continued my hero.

"Get rid of this!" I was suitably shaken. "Why you never know when the Brownie troop might need two square yards of pink brocade or a juice can full of yellow sequins. Which reminds me, have you any chicken wire in the basement?"

Now it was his turn to be shaken. "I thought we decided absolutely no more pets until springtime!"

"For wreaths, silly. There are hundreds of pine cones somewhere in a big shopping bag, if I could just find that shopping bag."

He began to wilt visibly. In another two weeks he will be drilling holes in Yule logs to hold candles and perhaps even stringing pinecones with the rest of us.

All the world loves a do-it-yourselfer.

The dime stores are filled with styrofoam in a hundred different shapes and sizes.

There are a dozen books on the newsstand telling how to build everything from a dollhouse to a miniature gumdrop castle. People build whole careers on dreaming up projects for other people.

My earliest memories of the holiday season are of my own mother hastening through the pre-dawn knitting the last sleeve, sewing tiny buttons on miniscule doll clothes or spraying the last gilt angel.

Last year our own girls took up crepe paper wreath making. We had wreaths of every color hanging from every picture hook and ledge in the house.

This year it's folded trees made from Reader's Digests. There must be two dozen trees in various stages of folding and spraying. Who ever heard of a pale blue Reader's Digest tree?

Remember the year of the toothpick trees?

And the year we saved 74 empty juice cans and forgot what we had planned to make with them?

This must be the holiday I finish Dear Friend's Finnish sweater, started and promised two years ago. Somehow it doesn't mean much anymore when I tell him he would have to pay fifty dollars for that sweater in a Carnaby Street Shop. (I dare not think of the three half-finished pairs of wool socks buried somewhere in the bottom drawer. Maybe I can find some dachshund owners who would like argyle sweaters for their pets.

I've discovered a marvelous pattern for a lacy stole, a breakfast tray and a seesaw. Himself is somewhat distraught. "Why should I make a see-saw? We don't know a soul we can give a see-saw to." He has lost his affinity for the aesthetic balance of a bright orange see-saw. I pull out my sympathetic Helen Hayes look, "Darling, why don't you make a drink and read the new Reader's Digest. There's a great article on archaeology."

"I can't," he announces glumly, "It's already folded and sprayed. Pink. Whoever heard of a pink tree?"

"M-o-t-h-e-r" comes a call from the bottom of the stairwell. "Where are the toothpicks? I have to take 190 tomorrow for a project in art class."

Our mantel will never hold all this!

Children Nourish the Wonder in World Around Us

March 5, 1967

Children nourish the wonder in us.

It begins when they are babies and while it may ebb and flow like tides through their growing years it continues to feed our needs in sweet surprise like the first spring flower or the first swift snowfall.

Their wonder about the world around them may be profound or funny. It may happen on hushed wintry afternoons or hot, crowded seashore afternoons.

The important thing ultimately is to be there when it does happen.

Recently while the television and stereo were competing with one another and the sounds of a continuing children's argument filled the hallway, I hurriedly cleared the table, trying not think of a meeting only twenty minutes away and another half-dozen things demanding my immediate attention.

"Come here, come here quick!" demanded one of the girls at the open back door, wintry wind rushing through the house.

"What is it?" I asked impatiently, annoyed at the interruption in my hasty mental rushing about.

"Just come here—please," the child persisted, lapsing into a hush.

I went to the open back door. The winter twilight was a fading blaze of pink and lavender, like aged velvet falling beneath the dark blanket of night sky. The moon, already high in the southern sky, was a huge silver bowl spilling a strand of stars onto the dark blanket.

There was no need of words. We stood for a moment in the cold winter air, sealed for second in an envelope of wonder, the noises of daily living dimmed and put aside.

Another afternoon all the children watched with tightly controlled breath and glee while the gray squirrel who lives in the oak pranced smartly up to the front door, tilted his head and inspected all of us with bright eyes wary and tail twitching nervously.

He quickly snatched a peanut from the doormat and zoomed toward a nearby patch of ivy. Turning around to make sure he was being observed from a distance, he carefully buried it.

He came back again and again, making endless trips, finally resting on the porch chair to eat on and throw the shells with unexpected abandon into the potted geraniums.

For almost an hour we were brought from separate moods and separate undertakings to share the warmth of another cocoon of wonder.

While parents carefully contrive to find moments of wonder on carefully planned trips to museum and zoos, they are apt to be frustrated and disappointed.

The unexpected moment of wonder is the premium, the prize.

One evening our eldest daughter disengaged herself from her record player and the Monkees long enough to join us at a symphony. Usually tapping her foot to the thrum-drumming of a rock-and-roll beat, she was subdued and thoughtful as she watched the venerable old concert hall fill with people.

The conductor appeared impeccable and restrained in his white tie and tails. Lights dimmed and there were preparatory coughs here and there.

The music began softly at first and then surged in great waves over the chandeliers and gilded boxes above us. For some unaccountable reason I was aware of a brass rail running beneath the row of seats before us. We had all automatically fastened our heels around the rail and the music was quivering and trembling through the vibrations of the rail. I looked sideways. Her eyes were large and luminous in the dark, and I saw quiet tears falling across her flushed cheeks.

At times like this it is not wise on the part of a parent to record the instance with the weight of words. Rather to tuck it away in a pocket of one's heart for that time when the children have grown and are gathering wonders of their own.

'Sound of Music'
Complicates Life for Busy
Mother

March 26, 1967

For a long time I was sure I was probably the only person in this country who had not seen "The Sound of Music."

Oh, I knew a great deal about the film and knew most of the music by heart (as who wouldn't after having been exposed to the record dozens of times a day for a year or more!)

But I had never been exposed first hand to the effervescent charm, which led moviegoers back for second, third and thirty-third repeats of the film.

My children worried. How could I cope daily with the mechanics of living, never having seen Maria?

Finally on a rainy Saturday night the children took their jaded, slightly weary parents to see Miss Andrews as Maria. We stood patiently in line under a chain of rain-wet umbrellas before our neighborhood cinema. A young teen couple engaged in a cheerful patter behind us. This was her fourth trip, his second to see the film.

We settled into our seats at last, the children in front of us, barely able to contain their excitement. Every few seconds one or another would turn around to whisper, "Wait, just wait, you'll really love it!"

When the group of people in nearby seats discovered this was our first time, they offered us bits of advice and generous smiles such as novice voyagers get from seasoned travelers on the first trip abroad.

Lights dimmed, a burst of music filled the theatre and we succumbed with the rest of the world to the beauty of the Alps and the magic of Maria.

Life, since then, has never been quite the same.

Miss Andrews, wherever you are, will you kindly tell my children that everyone cannot spend a spring thunder shower dancing on the bed and singing in sweet harmony while the lightning flashes and thunder booms?

I felt confident, I really did, all the way home, splashing through the midnight puddles with the children singing "Do-Re-Mi" in sleepy good humor.

I felt sheltered and warmed in the glow of lingering melodies. The next morning someone burned the toast and there was a terrible tussle about a caterpillar in a jar in the refrigerator. I felt most un-Julie Andrews-like, quite peeved and disgruntled. And I wouldn't have torn down anyone's draperies to make play clothes for that group of ill-tempered children.

We trekked through the parking lot filled with charcoal grills and most of the U.S. population under 12. I found the picnic hamper getting heavy. All I could think of was Miss Andrews and her brood cheerfully swinging across the mountaintops showing no signs of tiring or crossness.

I was in fact completely gay and cheerful until I tripped and fell over a little boy setting off a firecracker. "Hey, watch where you're goin'!" he yelled.

Once again the magic left me. I growled at one of the children in a most un-Julie way to help me with the damned picnic hamper, for heaven's sake!

It has been like this ever since. Some days I make the beds, smilingly ignore quarrels, and sing all the way through the pile of dirty socks.

Then I have a bad day when I snarl at the children, stomp about and sing not a note, feeling almost immediately remorseful and slightly guilty.

I never felt this way after Mary Poppins. I can't understand it, but I know one thing, you aren't about to get me back to see that movie again! My life is complicated enough!

Inquisitive Kids Hinder Father in Spring Chores

April 23, 1967

Last evening our budding adolescent collapsed into a living room chair, hooked his legs over the arm and proceeded to pick the sole off his sneaker.

"Where'd you go?" murmured hubby from behind the newspaper.

"What did you do?" continued his Dad.

"Nothin'."

"That so?" came the answer.

Now this is not a notable or original conversation, but what makes it significant is that two weeks ago it could not have taken place. Such remarkable disinterest would have been totally unacceptable, but it so happens that friend husband is still recovering from a harrowing Saturday full of questions. He is still "healing" and hence tolerates the oblique answers and half-formed questions.

It began on one of those golden Saturday spring mornings when even the dogs tolerate English sparrows and foolish mortals that we be, we try to jam eight weeks worth of chores into eight hours.

"I think I'll dig up the garden, then put a coat of paint on the back porch," announced Himself, beaming at me over the breakfast table.

"What are those kids doing on the back porch," he asked. There were five or six tots and toddlers pressed against the screen door.

"Oh? They're everyone's little sister and brothers. Nothing much they can do like going down to the ball field. They're just around."

"Hi!" offered hubby in his best diplomatic manner.

They glowed and wriggled and grinned. "Hi! What 'cha eating? Can you come out soon?" A chorus of eager questions flooded the breakfast air.

"Well, I'm just getting ready to dig the garden, and you may watch if you like," answered the benevolent prime minister of the peat moss.

And it began. The sun rose high over the roof, and the five or six children multiplied to 10 or 12 as hubby bent and shoveled and stooped and shoveled some more. "Why are you digging so deep? Where'd you get the shovel? Can I help? Are you going to dig to China?"

He paused to wipe his brow and tried to sort out the questions but they were 20 ahead of him by this time.

"Why are you sweating so? Are you going to get sick from sunburn the way I did once? Does your back hurt? Are you going to grow beans and giants and stuff?"

He came into the house to wash his hands. Anxious faces pressed to the screen door. "Are you coming right back? Do you have to take a nap?"

He sighed. "I didn't have to answer that many questions when I was drafted," he whispered to me.

He returned to the back yard and the car. There were dismayed. "Where you goin'? Will you be gone long? Are you going to the store? When you comin' back?"

When he returned from the paint store, the back yard was oddly quiet. "What happened to the C.I.A.?" he asked.

"Naptime. They all have to rest for an hour."

"It makes me kind of uneasy, now that I don't have to explain every move I make and answer all those questions. Make me a sandwich, if you would, and I'll mix the paint."

Later he claimed they came from miles around to watch him paint, but one went home with a green hand or a green nose.

"How come you're painting so fast? Is it sticky? When can we walk on it? What's your mother doin'?" The investigations force grew in numbers and their curiosity rose like a mushroom over the group.

Hubby discovered it might be easier to anticipate questions and he began to explain everything he did. "First I'm going to sand the rough spots and then I'll paint."

"I have to paint in one direction so it will come out evenly." And so forth. And so forth for an entire Saturday afternoon.

The funny thing was the following Monday I happened to see his secretary downtown on her lunch hour.

She asked, "Is your husband feeling all right today?"

"Yes, I think so, why?"

"Well, he keeps explaining. Like this morning he said, now I'm going to sharpen some pencils, then I'll write my report, then maybe I'll go to the coffee shop. He doesn't have to explain everything to me."

"Well," I smiled, "you just get that way when you're around the K.I.C. a lot."

"The K.I.C.?"

"The Kindergarten Investigation Corps?"

Guitar-Carrying Mother Rejects Folk Singer Role

May 14, 1967

My son the folk singer had broken a string on his guitar.

He wanted to take it to the music shop to have it repaired, but didn't want to be seen carrying it about the shopping center.

"What if someone I know from school sees me?" he lamented.

"They'll just say hey there goes that long-haired folk singer," I retorted, receiving in return a dirty look.

"Would you take it to the shop for me?" he pleaded.

"I would, but right now I am decoding a message from your sister with my genuine Sly Sam Code Ring which we got with 14 frostie toastie box tops."

"That's all right, Mommy," interrupted Miss Sly Sam code-sender. "If you go the shopping center you can turn in my Barbie doll for the new one with joints that bend."

"Which is, you see," said the lunatic, "how I happened to be strolling down the mall of the local shopping center one Saturday afternoon carrying a folk guitar, a slightly bedraggled Barbie doll and wearing my Sly Sam code ring.

The first person I encountered was the president of the P.T.A., looking very dapper in a porkpie hat and country squire tweed sport coat.

"Hi there," he said, feigning nonchalance. I shifted to the other arm and tucked Barbie under one elbow. "Hi! Say, I hear we're getting a fine carousel for the spring fair."

He looked bemused and answered slowly and distinctly, as one might with a very young or very old person: "Oh yes! Yes, indeed, in fact, I know you will enjoy our merry-go-round."

It occurred to me that my appearance was causing him some disconcertion, and I laid my hand gently on his arm to tell him the circumstances. The sun blinked on my Sly Sam spy ring and he, looking wildly about, tipped his hat and disappeared into the gift shop.

The next person I met was one of the children's teachers who never raises her voice and speaks continually of the children as "our little people." My girls adore the ground she walks on and decorate my most hectic days with endless tales of her never-ending graces. She was wearing a smart looking summery dress and carrying an armful of books from the village library.

Again, I had the problem with re-arranging the guitar and the Barbie doll. "Hello there," I called to her. "How are you?"

She stopped dead in her tracks. "Oh, I'm fine. How are you my dear," she asked in an ominously solicitous tone of voice.

"Oh, I'm fine, at least as soon as I trade in my doll and get my strings fixed, I'll be fine."

She put her arm gently around me, "My dear, it is so hot, wouldn't you like to come in out of the sun, and have a nice glass of iced tea with me."

"Golly," I answered." I certainly would love to, but this code ring is beginning to hurt like mad and I better get home before it gets stuck on my finger."

She took refuge in the gift shop also.

The third person I saw was a new neighbor whom I had met once since she moved in the neighborhood. "Hi there," I called out.

I stood smiling with Barbie staring vacantly at the sidewalk and the sun reflecting off my gold spy ring. She glanced quickly at me and darted in a very feminine fashion into the gift shop.

That gift shop was doing a great business since I appeared on the scene. I wondered if they were inside deciding whether to call my husband, my children or the paddy wagon.

Gratefully I deposited the guitar with the broken string on the counter in the music store and explained the problem. While they were fixing it, I dropped in the drug store for a coke and ran into someone who looked vaguely familiar and turned out to be the wife of one of the officials in hubby's business.

We chatted brightly about the weather, and I was careful to keep my hand with the Sly Sam spy ring tucked behind me. A young fellow who works in the music shop stopped by and apologized for interrupting our conversation. He handed me Barbie in her black and white striped bathing suit. "Thought you might need this," he explained. "It was on the counter where you left it."

As always in situations of this nature, explaining only makes it worse. I laid my hand with the gold spy ring on my friend's arm and said as gently as possible, "It has been lovely talking to you but now that my strings are re-strung I must go home and de-code a message from a spy that has come directly to me from Bulgaria in the backyard."

I didn't even turn around to see if she went in the gift shop. There are problems I don't have time for.

That evening my husband asked me to run down to the shopping center to pick him up a can of turpentine.

"I can't possibly," I squealed. "My hair is a sight! What if I should see someone I know!"

Barbecue Culture Aims to Bedazzle Guests

July 16, 1967

Remember "weinie roasts?" That was before the present day of glorified patio-dom with its miracle marinades and electric rotisseries.

We used to sit around a small fire and toast our hot dogs on the ends of long sticks until they sizzled and popped. We might have a bag of potato chips and some lemonade if there were lemons left in the icebox. Special days we mixed up a bowl of salad.

That was BB (before barbecues).

We now have a Barbecue Culture with its accompanying tribalistic rituals, costumes, folklore and written history. Invite us to a champagne dinner and we are impressed but hardly nervous. Begin with the spoon on the right and progress inward. Wear pearls. White wine with the fish sauce.

But, invite us to a barbecue, and we immediately find our palms damp with nervous perspiration. We dash to our closet to find out what is available, then to the phone to find out what everyone else is wearing.

The hostess might appear in a hot pink satin jumpsuit, pop art culottes or her country tweed Bermudas and cardigan from Scotland.

"Come casual" was the blithe instruction from a recent hostess. She dazzled everyone with her red, white and blue butcher apron and matching leotard. In my standard suburban blue Bermudas and starched white blouse I felt like someone's visiting aunt from Kansas City.

I haven't had an honest-to-goodness simple hamburger at a patio party in more than a year. I have had curried lamb, veal delight and beef in a variety of 500 marinades (at separate times, thank heavens!)

Cheese imported from Holland, salad from someone's secret Peruvian recipe, ham cooked in a stocking—and holy of holies, the shish kebab, flaming delight of the Orient—all these have paraded before my barbecue-bedazzled eyes.

After a summer of this I had no recourse but to go out and buy a barbecue cookbook. There are a dozen to choose from. The pictures are magnificent, and with reluctant candor, I admit that I've tried few recipes, but it makes great reading on rainy Saturday nights when the late show is a bore. (Ray Milland and Betty Hutton[32] on a balcony in midtown Manhattan and me with my barbecue cookbook poking hubby and saying, "Hey, sweeties, doesn't glazed-honey-dipped-smoked-chicken-wings sound divine?")

The barbecue cookbook became a status symbol.

Visiting the kitchen of my hostess in search of a simple glass of ice water, I found her husband carefully sifting through half-a-dozen bowls of marinade hunting his cigarette lighter. He spoke in a hushed voice. "If I mix the bowls up it will throw her schedule off and she'll be confused." I was confused too. I don't know if we had beef tarragaon or sweet and sour pork. Maybe it was curried hot dogs, heaven forbid!

The husband of a friend mentioned casually to her before bed on Wednesday that he had invited his bowling league over for a "cook-out" on Friday. Before fainting, his wife inquired sweetly (it was almost their last communication), "How many?"

"Oh about 34," he yawned. "Not counting kids, of course," he added. Noting her shock-glazed eyes, he soothed: "Now nothing special, just hot dogs and hamburgers and maybe some potato salad if you feel up to it."

"Oh Jimmy, why didn't you invite them to dinner? It would have been so much easier," she sobbed, slamming the closet door on her hand.

Last I saw her she was in the kitchen with my beautiful barbecue cookbook grinding peppers and shaking vinegar bottles and chopping mushrooms. I went home and made a simple American cheese sandwich. Best thing I've had to eat in ages.

Fall Pilgrimage Is a Real Joy; Educational, Too

October 22, 1967

Autumn is a time for pilgrimages.

With a smoky blue haze over the mountains we headed south where the hillsides already were covered with red and gold patterns of color and the air was filled with the scent of falling leaves and morning dew.

In the orchards the trees were bending with the weight of apples and roadside stands abounded in the fall harvest—gallon jugs of cider, red and yellow apples, brilliant orange pumpkins, Indian corn and jars of homemade jelly.

Lunch was served on a fallen log 3,000 feet above sea level, with the valley set before us emerging from the morning mist like some lovely pastoral. A new and interesting insect, sculptured like a Giacometti, dropped on the log and explored its far reaches as we watched fascinated.

There were the trees, the air, the valleys and the colors. We felt no need of "civilization's" dubious assets at this particular moment.

As the afternoon sun crossed the sky we hiked deep into a gorge to watch the final spectacular descent of splashing white falls. Breathless and awed, we sat on boulders and listened only to the water's excited babbling. The hike back up the mountainside was a gallant affair, punctuated only by groans and puffing. We knew why the Indians were reputedly so quiet!

Dinner was cooked as the moon rose in a white arc over the valley below, and a fox ran across the road, drawn to the smell of our campfire. Temperatures drop fast in the mountains, and before dinner was fully done we were huddled under blankets gratefully drinking hot chocolate with marshmallows.

By the time we had doused the campfire and put away our gear, it was very late, and cold and tired, we were looking forward to the 20th century motel that beckoned at the end of the mountain range.

"You may watch television as long as you like after you are ready or bed," came the blessing. There were sighs of delight.

Like eerie refugees from a sooty campfire we arrived at the motel, clad in our rugged mountain clothes, to mingle with the local people who were in best "bib and ticker" for a Saturday evening. Never had hot baths and central heating felt so good!

Sleepy heads were nodding on the pillow when the Saturday night movie came on the television screen. Five minutes later there wasn't an open eye in the room. I crept to the wide picture window and watched the neon blinking of a dozen signs. Beyond were the mountains and the haze, but nothing was visible. "Civilization" had usurped its rights.

Sunday was for heroes.

We walked the brick sidewalks of historic little towns where patriots were born and raised and fought. We read historic plaques and gazed at statues. We walked the beautiful green fields where Civil War battles were won and lost and the destinies of men decided.

High on a Virginia mountaintop the children found a hero in the Monticello home of Thomas Jefferson. A name in a history book, he came alive to them in the beds of lovely blue wildflowers and the meticulous letters written to his daughter—all preserved with grace and love for this generation to see.

There on the mountaintop, with visitors from Korea before us and students in chic mod clothing behind us, we all felt the invisible breath of history draw us close and nearer to those dear to us.

Jefferson only wanted to be remembered for three things, the gentle lady in gray told us. He was the builder of the University of Virginia, the author of the Virginia Religious Liberty Law and the author of the Declaration of Independence. These were his gifts to the people. All the other things that happened to this statesman he considered as gifts from the people to him.

There were few dry eyes left in the room.

In the late afternoon happy sunset of an autumn weekend we each stayed quiet in the cocoon of our separate thoughts. History had touched us. The mountains had touched us. For a short time we had loved this land in a way unique, one which cannot be described in a 60-second television commercial or a rhyming jingle promising riches at the nearest gas station.

'Essence of Soul' Creates
Hermit in Electric Age

December 1967

Since assorted personages such as the Monkees and the Beatles and the Association have been usurping our silence (yes, Marshall McLuhan[33], this is an electric age!) for some time, I decided to invade theirs.

There was to be a fall dance at the junior high school, and one of our many guitar-playing neighbor friends was in a band competing for first place. Three bands would participate, and the winning group would get the Christmas dance contract. They had spent hours and hours rehearsing, and pooled their resources when a piece of equipment gave out or needed repairs. The mothers had been drafted only to buy matching shirts for the boys.

The matching shirts were a nice idea, but since I find it difficult to tell one 14-year-old boy from another, beneath their bangs, it seemed a bit unnecessary.

Now, it is a well-established fact that our teen offspring would much prefer we not visit them at (a) school, (b) dances or (c) parties. In fact, they would just as soon we pick them up incognito and as unobtrusively as possible when they are visiting the dentist or the local shopping center.

The PTA even sends letters home to let the parents know when meetings are to be held. They know their teenagers well!

Thus my announcement that I planned to visit the battle of the bands came as a shock and was received with about as much enthusiasm as the news that the last of the Beatles would be married.

"You're not serious?" asked my daughter who was creaming her face with my cream and drying her hair and polishing her nails with my nail polish.

"Well, I thought I would wear your fish-net hose, and my miniskirt and maybe those false eyelashes," I answered demurely. Everyone looked anguished. They could not have been more disturbed had I announced I was entertaining the Watusi contest in Macy's front window.

Dance night came, the giggling gaggle of girls departed, and I, having promised faithfully on all my hand-made potholders that I would "not make a scene by showing up in a miniskirt," left also for the school gymnasium. (In a gray flannel skirt and round-collared blouse that fairly shouted "M-O-M!")

"You're not really going?" asked hubby.

"Of course I am. I have been listening to that child practice for five years. Now I want to hear him in live action!"

The name of the band, ten in number, (not counting amplifiers), was "Essence of Soul!" The essence of soul, it would appear, is noise. And more noise.

The parking lot of the good gray school was fairly rattling with the steady throbbing of a million kettledrums. Walls trembled when I opened the door and the soles of my feet were stuck with the floor tiles reverberating to the biggest beat I had ever heard.

I crept furtively down the hall, joined by several other M-O-Ms. At the end of the hall were the coat racks holding about 500 coats. Several hundred more were on the windowsills, floor, bookshelves and counters. I was thinking of the $40 coat my darling daughter had eyed with lingering love in a department store only the evening before.

In the gym several hundred teen-agers were dancing in some primitive tribal dance with the most intricate and fanciful footwork I have ever seen!

It seems that amplifiers have little amplifiers and the world is just one big amplifier where this music is concerned. "You can't really feel it if your eardrum punctures," one of the parents shouted into my coat collar.

I was astonished to see our daughter engaged in an intricate line dance with much finger snapping and elbow jerking. Fred Astaire would have been mildly pleased. I was dumbfounded. Here was a child who could not get up and down the stairs without falling part way, dancing as though the night would never end. There were dozens of others who at day's end were so tired it was difficult to open the back door for their mothers when they came home carrying five sacks of groceries. But their energy had returned marvelously, thanks to the "Essence of Soul," and they were jumping, jiggling, jouncing and jigging, as though 10,000 red ants had been let loose in the school gymnasium!

I met the mother of the drummer, the one with the white hair, tired eyes and earmuffs. I met the father of the amplifiers (He put up the loan). I waved at our friend the guitar player. He seemed most relieved I had my mother costume on and not the Twiggy outfit.

There was a stunning young miss in platinum hair doing the shag or something like that. She teaches English. There was a tall handsome fellow doing the hurly-burley or something like that. He teaches algebra.

After twenty minutes of soul, I crept back down the hall and into the dark blue silent night. The silence made me uneasy. I looked in the back seat of the car to make sure there weren't any hidden amplifiers. Then I stopped at the shopping center and bought a pint of butter pecan ice cream, went home and put away all the records on the floor and put three Mancini records on the stereo. Mr. McLuhan, you may think it's necessary to become involved in this electric age. But I, sir, have just become a hermit in the electric age. Think of it, an electric hermit!

PART III

Having Teen-Age Children Is What Causes Middle Age

1968–1972

Intellectual Elf Sheds Her Image as Miss Tagalong

1968

Miss Tagalong, the youngest in this household of individualists, has decided lately she will no longer tag along.

Definitive and decisive at age 11, she let it be known that she preferred dark frames for glasses despite what the rest of the family liked. The fact that her sister declared it made her look like an intellectual elf caused her no more worry than a dangling participle. Besides, what's so terrible about an intellectual elf?

Concentration is her forte. This was inevitable since she grew up in the midst of pandemonium, auditory, physical and otherwise, while her father and brother sit in vocal concentration before the football game on television and her sister plays the transistor radio at so many annoying decibels, she sits curled in the big green armchair traveling with Nancy Drew through this week's mystery maze.

She began to cook when she was old enough to climb on a kitchen chair and stir the cookie dough or the cake batter or the mixture of the moment. Addicted to gingerbread, warm and fragrant, topped with peaks of whipped cream, she will mix up gingerbread from a mix and have it in the oven before bedtime snack time. It still annoys her that she is not yet considered old enough to light the oven herself.

Perhaps because she is of a quiet bent, a bit shy, pretty much the introvert, she has developed a passion for wild colors. The province of psychedelic color patterns was hers before the hippies took over. Call it purple and hot pink, citrus orange and violent purple, but call it hers.

Now that she is sewing, she runs straight as an arrow to the "wildest" display of fabrics. But as she keeps telling us, it is her money and her taste, and if we prefer those quiet browns and greens, so much the sadder for us. She would rather play cards with her Dad than straighten her closet shelves, which somehow look as though they were about to come down or had just been installed. Her sock drawer is likely to contain acorns and bits of ribbon and old spelling papers. Her "project box" is so big now it won't begin to fit under her bed.

Under way are a seascape in oils, a muffler in red and white, printed signs, crocheted doilies, a sampler or two and too many tangled things to mention. But she is a finisher. Every few weeks or so, from this massive heap of handicraft, emerges a finished project. Which, as her father relentlessly points out, is a far better average than her mother has been maintaining over the years of Unfinished Projects.

She is the first to finish the dishes when her turn comes along, and is apt to have to do a few over again, when checked. Somewhere along the line, she got drafted into taking the venerable "old dog" (as called by our dismayed allergist friend) for her morning constitutional before the morning dew has left the grass.

While the milkman finishes his neighborhood route and the early birds are arriving at the school down the street, our intellectual elf and venerable dog trot to the soccer field, once around, and born again.

There has been, I understand, a "meeting of the minds" because of these morning strolls. It is getting chilly now and foggy and the elf likes to stay nestled in her warm bed longer than usual, which means the length of the walk must be cut down.

When the elf has not arisen by 8 a.m., old dog is sitting by her bed, waiting, eyes properly martyred, tilt of the head, properly suggesting patience and expectation. She follows Miss-Used-To-Be-Tagalong to the kitchen where she again sits in martyred silence while breakfast is consumed. At last they break into a trot and start down the street, the cocker's ears flying in the wind, dear one huddled in her early-morning sweater.

At the soccer field they cannot agree. Pooch would continue. Miss Elf would return to the warm kitchen. They stand and stare and utter not a word. There is a wall of silence. Pooch will not plead. Miss Elf is adamant. She turns, starts home, and with a backward glance over a flying ear, pooch bounds along, too.

It is to the best of our knowledge, the first time in this long association of canine-family relationship, that pooch has given in to family. Run this girl for president, I keep telling the rest of the folks over the burned toast and sticky strawberry jam and spilled milk.

But she is deep in a crossword puzzle, and cannot hear me, or will not hear me. The pooch is resting her white-tipped head on Miss Elf's independent little lap.

Drumless Combo Makes Good Use of Trash Can Lid

March 24, 1968

While the rest of the children are pressing their noses to the large plate glass window of the pet shop, our 15-year old is in the nearby music shop gazing blissfully at ominous looking electronic equipment.

"Let the boy dream," sides his father, who, nevertheless, cringes when the living room is filled with a record advertising the manic sounds of half-a-dozen wailing electric guitars.

"I would prefer that he dream of something less audible," I sigh, "like lemon meringue pie and weekend camping trips.

It is not so much that I dislike all that electronic gear cluttering up the scene for our younger generation. It is just that their determination in the face of insurmountable challenges gratifies me.

Case in point: the trash can man!

For some months now, the boys have talked of nothing but assembling a "group." Since there now must be 147 other such "groups" in their age bracket alone, such discussion was accepted for digestion and then forgotten. One of the boys continued to play rhythm and the other, melody. It was a pleasing, easy arrangement.

Last week they came home jubilant. The third member of the group had been discovered! A quiet lad, not given to boasting, his talent has been noticed as he drummed on a lab table during a biology lecture. "Do you play the drums?" they asked elatedly. He blushed and beat out a quick tattoo with a jazz coda.

I interrupted like a rude parent: "Where are you practicing?" I asked.

"Here, Mom, here," cheered the gang twirling me around in the kitchen. "From one to five on Saturday afternoon and from 7:30 to 10 in the evening."

"That's nice," I squeaked, wondering how far the patience of our frazzled neighbors would stretch during these "growing years" (commonly known as the "noisy ones.")

Saturday chores were accomplished with unbelievable enthusiasm, in preparation for the arrival of the drummer. He was tall and gangly and had never heard of Gene Krupa.

"Where are his drums?" I asked innocently.

"Didn't we tell you?" he hasn't got them yet. He's getting them for his birthday in August. His parents promised!"

"What does he play on then?"

"Trash can lids!" they crowed all in a voice.

You know, the funny thing is, they didn't seem to sound half-bad. Bass blues, six-string melody and pastry brushes on trash can lids—not quite bluegrass and not quite folk rock, but interesting!

Hence it is that I view with alarm these yearnings over amplifiers and the like. Perhaps, somewhere, back in my primitive parental psyche, is the fear of being replaced by 1500 amps.

◆   ◆   ◆

Dining out at an old German restaurant on Dad's birthday, our 10-year-old was enthralled with a ball of twine representing $18,000,000 worth of napkins. Some unknown person had saved the twine that wraps the napkins as they are returned from the laundry.

The finished ball measured almost three feet in circumference. If her older brother can be window-gazing at the music shop, then why can't she go about the neighborhood gathering up odd pieces of string and yarn? A charmingly uncomplicated girl, why in the world has she taken it into her mind that she, too, can save 18 million dollars worth of string?

The same little miss has recovered all her school books in bright yellow with the notation in broad black letters: CLOSED WEEK-ENDS.

◆   ◆   ◆

Call it the eerie influence of the equinox, or call it what you will, the entire family has come down with jigsaw puzzlephoria.

The addiction leaves little time for other communal activities such as eating. Comfortingly enough, it has come to supercede television as it is possible to listen to all the dialogue and leave one's eyes and hands free for the intricate contours of unbroken blue sky and mazes of azaleas.

While no formal societies have been formed, it is possible to meet other puzzle maniacs on buses, at meetings, in school. We have not been able to cure one another yet, but we have exchanged symptoms and puzzles.

While the round puzzles are interesting, somehow the challenge of finding the corner piece is lost and there is a vaguely dissatisfied feeling! Puzzle-lovers are insomniacs as well. How could one possibly go to sleep with only 47 pieces to fit into that pattern of choppy sea.

And curses on the person who lost the orange piece from the middle of the sailboat. The entire house is turned upside down at 2 a.m. in search of the missing link.

A black day in the history of the family was the day I tripped over the dog, fell into the card table and upset twenty hours of careful work on a Riviera beach scene. Banished from the playroom, it was for me an oddly sad time sitting upstairs reading the weekly magazines and hearing the groans and sighs coming from the puzzle room.

Father's Day ... A Message to a Son Growing up

June 16, 1968

This is a letter to a son.

Today is Father's Day 1968. Because of the sad events of the last ten days [the assassination of U.S. Senator Robert F. Kennedy on June 6], the holiday takes on a different dimension of meaning, a special quality far removed somehow from the frivolous ties in gift-wrapped boxes and witty art cards we have come to expect.

Today you are the son. Sometime in our tomorrows, in our tomorrows, you will be a father. The chains of family continue on, and even now we are weaving together the legacies of tomorrow.

We would wish you these.

We would wish you love, not the wailing love your records shriek of, but the strong current of love that binds men to their families and to their county and makes them giants. Just as you have seen your country mourn, you have seen them join in one outpouring of unaffected love. Take pride in this.

We would wish you compassion.

And tenderness.

We would wish that your determination of purpose be tempered with the gentle winds of compassion, for it is the tree that bends which grows tall and supple and will not snap in brittle frustration.

We would wish you valor.

And honor.

Old-fashioned words in an up-tight world, but yours is the generation of lyrical words, of innovation, of imagination and introspection.
Take honor and valor into your heart.

We would wish you belief in the individual.

A well-worn saying from the Chinese admonished that a journey
of a thousand miles must begin with a single step.

In your lifetime you have seen national mourning three times over,
repeating the seemingly endless cadences and codas of shock and
grief. You have had to leave the ball fields and playgrounds early
because of rioting in city streets. You have seen college students
invade their president's office, and you have seen older brothers leave
for war. Sheltered in an affluent society, weaned on television, you
have been buffeted by tides of violence.

We wish you justice.

And justice, particularly for you, must begin with a single step.

It means adhering to the truth, refusing to take the easy way out. It
means not copying another's homework, being strong enough to
stand up for your beliefs though you disagree with the crowd. It
means sacrificing some of your own comforts and looking about you
at the inequalities not ten miles from where you live in the lives of
those less fortunate.

This will take courage.

Justice is not reserved for that white-columned building you visited with awe so many years ago. Justice is a living, breathing part of
you, which should be with you from the moment you turn off the
alarm each day until you finish the work and play and problems of
that day.

We would wish you understanding.

And respect for wisdom. An open mind. What a beautiful pure
expression, and what labor to achieve!

We struggle, now, you and I. You are growing upward and out-
ward in a million ways. You disagree. You fret. You are stirred and
troubled and torn in ways you cannot understand. You resent this
generation's attempt to "understand" their mistakes, their burdens.

There is a bridge we have been watching now for more than a year. It is on the winding road through marshes and truck gardens and factory districts that takes us finally to the beach. We have come to know the road well and to watch with some interest the progress of the steel girders as they have been erected.

There is an imposing sweep of steel, a breathless drop over choppy waters, the mastery of men and material. But what amazes us most is that the bridge was begun on both sides of the crossing. We joked about this. Would the two spans meet or would they bypass one another in the middle?

We are a great deal like those two spans. In the middle the widely ballyhooed "generation gap." But both spans have been built with care and precision. And someday the bridge will be one.

We would wish you all this, and above all we would wish that you light a candle, take one step, look around you and share your vision.

You have mourned and I have mourned.

Now it is time to light a candle of justice, to build another cable in our bridge still unfinished, to use the gift of today.

Saturday Gives Grounded Family Rough Weekend

August 11, 1968

"Saturday" is a parakeet with the spirit of an eagle and the aeronautical audacity of a Boeing 707.

He came on a Saturday and left on Saturday.

Bright green in plumage, he boasted a canary yellow head and lovely long tail. Mercurial of mood, he would sit for pensive minutes watching the family activities then, quick as a flash, dart to the top of his cage to stage an impromptu boxing bout with his silver bell.

His first trick was to learn to unhinge the door to his cage and open it. Thereafter it was rarely closed. Ignoring the fancy trappings of his cage with its bells and parakeet toys, he took up a stand on the dining room windowsill fencing with the lock and pressing his head against the glass to watch the sparrows and murmur to them in a dove-like voice.

As he matured he developed a dogmatic personality. Refusing all coaxing to emit some inane phrase repeated 1,000 times before his cage by a human he merely tolerated, he spent a large part of the morning rearranging his cage, tossing out the lettuce leaves he disliked and rolling up the paper towel covering if the color was not to his pleasure.

Strangers walking down the street paused to wave to him. Small children stopped and giggled. Oblivious to all, he fell madly in love with his echo. Perching on the tall glass chimney of a white milk glass hurricane lamp, he discovered how to lower his head and chest into the hollow part of the lamp and by murmuring to himself create an echo.

Then one day he lost footing and fell into the lamp. As he was extricated gingerly, he squawked angrily at the family, blaming it for his discomfort and embarrassment. Occasionally he would fall in again, and we would hear a pleading murmur to his echo and gain, the gentle extrication would begin.

Second only to this was his fascination with his reflection in the hall mirror where he spent countless hours preening and admiring and tapping his beak against the parakeet image. It was dangerously close to the front door, but he never flew in that direction.

But something inside "Saturday" yearned for the free air, and one Saturday morning as he sunned in the backyard while his friends the sparrows had lunch, he freed himself and soared into the nearest maple tree, and from thence over the treetops.

First came incredulity. Then came the deluge of tears.

All activity ceased as we paced the neighborhood from block to block watching for a flash of green in the jungle of August greenery above us. It was a futile attempt. Then, hours later, his bright arrogant chirp was heard just a street away in the top of a young oak tree.

We assembled beneath the tree, a motley crew: dogs with wagging tails, youngsters in bare feet with tear-streaked faces, neighbor's children.

There were adults with paintbrushes and tea towels in hand, their projects abandoned behind them. Someone brought a ladder, and someone else brought Saturday's empty cage (no temptation at all to him!) Still another brought a pet parakeet hoping to lure him with friendship. We had thought of acquiring a friend for him and naming her "Sunday," but he was an independent individualist in love with his own fine echo.

Perched in the lofty treetops, Saturday watched the activity beneath him, for a time distracted from the preening of his feathers. Bored, finally, he soared off to another tree and the growing crowd chased him down one street and then another. An ice cream man stopped to replenish the troops. Everyone had a parakeet story to tell. Hours passed. Morale sagged. Dinnertime came. The search, now merely a token gesture, was abandoned temporarily.

That evening there was a woeful lapse in the contrapuntal beat and sounds of a family gathering for dinner and talk.

Sunday came and went.

Monday morning before the sun had burned away the early haze a tyke knocked on the door and announced solemnly that the vagabond was home. "He's in your very own tree." And so he was. I climbed a ladder with his cage and cautiously tinkled the silver bell. He tilted his head and then with absurd dignity walked down a low-hanging branch, paused, looked at me, and walked directly into his feeding tray, where he pressed his face against the tiny mirror, perhaps to reassure himself of his individual existence after 48 hours in the vast green outside with its unknown terrors.

Unearthly docile and quiet he submitted to our welcomes and caresses, then slept for several hours. He was unnaturally quiet, but the next morning he began with a loud squawk chorus, buzzed the Baron at breakfast, and landed on the hurricane light with a great crashing halt. Once again, Saturday was king of the hill. Of his hill.

'New' Pants Look Proves You Must Go "Out" to Be 'In'

September 29, 1968

Yves St. Laurent opened his new boutique, Rive Gauche, in New York, and the police had to control a mob of 20,000 who turned out to see his "new" pants look. Incredibly shy and boyish in tousled hair and horn-rimmed glasses, St. Laurent appeared in a paisley shirt, colorful tie and many strings of chains about his neck.

Makes you think about the mornings you send the boys back upstairs to change and they come to the breakfast table with striped shirts and plaid trousers, doesn't it?

It is becoming more and more difficult to stay "in," because, essentially you see, you must go further "out" in order to be "in." Just when I am getting up the courage to shorten my fall skirts by two inches, everything is pant! Just when I have saved enough labels to send away for my genuine plastic, see-through, soup-can pillow, Emile Zola posters become very "in" and the soup cans are "out."

Barbara Streisand started the big rush to the thrift shops for faded boas to wrap around the 1920-style beaded dress. Now I can buy feathered boas (imitation, of course, how many boas do you think there can be!) in seven different shades in my favorite yard goods department. I can also buy imitation rattlesnake skin and fake fur and fake leather. The prices are real.

Early in the summer our eldest asked me to make a Nehru-type shirt with Dr. Zhivago-type embroidery. There were no patterns at that time, and the weeks melted together. Now there are patterns and he tells me instead he wants an American Indian shirt and real moccasins. In six weeks we have jumped two cultures.

Peacock feathers are on sale in our local supermarket, and I keep worrying about the peacocks. Did they shed them, or were they forced to part with their beautifully elegant feathers with the purplish eye on the tip. In order to fill the fireplace with peacock feathers and cat-o-nine tails it would cost me about as much as importing a peacock from wherever it is one imports peacocks!

At a recent gathering I was the only person with ordinary-toned stockings. Preference ran to off-white, which gives one the appearance of a rejuvenated corpse. All this is happening when I am still learning how to apply eyeliner that will make my eyes three times as large. With the ineptitude at cosmetics resulting in black smudged eyes I can only assume that wearing pale pink stockings might add to the general impression of impending illness.

Our girls change their bulletin board weekly and sometimes more often. There may be pictures of favorite recording artists interspersed with psychedelic artwork and postcards from summer trips. My bulletin board in the kitchen still holds a dental appointment card from 1966. It takes so much time to stay "with it."

The hippies discovered (or so they thought) the Army-Navy surplus store. Happy as children, they bought up old fatigue shirts and durable winter jackets. What they don't remember is that their mamas were trekking to the surplus stores to buy canteens and mess kits for their Boy Scout days, ten-cent bandanna handkerchiefs for their sisters and other assorted interesting things from camping lanterns to camouflage tents! This was long before it was fashionable.

What really hurt was to discover I was the only person in the beauty shop, other than the operator! Every other chair was occupied by a wig or wiglet, while its mistress was apparently home waxing the floors or out shopping for bargains.

There I was wig-less and eyelash-less, enough labels in my pocket-book (which by the way is Nantucket, circa 1939) to send for the genuine plastic see-through soup-can pillow, and then I noticed! I was the only female in the room with a skirt on. Cute little blondes in culottes and svelte brunettes in black jump suits glided about affixing curlers and drinking diet drinks and talking about their boyfriends.

Is this the real world I asked myself! It upset me so much I almost bought one of those genuine gold mesh Indian headbands to wear to the next meeting of our Tuesday Quilting Club party! (Except that the Tuesday Quilting Club is now down at the new place in town where they teach housewives the newest psychedelic dance steps. They even have a cut-rate package where you can learn to bowl, dance and get a massage.)

It is not enough I must keep up with the music, the clothes and the art of our day-to-day culture. Now I cannot even read a good book in peaceful solitude. New books are creations of sight, sound and smell, the "reading" of which may require paper folding, incense burning and tape recordings. Enough is enough! I have been through the sight, sound, smell, show-and-tell years of three children's infancy years. Please, 1969, let a book be a book be a book!

Today's Upbeat Heroes Prompt Escape into Nostalgia

December 1, 1968

"But you said," he insisted with aggravated adolescent dignity, "that we could always buy whatever we wanted with our own money."

I was gazing at the pristine white surface of a double record album by an internationally known British rock and roll group. It boasted a glossy album picture (perhaps on the thesis of reverse snobbery, that is, their fame is so great, no picture would be necessary to sell the album). Inside were four moderate-sized pictures of the recording arts, a large poster, the lyrics to all the songs, including something about a glass onion, something about a girl named Sadie, and something about the USSR. I read all the lyrics carefully over coffee and cake, trying to remember that Leonard Bernstein[34], who, as everyone knows, is great, thinks THEY are great. It didn't work.

The metaphors were inventive, the images elusive, and I felt as though I were shadow boxing with a cynical guru. The beat, as always, was methodically deafening.

I began to tell him about the theater of the absurd. It trailed away into nothingness, as the weight of my thirty-odd years identification with Ella Fitzgerald and Frank Sinatra put me into the category of People Whose Opinions Don't Count.

Meanwhile, upstairs, the girls were patching their sneakers with adhesive tape prior to basketball practice. The older one was dabbling her newest skin cream on assorted spots, and her sister was reading upside down on the bed.

"Turn on a light, you'll ruin your eyes," I said automatically, hunting for my bath salts on their bureaus and quietly returning the talcum powder I had borrowed the day before. The dog was placidly sitting by the wastebasket waiting for everyone to turn around so she could upset it and run away with the candy wrappers.

"All the cream in the world won't help if you don't eat enough fresh vegetables and fruit and get enough sleep," I said, thinking to myself, "This is a recorded announcement."

Eyes rolled skyward.

They are already putting the finishing touches on holiday gifts and wrappings they have made and finished themselves with materials purchased from allowance money. I am still running around ten lists in my head, 15 lists on paper and a pin in my slip. I could cry.

It is almost time for the grievance committee to meet. The grievance committee meets on alternate evenings or on those occasions when Mother has had a fairly peaceful day and is not apt to turn it into a reverse-play "Now-it's-my-turn!" hearing.

"Make her clean up her half of the room." I look about. There are only three skirts, two sweaters, two stuffed dogs and a pair of shoes on the bed. I make a note. "Make her stop calling me 'Ole Wart-Nose,'" Sympathy is nine-tenths of the court's decision in this case. I cluck quietly and shake my head.

Their brother appears. "Make him stop putting his old junk in our room," they complain. He groans, smiting his forehead in full Shakespearean splendor. "Do you think I need to shave this winter?" he asks, thrusting his smooth jaw forward.

In the basement, the Baron is puttering happily with unfinished projects. A million tiny parts, all electrical or wooden, all ominous, lay about on the floor, and he is whistling happily as the World War II radio plays World War II love songs with sentimental lyrics and unbelievable violin background. "It's rather quiet here, isn't it," I say, pushing aside some condensers and tubes and things, and sitting on the couch.

He smiles, pointing to the acoustical ceiling. "Best thing we ever did," he adds. "Aside from braces and piano lessons and so forth."

We talk about heroes, the gas bill, college, heroes, the telephone bill, the almanac, Glenn Miller[35]. Funny how many heroes today have bushy hair and droopy mustaches and use music and enigmatic tone poems to wrest the nickels and dimes and quarters from all those boys and girls trying to prove they are different from all the other generations that came and went and came and went before.

"There is an Old Gary Cooper western at the shopping center theater," the Baron offers. Nostalgia to soothe the ragged edges of our philosophizing.

"The children say if it isn't Peter Sellers[36], it isn't worth going to."

"Drat the children," he said. It's my allowance and I like Gary Cooper!"

We joined hands, stepped over a meandering mountain of wood shavings and walked silently under the acoustical ceiling upstairs, past the electric beat, Ole Wart-Nose, smiling dog and everyone. In the distance, just behind the drummer in six-eight time, I thought I could hear a violin.

Monday Morning Just Isn't the Right Time to Enjoy Stereo

January 12, 1969

Monday morning comes sliding in palely beneath the bedroom curtains. There is a squirrel running on the roof or perhaps just dry twigs blowing about. I cushion myself in the cocoon of silence and dread the wakening of senses to percolators and alarms and morning sounds.

Creeping downstairs, a sleepy dog swaying and yawning behind me, I put Segovia on the stereo, turn it down low and curl on the sofa to fall into the perfect sounds. The bird murmurs sleepily beneath the cover of his cage.

How lovely to be warm, I think. How lovely to be quiet. How lovely.

An electric alarm zings wildly through the bedroom crashing heedlessly through my silence. Annoyed feet strike, the floor, a door slams, the seven o'clock news intones the current crises.

I shuffle to the kitchen and smell the coffee canister thinking about all those green warm coffee plantations in South America and what the coffee pot says as it pop-pop-pops.

"Mommy, it's raining in the living room," says my 11-year-old, sleepy serious behind her glasses.

"Don't be silly, darling, that's just Daddy taking a shower."

"I know it's just Daddy taking a shower, I hear him singing. But it is still raining in the living room." She yawns.

I go to the doorway. Indeed it is raining in the living room, splashing merrily on the deep gold rug, throwing up little sprays of mist against the walls, gathering in tiny drops on the white ceiling.

"Can we have warm buns for breakfast?" she asks, nestling in a corner of a chair away from the rainstorm.

"Maybe, yes, I don't know," I say, taking the steps two at a time and pounding on the bathroom door.

"What now?" comes the answer. Good heavens, an executive already before the white shirt is ironed and the cuff link inserted.

"Darling it's raining ..."

"... So I'll wear my raincoat!"

"In the living room?"

"Where?"

"We all run down the steps together, the dog barking happily, stereo whirring pleasantly, coffee pot perking and doorbell ringing. The doorbell ringing belongs to the milkman. He tells me I can't keep the Christmas greens in the milkbox anymore. Of course, I reply, hunting an umbrella.

"Lady," he says, "does it often rain in your house?" I smile reassuringly and give him my Greer Garson[37] eyelash-batting trick. "Hardly ever in the summertime," I say.

"Mommy," interrupts the 11-year-old, "there is a strange dog in the backyard. He climbed the fence all by himself."

I run through the house, tripping over things, bumping into tables, trailing my good orange hostess gown.

It may be a dog with amorous intent and that is simply not in the plans this year! Out over the icy porch I fly, through the air now, down the back steps, one at a time, and make a bumpy three-point landing on a patch of icy grass.

The dog and her admirer canine friend look at me with friendly interest. A neighbor passing down the street tips his hat politely and mentions the freezing rain we had in the night.

"My eggs have turned to stone," complains Number One Son, attacking his plate with a knife and fork. "And the butter is cold and hard," adds his father, tacking on, "and have you ironed a shirt for me?"

Down the steps I fly two at a time, plugging in the iron, tuning in the rock-and-roll station on the radio (can iron twice as fast), and praying for clean white shirts in the bottom of the laundry basket. The dog leaps up upon the studio couch and watches with detached amusement. "For you I would have broken both legs," I snarl at her. She wags her tail enthusiastically. "I could be in bed for months! In traction!" She pants hopefully.

Shirt ironed, lunch bags packed, Segovia rescued, rainstorm abated, I pause to take an aspirin.

"You take too many of those things," comments my impeccably groomed, well-fed, disgustingly cheerful husband.

I can't help it. I'm a shrew by now. "The ceiling will probably collapse by nightfall," I say. He doesn't answer.

Then he asks, "By the way, what is that pound of bacon doing defrosting on our bureau. It is with your powder and perfume."

And my darling daughter adds, "Mommy you put a pair of socks in my lunch! I wanted a bologna sandwich."

Clutching Segovia and basting back my ragged hairline with three bobby pins, I march over the damp towels covering the gold rug, take the greens out of the mailbox, wave to a complete stranger passing by, and then I sit by the window to watch the morning sun rise on another quiet humdrum morning.

The Best Part of a Snowfall Is Going Inside to Warm up

March 9, 1969

Snow!

When the snow shovel had been put away and when the first orange-yellow crocus was poking its head through the mulch, it came. Great white flakes drifting down silently and making a white blur out of the horizon. Little ladders of intricate snowflakes climbed the windowpanes, and bridges of snow lace chained from branch to branch of the shrubs beneath the windows.

But it came on a Saturday.

Why not on a Monday? The children moaned. The roads will be clear by school time!

Driving through the onrushing white, our windshield wiper made a happy steady whoosh-whoosh through the gathering accumulation. In the village library there were dozens of rosy-cheeked children in ski hats and high boots, gathering goodies for the weekend.

Through the floor to ceiling windows the trees were a white winter wonderland. Arms full of Styron and Stravinsky, Gold and Grieg, Byron and Bach, we staggered back to the car, laughing and tasting the snow.

Snow makes people hungry. Just the sight of all that great soft whiteness, silent and beautiful, sends people dashing to the groceries for brown sugar and cinnamon, chocolate and marshmallow.

It sends the Baron to the kitchen for his semi-annual fudge production. And a production it is! Lovingly, jars of peanut butter and marshmallow and tins of chocolate are placed on the cupboard. The pans are buttered and lined in a row. The children are lined all in a row. "Can I lick the beaters? It's my turn, my turn!"

Outside, the hush of snow-covered streets, lamps throwing yellow circles on the road. Inside the heady warm smell of fudge coming to a soft boil. Gallons of fudge.

How will we ever eat all that fudge? "We'll manage!"

There is something about playing in the snow at midnight in the frosty silence that is absolutely intoxicating.

The children jumped from the porch into giant snow banks; they flopped with slow-motion elegance into fresh snow, making "snow angels" everywhere. Then they leaped and did cartwheels, their squeals echoing across the open spaces.

Lastly they built a giant nine-foot snowman in the middle of the alleyway." The Abominable Snowman" they crowned him, and ominous he was, looming over the shadows and shapes of the midnight sky, his solid bulk gathering little flakes on the edges. Larger than life, ludicrous, lopsided and completely endearing.

How will we move the car?

Must we move the car?

Can't we play in the snow forever and ever and never go to another place again?

The railings are covered with sodden heaps of sweaters and ski pants. Boots stand dripping on all the newspaper we could muster to place before the heaters. Two dozen dripping mittens lazily drip water onto the basement floor.

Steam rises steadily from beneath the bathroom door while showers are taken and heads shampooed. Then in heavy robes and slippers they gather for the late show with a pan of still-cooking fudge.

Sleep conquers all, and in the space of 15 minutes there are peaceful childlike snores from all comfortable chairs and sofa. One is asleep on the floor, her head propped solidly on the sleeping back of an exhausted cocker spaniel.

Then I know what it is I love best about this snow, this insular warmth, island light of love.

King Constantine Given Blame for Easter Week Mess in Dining Room

April 6, 1969

I guess we can in some oblique way blame King Constantine for all the mess in our dining room this week.

King Constantine, because it was he who originated the custom of wearing all new apparel during the Easter season, and clutter in the dining room since the girls entered high couture in the midst of the African violets and geraniums where the light is best.

When they asked if they might make new outfits this year no one could have been happier. Except, perhaps, their father, who has to take a three-hour nap after shopping expeditions with either one of them.

"Isn't it marvelous how much money we're saving you, Daddy?" each of them would ask, trailing bits of thread through the living room, holding swaths of material before themselves in front of the hall mirror.

They moved the sewing machine into the dining room where the light is best and where the large oval table with its cushioned mat could be used for cutting and pinning.

Their father appeared a bit put off when he assumed his regular place at the head of the table and had to dodge not only the birdcage and the plants, but also the sewing machine and large soft piles of basted fabrics. "There won't be any straight pins in the salad, I trust," he said dryly.

One of the girls, the youngest, had undertaken a lime green suit with lining to match the blouse. (She will, undoubtedly begin her world travels by climbing Everest.)

Her sister chose a billowy pink creation with flowing sleeves and lined body, definitely very Loretta Youngish.

It would have been so lovely if they had at least chosen the same colors. Most evenings there was a scheduling problem with time at the sewing machine—AFTER the fight over dishes and kitchen clean-up time. "What the devil are you LOOKING for?" their father would shout as he was moved from chair to chair as we took up cushions and crawled around on all fours looking under chairs. "A bobbin, darling, a pink bobbin."

"What the DEVIL is a pink bobbin and does it bite?"

My specialty became ripping out seams and putting in zippers. I became the local home champion of putting in zippers. Because I would have preferred reading that new novel from the library or walking the pooch in the park, I became the Martyr Who Puts in Zippers.

A suit began to take form, a sleeve quite naturally just went into a bodice after four or five tries. (If you have never tried to put a right and left sleeve into a perfectly beautiful bodice, you don't know what I mean, but accomplishing this small detail has been known to make strong women weep and weak women faint! Sleeves, in case, you don't know it, are EASED into the body of a garment, something equivalent to parking a family-sized sedan in a space big enough for a shopping cart.)

The dining room rug was now dense with tiny bits of thread, pieces of pattern and the scraps from large lavender tissue paper flowers and origami birds (our "mod" Easter decorations this year)

"Didn't I buy you a vacuum cleaner couple of years back?" asked the Baron hopefully. "Daddy," one of the girls chimed in, "wouldn't it be great if we had TWO sewing machines?"

"What's wrong with one of you vacuuming while the other sews?" he asked rather grimly. Silence.

"But THINK of all the money we are saving you by sewing our own things!" came back like a Gregorian chant from all corners of the house every time a new length of lace or interfacing or zipper was to be purchased.

Like skiers rapt with the first run down the slope they are already swooping ahead in their enthusiasm, planning full-scale summer wardrobes. A summer shift was cut out in a morning, and that afternoon, material purchased for a pair of bell-bottom pants.

"One thing, though," their father said smiling, with his Friendly Philosopher face, "maybe now I'll get buttons sewn on all those shirts."

I wouldn't count on it, sweetie, I just wouldn't count on it!"

Influence of Miss Bozwell
Keeps Entire Household on
Its Collective Toes

April 13, 1969

Before Miss Bozwell I was just a simple everyday housewife struggling with the ground beef and trying to ignore the ironing.

Now I'm a reject.

Before Miss Bozwell, our budding, boisterous hoyden of 13 (AND one-half), was content to beat the boys at football and hang around the soccer field in a college sweatshirt.

Miss Bozwell is her home-ec teacher. I've not met Miss Bozwell yet, but I've heard numerous descriptions all of which conclude with pretty, smart and talented.

The hoyden now washes her hair every other day, smells like violets and notices things.

Monday, coming into the living room: "Mother! That blue velvet cushion on the rocker is really very good. You've provided a focal point for the living room."

"I have? Your father says it's lumpy and comfortable to sit on."

Rather shyly, a bit later, she gave me graph sheets and cutout pictures of basic furniture pieces. "Maybe you could rearrange things the way Miss Bozwell does—on paper—instead of shoving all that furniture around and getting mad." Lead hints.

Tuesday, our young miss appeared with shining hair flipped back over her forehead. A style, I might add, which I had been trying to encourage her to wear for more than a year.

Demurely now, "Miss Bozwell says I have a perfect oval face and should wear my hair this way. Do you like it?"

Wednesday was chicken noodle soup day. "Mom, why didn't you ever tell me that when a person eats soup he goes from front to back with the soup?"

(It occurred to me quite idly that there were days she was in such a rush to get back outside that she DRANK the soup from the bowl, but I hedged.)

Thursday she made dinner, set the table, lighted the tapers, and planned dinner music, "Mother! We don't have any paprika!"

"You always said you didn't like paprika."

"But Miss Bozwell says it is the essence of this recipe." She went next door to borrow paprika. Maybe to dispense with decorating advice, gratis, heaven forbid.

She saw the rest of the family in a new light. This is an ominous experience. One becomes awkward, constrained, aware that the hand must rest in the lap while dining, aware that last month's haircut looks shabby, aware that last year's draperies are limp. I began to see the entire world through the bright fearless eyes of Miss Bozwell.

To husband: "Why don't you THROW AWAY those ratty-looking ties," he, offended, asks why. "Because Miss Bozwell would say they were tacky, that's why!" he is mystified, and I querulous.

To son: "Do you have to WOLF your food down? No one is going to take your plate. Eat slowly!" he is chagrined, his basic premise threatened (Premise number one of all teen-age boys: He that eats the fastest gets the most.)

"Miss Bozwell says ..." became the touchstone of our daily lives. She was civilizing us by degrees by remote control.

On bright spring days when the dust balls came out from under the beds to play and the ironing mounted to the ceiling, I became fidgety and depressed. I knew Miss Bozwell's floors were covered with sunshine and wax and that her ironing was starched and smelled of violets and hung in her closets.

Then friend husband reminded me of Mr. Gordon. Mr. Gordon was the Cub Scout leader not too many years back and could build the best kites in town. He knew how to make the best beef stew in town. He knew karate and judo and played the guitar.

I wonder whatever became of Mr. Gordon. Our ex-Cub Scout no longer flies kites, but he still loves beef stew and plays a pretty mean guitar after dabbling in karate and judo lessons at the "Y."

"Thank heaven," I sighed, "for all the Mr. Gordons and Miss Bozwells of the world. They tame. They cajole. They keep us on our toes.

This month I'll meet Miss Bozwell at the Spring Fair PTA. But first I must get a haircut and do something about my nails.

Image of Mother Usually Distorted

May 11, 1969

I have news for the television industry.

The American mother is not that Doris Day type running around with a bubbly laugh and trim figure. Neither is she the hysterical Martha Raye[38] type done up in plastic curlers and hugging her sagging sweater about her. Nor is she the svelte young model who runs through fields of clover with her long shining hair bouncing in the wind.

The American mother is that gal in the faded denim sneakers and worn-out slacks hunting for the socks that never match at 6:30 a.m. in the morning.

She's the woman lugging in seven bags of provisions from the supermarket and praying they last the week.

She's the one who gets up with the sick puppy in the middle of the night and saves the guppies from their mother.

She knows the lyrics to the latest Beatles record and can't remember a line from her college literature courses.

She cries at the movies and when the children are sick. Nothing in her education has prepared her adequately for this elaborate ritual of motherhood, its paradoxes and problems. When she should have been taking a casserole cookery course she was Berlitzing her way through Spanish and when she should have been doing some research on faulty plumbing and wiring, she was designing jewelry.

When the babies were born she worried about their eating patterns, coaxing mouthfuls of Gerber's into their impatient mouths. When they became gangling teenagers she feared they would never stop eating and the refrigerator would wear out before they married.

When they were very little Dr. Spock and toilet training manuals occupied her thoughts. Now that they are teenagers she thinks they live in the bathroom before the mirror combing and primping and preparing for dates four days ahead of time. Dr. Spock has problems of his own.

When they were little she worried about their walking. She still worries. They simply don't like to walk anywhere. Drive, yes. Walk? No.

When they were little she starched their petticoats and ironed them until they stood out in pleats. Now they iron their hair and nothing else.

Her sons would prefer her to lose twenty pounds but bake more. Her daughters declare her skirts are too long and her hair too short. They wish she would do the dishes more often and increase the allowances.

Her husband, whom she sees mostly under impossible conditions, wonders where she gets her energy. When he takes her to the neighborhood movie, she falls asleep before the Indians reach the mountaintop, and he wonders why.

He expects her to turn out seven white shirts a week, starched to a fine line between discomfort and despair. He accepts her quiche lorraine without an after-thought and sees nothing upsetting about bringing home dinner guests when the children have chicken pox and the furniture is being recovered. He even fails to notice when her temples begin to gray. And that is, she supposes, one of the reasons she still makes him quiche lorraine.

She has stopped writing to college friends because she is always on the highway driving someone to a dentist appointment or piano lesson. She has briefly considered yoga and has given it up when the mint took over the flowerbeds. She would love to go away with her husband for a weekend without the children but she can't really stand to be away from them for more than a few hours at a time.

Nothing much upsets her anymore. Broken noses and broken table legs all go by the board. Empty ice cube trays and endless processions of socks with holes in their toes and no mates mark her days. Suddenly the children are taller than she, but they still forget to take out the trash. Suddenly the daughters grow beautiful and the sons grow handsome but when they fall sick it is the old lullabies from a thousand nights before they want to hear in the fevered middle of the night.

Magician, mechanic, master-chef, mother?

Save the frilly expensive robes for later. They're not the thing for taking down the laundry at 6 a.m. or cleaning up after the puppies. Save also the expensive sentimental card and the elaborate box of chocolates. Draw her a picture, crayon your name, and she will save it forever in the bottom of her drawer beneath the pictures of yesteryear.

Psychiatrist Needed as Philodendron Shows Serious Withdrawal Signs

June 15, 1969

Do plants have emotions? Are they capable of love, affection, distrust, envy, greed?

Of course they are. You may not subscribe to this theory, despite its many vociferous advocates, but it's perfectly obvious to me that my plants have total personalities. (Yes, and some have split personalities, too.) What I haven't figured out is why little old ladies and toddlers and stray animals love me without question, but why some of the plants in my garden can scarcely control their disaffection!

I have never really made it big on the houseplant scene. "You move them around too much," advises my mother whose philodendron grows while you watch and entwines itself lovingly around anything in its way. Meanwhile my philodendron droops sadly in a corner of the living room showing serious withdrawal symptoms.

Actually, if you want the whole truth, the only group that REALLY accepts me for what I am are the petunias. They just bloom and bloom, sending out trailers after one another and smiling up at the morning sun.

The marigolds are disdainful, and the rose bushes downright suspicious.

I have a friend who talks to her plants every morning, reassuring them that all is right with the world. I tried this for a morning or two, but let me tell you something, it's pretty darn hard arranging to be in the garden when nobody is leaving for work or hanging out the laundry. There is always some nosy little kid of three on a tricycle who says, "Hey, lady, whatcha doin' talkin' to your flowers like that for?"

Then I have this problem with apathetic ivy. Everyone in the neighborhood has lush shiny green ivy climbing up lampposts, porch railings, brick walls, and so forth. It is rumored that if you stand around too long in one place, you should watch out for the ivy. Not my ivy.

My ivy wanders up and down one narrow path on the hillside and cowers when a chipmunk comes near. Fortunately the neighbor's ivy is friendly and has begun to send trailing fronds across the lawn.

Plastic flowers I can barely tolerate, but sometimes, in secret, I threaten the geraniums thusly: "Listen, you guys, either you bloom by the weekend, or I'm going out and buy the biggest bunch of fake geraniums you've ever seen!" Sometimes it works.

Someone said, grow hydrangeas. The flowers are beautiful, the bushes large, and they require so little care.

I would like you to know that last year we had the biggest hydrangea bushes in the neighborhood, the only ones, I might add, without any blooms.

Not too long ago I had to remove, almost by surgery, a baseball mitt that had been tossed in the African violet plant, which had been placed n a new place because the bird was trying to build a nest or a bridge out of its leaves. I was terribly discouraged.

Then my waning faith was redeemed just a bit.

To begin with, there was this shoot of philodendron on my desk in the bedroom, covered last February with a landslide of clippings, books and skirts to be hemmed. One day not too long ago I discovered a dusty, but thriving spiral of green twining in and round everything. The philodendron was growing, and it obviously felt quite at home in the clutter. I tiptoed quietly away and let it do its own thing.

Then, outside, in the garden I discovered this luxuriant growth of vine in and around the fence, lacing itself intricately with some kind of inner precision. Occasionally there were some timidly pale blue flowers. Every time someone tried to leave or enter the yard, the vine would tap them on the leg or send them sprawling into the great black iron pot holding the geraniums who sniffed derisively.

The Baron began to chop away at the vine with the clippers. "What are you DOING?" I screamed.

"It's only a weed," he answered, astonished.

"But can't you tell," I sobbed, "It LIKES us!"

Tennis Season Loses Its Bounce When Game Falls Short of 'Image'

June 29, 1969

In our neighborhood if you don't play tennis, you are a real dropout.

Meet a dropout.

I certainly would love to play tennis—I think. But I have this problem. Delusions, it's called. I have this mental image of a lithe-limbed athlete in a smart, spanking-white sharkskin tennis dress sailing around the courts and sipping gin and tonic in the early evening cool under the trees.

It doesn't work.

To begin with, people around here take their tennis seriously. Like the French and Indian War. Like existentialism. The clinics for the little kids begin at 8 a.m. when the first batch of athletic instructors bound across the courts in their whites, tossing fresh cans of balls to team captains. From then until midnight, it's all business. At dark there are lights that can be turned on for the diehards.

I might mention that I am married to a diehard.

When tennis season begins I see him for a blurred moment in the morning as he is hunting socks that match (at an hour when I can't even see shapes, let alone colors) and then again at dinner for 15 minutes and finally about 11 p.m. when someone loses the last tennis ball.

I understand their zeal.

I understand the game. Well, pretty much.

The game doesn't understand me. For so many years now I have thought of sunshine as something good to hang clothes in on laundry day and to help the flowerbed prosper. I haven't been in the habit of thinking of sunshine as something to run around in at high speed, tracing the path of a sneaky white ball so that you are too tired to do laundry or gardening.

I get blotchy.

My ankles swell up. My eyes water.

My tennis dress looks like something discarded by a 13-year-old who has outgrown the Chubby Girls Department.

Ginger Rogers[39] (and you know how old she is!) plays tennis faithfully every morning. Ethel Kennedy[40] plays several times a day. I play once a week and everyone thinks Agnes Moorehead[41] is doing her famous invalid scene in our living room. Instead of sitting under the trees and sipping gin and tonic, I am in the bathroom smearing liniment on the places where muscles dissolved years ago.

My children, who say it is too hot to cut the grass, are up before breakfast, tearing around the courts and sweating like stevedores. The love of my life, who hasn't shopped for a new suit in two years, has spent weeks going from store to store to contemplate the new metal racquets, testing each one thoughtfully for balance, strength and price while I rummage through endless piles of bowling shoes, lacrosse sticks and barbells, the romantic stuff of which sporting goods shops are made.

He, truthfully, did not spend that much time picking out the house we were going to live in for the rest of our lives.

And he continues to play in red tennis shoes that were on sale (naturally) two years ago in a flea market. It is a 'camp' style, which brings him laughs and throws his opponents off guard.

Every winter, couples we know take romantic weekends to New York to sip sherry in oak-paneled dining rooms and see the latest openings on Broadway. We go to a neck-breaking weekend of watching professional tennis for 16 hours at a stretch.

Our dinner conversations dwell these days on serious philosophical matters. Like what's wrong with Arthur's forehand and why Mark psyched our Bill on the last set in Tuesday's final. Imperial gut. Cat gut. Taped wrists. Clay courts.

"What do you think of the Supreme Court decisions? How do you like the dressing on the asparagus?" I asked.

"Mother you really ought to take off 15 pounds and then you could get around the courts better."

I keep thinking of that woman in the back of my mind.

She's sleek, trim and thin, and she flies over the net in one graceful leap after three sets of tennis before breakfast with her husband. (Who, by the way, resembles Paul Newman.) She lives in the back of my mind. My tennis ego.

Then I catch a glimpse of myself in a three-way mirror or I skin both knees in the first game of a set and have to crawl around with band-aids on both knees like a clumsy five-year-old. My tennis ego refuses to merge with me.

So maybe I'll take up chess. Or cake decorating. Or yoga.

They'll all be home in September. Right before football season.

Search for Quiet

July 6, 1969

Men need noise.

Why else do little boys run imaginary motor boats around their bedrooms, making putt-putt noises while little girls sit looking at pictures in magazines?

Why else do ten-year-old boys run up the stairs like a herd of wild elephants and slam screen doors like an exploding firecracker?

Why else do men whisper in church like hoarse frogs so they can be heard all the way up to the front of the altar?

These are the things I told myself last evening while being pursued relentlessly by a transistor radio attached to the male of my house. (The other male had left the house earlier with guitar, amplifier and other equipment designed to drive another mother crazy for the evening.)

In the cool dryness of the basement playroom I was tackling the basket of laundry marked April and listening to some soft music when the Baron appeared, restlessly clattering down the steps and spilling ten pounds of potatoes clunkety-clunk down the steps with him.

He switched off the radio and switched on an FM tuner that he had just bought second-hand.

"Great bargain!" he enthused at the time. "Great bargain!" boomed his son as they dragged in more electronic equipment and bits of wires. It makes a noise that is a cross between the Metroliner on its way to New York and a crazed lion.

In the basement while I ironed a shirt he began connecting wires and disconnecting wires, making science fiction noises and stirring up my already skittish nerves. Suddenly, he came across the ballgame, which he turned up to a nice medium loud range so the folks down the road could listen too.

I unplugged the iron cord and fled to the back porch where I could hear nothing but the steady throbbing of the neighbor's air-conditioning equipment.

To the front porch this time. A car with a tired muffler passed. A mockingbird trilled a little night solo and the baby birds in the bushes near the porch whimpered an answer, I was beginning to feel the ends of nerves unclenching.

The front door slammed. It was our 14-year-old, her hair in curlers, a transistor pressed to her ear with electric rock pouring forth in tortured tones. The Baron, jiggling ice cubes and humming a Bavarian drinking song, came out to the porch, took her transistor with a beatific smile and changed the station to the baseball game. He turned the volume up the tiniest bit so the folks down the way wouldn't miss a play.

Daughter rolled her eyes. I shrugged. The Baron smiled even more as a home run was hit and the score tied up. The commercial woke up the birds in the bushes again and three cars with loose carburetors came clanking by.

Our son was in one of the cars. And his friends. And their amplifiers. These days ALL his friends have amplifiers.

But he did have a haircut, and they all looked so healthy and fresh and excited. "We have a new arrangement," they cried.

So in the basement we had folk rock and on the front porch we had the eleventh inning of a cliffhanger. Upstairs we had a radio talk show and in the back yard we had the throb of a hundred air-conditioners straining to out-watt each other.

Even the hot water pipes began to talk to one another.

I was in dire need of Q-U-I-E-T.

I put cotton in my ears, plugged in the hair dryer—which gives the same effect as the "white" noise still used by some dentists—and shut myself in the bedroom to read.

Some time later, while sleeping my way peacefully through a Russian novelist, everything was disconnected, and the Baron stood there with the plug to the dryer in his hands, demanding, "Hey, do you know that thing makes a heck of a noise and it's almost midnight?"

"Really?" I said yawning. "Where is everyone?"

"In bed. Want some lemonade?"

We dropped two trays of ice cubes on the kitchen floor, slammed the kitchen cupboard doors and tripped over the dog sleeping, naturally, in the middle of the upstairs hallway, who immediately yowled like a terrified medieval princess.

"Gee whiz," came three tousled heads from bedroom doors. "Do you guys HAVE to make so much noise?"

Later, while the house slept, there was only the sound of dry leaves brushing against one another in the tall oaks outside and an occasional faraway jet going somewhere mysterious across the night sky. And I couldn't sleep. They said, later, it must have been too quiet.

Moon Rediscovered Among the Dunes

July 20, 1969

As astronauts Armstrong, Aldrin and Collins[42] raced toward the moon's surface and we all shared that curiously heady sense of live history, we remembered walking on "moonpaths" just a few short weeks before at a picnic on the dunes.

This particular stretch of beach with its dunes and rough tall grass we still refer to as "ours" even though it is shared with occasional fishermen and a rowdy dog or two out for a run. We go there especially when the world is too much with us.

Last fall when everyone else was home stocking their woodpiles and knitting winter cardigans, we were there, scrubbing potatoes in the waters of the bay and roasting them in hot coals. Nestled in blankets, unwilling to surrender to the damp chill of fall, we ate and sighed and watched where the sky and horizon merge. The children lugged back great pieces of driftwood, and we built a roaring fire to toast marshmallows and to keep warm.

When the winter snows stopped and roads could be traveled, the first place the children wanted to go was the beach for a picnic. They raced like wild Indians, leaping and tumbling down the dunes, drunk with freedom from school and schedules.

Heads swathed in beach towels, we were Peter O'Toole, Lawrence of Arabia crossing the desert, falling on our knees and crawling toward the beckoning water.

We were Queen Isabella, launching three bits of driftwood on the water—the Nina, the Pinta and the Santa Maria. We watched them float out of sight under the drawbridge, followed jauntily by the new soccer ball that someone had forgotten to moor.

We were Marco Polo returning to Europe from the Orient with marvelous riches: a translucent peach-colored shell, a bit of driftwood shaped like a duck, a strange wildflower, a pointed stick for drawing in the sand.

Once more, as darkness fell and the cool night air settled in, coating our towels and blankets with tiny beads of moisture, there was the ritual of the fire, prepared more carefully this time, then watched until the last ember flickered and disappeared.

Then when glorious summer appeared what was the first thing the children wanted to do as we drove to the seashore, loaded down with enough equipment for a safari? Ride the ferris wheel? Try the shooting gallery? Eat cotton candy and caramel apples?

No. Go to the dunes and have a picnic. "Our" dunes. And so the preparations were dutifully made and the familiar trek undertaken. After football and soccer and tag, there were hamburgers and hot dogs and potato chips. The small fishing boats were returning to the docks as twilight fell with pleasant stillness.

One of the boys "surrendered" in remarkably presentable "Japanese" to a cabin cruiser as it swung its powerful headlamp over the water and beach. Perhaps they are still speculating over the sight of a young boy wit no shirt in tattered "cut-offs" yelling something out of a World War II late night movie.

The moon, a large orange beach ball, was rising behind us and swinging in a wide arc over the beach houses far away where lights had begun to twinkle.

Having been the only one never to walk all the way to the point, I was taken by the youngest and her father, hand in hand in hand, with a great sense of mystery, away from the fire, away from the voices, away from the lights of the bridge. The night was completely dark and still except for the orderly lapping of waves and the great globe of the moon, which hung directly before us. We walked on the hard-packed sand, not speaking at all.

Suddenly, as we turned a bend of the shoreline, the moon's light shone directly upon us, across the water, and across the sand—a spectacular shining path of light. We made footprints in the sand, solemn, then silly. A three-legged doodlebug? A giant monster with six feet? A dunes man with seven toes?

Across the water there were tiny red and green and blue lights from the boardwalk's attractions. Pretty, incongruous, man's toy.

Each footprint became a design. Each wave a homecoming. Each piece of driftwood a discovery. Each shell a present from the sea.

And the moon watched. Then we followed her path around the bend of shoreline, home, toward the flickering fire.

And it was enough.

Shakespeare Steals Scene as Teens Rate Movies 'Crummy to Groovy'

September 21, 1969

The discussion had turned to movies as it will whenever two or more 14-year-olds are gathered in the kitchen.

Reference was made to a film being shown at the neighborhood theatre. "It's rated 'G' but they are showing previews of an 'M' film," related one of the girls with a twinkle in her eye.

It was then decided that the rating code devised by the film industry was hardly an adequate service, unless of course it was something like "Dr. Doolittle" or "Mary Poppins" and your mother was going to make you take all your bratty cousins to the Saturday matinee.

With dedicated enthusiasm, they set about devising their own ratings, which went something like this:

C: Crummy, having trite plot, boring dialogue. "The Big 'C'" to be awarded annually to the really terrible movies.

P: Phony, cinematic hypocrisy, in which the viewer is entitled to smash his empty popcorn box on the floor, ignoring any anti-litter inhibitions.

B: Boring, with a capital "B", not to be confused with "C". This is a highly individual rating since obviously what is boring to one group may be another's chocolate pudding.

A: Adults will love it, meaning Katherine Hepburn or John Wayne is starring, there is a recognizable beginning and end, and the music is non-rock. This eliminates all beach party and motorcycle films.

G: Groovy, really groovy, something that is worth spending your allowance on, something that will have a sound track selling like hotcakes on records, and something without hypocrisy.

Want to know who got the really big "G", the super-groovy rating for 1969? Plot award goes to Bill Shakespeare, remember him? And the film award goes to "Romeo and Juliet."

We have continued with their classification system and find it handy for most situations.

Twice this week, both girls won the Messy Bureau Award for continued clutter, despite all efforts to unify and straighten bedrooms. One daughter received the Closed Door Award for a bedroom that had to be shuttered to the public eye. She was overcome with emotion as she received the award, sobbing that no one really understood her. We applauded gently, reminding her where the vacuum cleaner was kept.

The Implausible Parent Award went this week to Daddy Dear who managed to find either a football game or a baseball game on the television screen every night for five nights. Welcomed back into the embrace of his family (Remember the nice man, Philomena, he's your Daddy! Home at last from baseball season!), he jolted the entire family by trying to trade in the family pets for season tickets to professional football games. ("But darling, you'll never miss those silly tropical fish, and Mr. Bear has great seats for really big games!"

Impossible Dream awards went to me twice in one week for expecting a roast to last two meals and for planning a Saturday without errands. Other Impossible Dream awards were won by Dad who tried to get everyone to church on time and by Number One son who planned on going without a haircut for another three weeks.

The much-discussed Nervous Parent accolade went to Dad upon learning his son was now taking driver education and only a step away from borrowing the family car. Concurrent with this award, the only son was presented with the weekly Dusty Car accolade. Mother also received the Nervous Parent award upon discovering her youngest daughter is now old enough to attend afternoon dances in the school gym and wants an entire new wardrobe of teeny-bopper clothes.

"Cool Mom" for distinguished disregard during four hours of band rehearsal and a spaghetti dinner for 10 is a title I held dear to my heart for almost four days until it was replaced by "Mom Who Lost Her Cool" awards for screaming at the parakeet and upsetting a taping session of Donovan records borrowed from someone's wealthy brother-in-law.

Our own dog, long a revered member of the family, has just been granted the "Mean Mouth" title for six months running, having chased away the gas man, the newspaper delivery boy and Daddy's boss on the same Sunday morning. This was a neighborhood effort and the voting was unanimous. Unruffled by her award she continued to attack strange trash cans and wandering butterflies until time for her afternoon cookie and nap.

Friday night I threatened to name hubby a member of the select "Insensitive Clod" group of fellows, but just in time he pulled himself together and escorted me to a movie rated really "G" by the film experts in the household.

It was. Groovy, really groovy.

Mother's Hair Turns Gray as Son Who's Old Enough to Drive Takes Wheel

November 12, 1969

Middle age is having a son who is old enough to drive.

Just a healthy red-blooded American schoolboy with a dozen excuses why he shouldn't risk school on Monday morning (sore throat, fallen arches, misplaced protractor, strange dizziness, lost shows), he suddenly refuses to stay home from school, even with a slight temperature.

The reason? Driver education!

He's the driver, and I'm the one getting the education. And the gray hair. And the nervous tics.

From the back seat of the family automobile: "Mom, your hands just left the ten o'clock and two o'clock positions."

"Mom, want me to clean out the car for you?"

"Hey, Dad, can I drift the car down the driveway to wax the rear end?"

I don't believe it.

Why, his roller skates are still standing on the closet shelf, and his bicycle hardly has a scratch on it. (You KNOW who's going to be riding that now, don't you?" Just a few short years ago and he was talking about baseball mitts and matchbox cars, and now all he talks about are spark plugs and distributor caps.

His idea of a really exciting conversation these days is whether you shift into neutral before drive, and how many weeks it will be before he takes his test. I may take to my bed, that's what, I tell him.

This summer, in feeble attempts to prepare the way, his father allowed him to drive an electric golf cart at a posh golf course on the Atlantic seacoast.

"Gee, it was really neat," enthused the Stirling Moss[43] of the household. "We just soared over the greens."

"Yeah, va-room, va-room, almost right into the Atlantic Ocean," commented Dad, mixing himself a stabilizer.

Meanwhile we're poring over college catalogues and financial charts, and he is poring over the car operator's manual. There was a fleeting impression at the beginning of the year that he was exploring things like Spanish conversation and contemporary social problems, but no allusions have been made to such things in weeks.

"I'm getting old," I complain to dear old Dad after ole Stirling has given us the complete sales pitch on why we should buy a perfectly great rundown fourth-hand used foreign car.

"Nonsense," replied Dad.

"Then why are you smoking two cigarettes at once?" I asked.

It was only part of the large plan of things that the girls should take cooking at the same time. Therefore I discover that not only do I know little about driving, but also that my cooking skills are really primitive.

I began to notice the drivers in other cars approaching mine at traffic lights. How young they are! Baby sitters we used to call for, the newspaper boy down the street, why they're all driving. I began to have dreams of all the children zooming around Grand Prix courses in low-slung sports cars, flashing large white signs at me: "Hi, Mom!" "WHAT'S FOR DINNER?"

Remember when all they ever wanted was pony? A red wagon? A scooter?

"How can you be so CALM?" I shout at their father.

He smiles. "Well, first of all, there will be the insurance to pay for and then the gas, and before all, this, there will have to be a regular job to pay the bill for these small goodies.

Ah, the practicality of the American male!

Then, while stopping off at the cleaner's, which was on my way to the hardware store, I picked up a record at the music shop for Number One son who had asked me to do a few errands since I was really just going to the drug store and the book store. And the clear glorious light dawned.

My extracurricular career as the chief errand runner was drawing to a close. Those long, exciting evenings with 47 small errands to do were fading away. The world was preparing for a new chief errand runner. And I sighed, and said, resting my chin on my hands, "Tell me, son, tell me more about the spark plugs and distributor cap. It's fascinating. Simply fascinating!"

The Baron Takes up Jogging

November 29, 1970

Five years (and fifty gallons of ice cream) after the jogging craze seized the nation, the Baron has become a jogger.

He swears it has nothing to do with the fact that I stopped calling him "Sweetheart" and started calling him "Smiling Jack" when all the middle buttons on his shirt popped off.

He swears it has nothing to do with the fact that his new secretary is slim, svelte and size six.

He swears it has nothing to do with the fact that the last time he went to buy a pair of slacks, he was stopped in the aisles with the 32s and laughed down to the 38s by a slim-hipped young Edwardian sophomore in olive velvet.

But then I am neither here to question nor praise, and I just keep the telephone number of the doctor handy and the television warmed up for the nine o'clock game. (Remember when there used to be a nine o'clock movie? Cute as Joe Namath is, no one makes me cry like Gregory Peck!)

The physical fitness expert in the neighborhood marked out a mile course on a nearby muddy field, and ole Jack retrieved his sneakers from the dog's bed. The councilman for our district went along, but dropped out after the third night. No one could hear his speeches; the noise of their panting was too loud.

Jack walked back in the house, a nice eggplant shade, and soaking wet. He lighted a cigar in his best Bogart fashion and collapsed in the easy chair. "Why, darling, it's you," I said from the couch, where I was making do with a dish of gingerbread and whipped cream. "In this dim light I actually thought Paul Newman had dropped in to sit a spell.

The following morning Jack Armstrong[44] had dry cereal for breakfast despite what the government fears about dry cereal, and then he sprinted out to the car pool, holding in his stomach muscles, and smoothing down the graying sideburns. The dog ecstatically dragged his smelly sneakers back to her bed.

That evening before jogging time he had to fix the freezer, which first had to be moved like a recalcitrant moose from one side of the basement to the other. Next he had to help his daughter with graphing the migratory flights of birds. This was also like moving some intractable object. There was chicken for dinner, which he had already eaten for lunch.

He was not, shall we say, in a mood to become the body beautiful of middle America? But joggers are like weight watchers and parole boards. They never let you alone. His fellow joggers were on the telephone, then down at the corner waiting for him.

On Sunday he coaxed our youngest daughter to run with him, "In case I fall over, you can come home and tell your mother. I don't want to run alone."

"Don't fall over before one o'clock because I've got to finish the dumplings by then," I said.

I decided to rake the leaves while they were gone, and soon had worked up quite a steam and quite a mountain of fallen leaves. I watched them trotting up the street, the Baron a little behind our 13-year-old, who was skipping, her fair flying in the slight breeze.

He collapsed on the bench on the front lawn, and his jogging companion began leaping over the pile of leaves. "Do you have to do that?" he spoke rather sharply. She only grinned.

"Her," he said puffing and panting, "I don't need! My heart is pounding, my legs are killing me, and she is running around me and over park benches and over fences, and carrying on a conversation all the time.

Then the rainy spell came, and no one except diehards and astronauts were jogging. The Baron sat in his easy chair smiling through the cigar smoke and rather casually said, "Hey, anyone want to go for a little ride to the dairy store. Thought we'd have some ice cream."

He might as well have suggested a floating crap game at the annual church supper from the looks he got. He just tucked in his chin and said nothing. Then he noticed his belt buckle and the worn place where he used to fasten it. "Hey, hey, look, I've moved a notch!" Jubilation.

This morning he was singing La Traviata in the shower before he went jogging. I was thinking. They have these darling jogging outfits for women in powder blue, with monograms. I would do just about anything to be a size six, short of suicide of course.

The dog is going to hate me when I get my sneakers out of her bed too.

Mother of Adolescents Has Little Time for Self-Discovery

July 19, 1970

At poolside our slim new neighbor balanced a cooing baby on one hip, turning a creamy brown shoulder into the sun. "I mean it," she continued earnestly, "the years when children are in adolescence should be a time of self-discovery, a renewal of inner resources."

"Well, I discovered about thirty new white hairs last night," I volunteered. "Oh yes," I continued. "I discovered no one wears one-piece bathing suits anymore." I cast an apprehensive glance at my traditional one-piece navy blue bathing suit, which has the distinction of being rejected by every thrift shop in town.

My friend popped a pacifier into the peach-rimmed mouth of her baby. "When Jonathan reaches his middle adolescent years I expect to be well into a critical study of Jacobean poetry, and I intend to get down my loom and do some serious weaving. It's impossible now. He eats the yarn."

I watched my 15-year-old in her new bikini playing a vigorous game of water basketball. "Last night I spent three hours putting buttonholes in a bikini." I smiled hopefully.

"My goodness, how many buttonholes?"

"Only two, but I had to practice about 30 times and there were interruptions, like three extra boys for dinner."

She deftly opened a jar of baby applesauce and prepared to give Jonathan his lunch. My 12-year-old reminded me it had been an hour since their last hamburger, and were we out of orange juice already? All the cans in the refrigerator were empty.

Systematically spooning applesauce into Jonathan, my friend continued. "Seriously, have you considered studying some of the Eastern religions? It can do wonders for your contemplative powers." Jonathan hiccupped.

"Lately I haven't contemplated much except the empty orange juice cans in the refrigerator and the stubs in my checkbook," I admitted apologetically.

"There, you see," she glowed triumphantly. "All you need is a sense of direction, a determination of life values. After all, you have gobs and gobs of time!" I was reminded faintly of an old social studies instructor, and I began to count all the bikinis at poolside. It got confusing, and I decided to count one-piece bathing suits. That was easier. There were three in the toddlers' wading pool, a grandmother of eighty with gnarled legs and me and the thrift shop rejection.

Two boys were chasing one daughter around the pool, and her sister approached to tell me I was turning bright red and did I think I could spare another quarter for something from the snack bar?

Jonathan was placed in his bright yellow collapsible playpen for a nap while my friend lovingly coated her creamy golden tan with more baby oil and withdrew a notebook and pencil from her beach bag. "I write my plans in here everyday while Jennie sleeps, so when I reach middle-age I will continue to grow and stretch upward and not remain rooted in old patterns."

"Oh." I searched hopefully for thunderclouds, a child with a bleeding nose, any clear distraction.

"You know," she smiled, "if you don't put more lotion on your face you're going to have more of those little wrinkles around your eyes, and nothing in the world can be done about those."

"If people can't have that which they like, they like what they have," I said fatuously.

"What?"

"George Bernard Shaw[45]," I replied blithely gathering up my pasta cookbook, the handmade beach bag and the faded fringed towel with a sailboat forever tipping its keel into a faded lavender wave. I didn't tell her the girls' tennis instructor was majoring in Shaw and minoring in being nice to the mothers of teen-age girl athletes!

She adjusted Jonathan in his playpen, who drooled blissfully in his sleep. "I'm starting a yoga class for a few neighbors this evening if you would care to stop by. Jonnie goes to bed at 6:20 and I'm free from then on."

I picked thoughtfully at the next layer of skin peeling from my shoulder (does anyone ever get shoulder wrinkles?). "Gosh, I'd love to but I have to take the girls to their tennis lesson and there is an all-star softball game at 7 o'clock, and my son has invited three friends for dinner. Besides I haven't even made the beds or emptied last night's ashtrays."

But she was pondering her notebook. All the way home, I thought about increasing my contemplative powers and watching those eye wrinkles. Sunday's turkey was gone and there were three empty juice cans on the top shelf. In the evening paper there was an advertisement for a bikini sale.

I looked up Thrift Shops in the yellow pages, and then I tossed a coin to see if it would be Sartre or Shaw at the library. But the coin fell under the couch and lodged between three grimy tennis shoes. I just lay on the rug, contemplating the lone cobweb over the Chagall print and laughed and laughed. The Baron offered to mix me something long and cool. I accepted, graciously.

End of School Has Mother Longing for March Morns

June 28, 1970

Stumbling about the kitchen these long golden summer mornings, I illogically yearn for the gray foggy mornings of March.

School is over and "home has begun."

There are tadpoles in the basement, giggling girls tucked in sleeping bags in the playroom and the slam of the back screen door is like a metronome marking off my dwindling hours.

The bathroom is filled with damp, soggy towels and the lines in the garden are filled with damp, soggy bathing suits. Even the parakeet has become a little "tiddly," falling off his perch this week in fright over the raucous shouts of Joe Cocker or Janis Joplin.

The breadbox is empty, but the dining room table is filled with tennis balls and catcher's mitts. Someone is always leaving for a softball game, throwing kisses in the air, or returning home from a softball game, standing in limp disarray before the empty refrigerator door.

"I'm feeling very irreverent," I complain to hubby, scratching a new mosquito bite and trying not to hear the locusts' plaintive, dying hum.

"Don't you mean irrelevant?" he asked, scratching his poison ivy.

"Na, or maybe yes. It's just that the ice cube trays are always empty, the bathrooms are always full and the house is never quiet."

"I remember when you used to complain because the house was too quiet."

"It was a temporary aberration. Sometimes I heard the mockingbirds or the rustling of the sparrows in the rainspout. Now all I hear is the refrigerator whine and the agonies of some amplified rock group."

"You could devise a system, occupy the troops, scrub down the barracks."

"I've tried that. They can hide every piece of trivia in their closets in five minutes and then it's back to the Lucy reruns."

Monday the girls tried changing the color of their hair. It worked.

Tuesday the pickled eggs froze and the ice cream melted.

Wednesday the dog went in the bedroom closet and refused to come out even for a piece of chocolate. The vet says she is definitely neurotic, prescribed tranquilizers.

Thursday I ran a jitney service back and forth to the pool and the softball fields. I contemplated taking one of the dog tranquilizers. Discovered I drove 40 minutes with the brake on. Wonder how long before the weed-killer takes effect on the backyard. Company coming Sunday. If they don't notice the weeds they're sure to notice our poison ivy. Everyone scratching all the time. Only the dog is relaxed.

Friday the children invite eight friends in for hot dogs. There are only six hot dogs. At least soup stretches, but how do you "stretch" a hot dog?

Saturday the children made their own dinner and we went out with the grown-ups for dinner in a restaurant. No one spilled his milk. I fell asleep during the most exciting moments of the most controversial political film of the year. Apologized half-heartedly. Slept all the way home. Everyone was in bed at home. No key. Rang the doorbell. No answer. Even the dog hypnotized into heavy sleep by her medication, does not bark. No signs of anyone getting up to let Mom and Dad in the house.

We sit on the cool front steps and look at the moon through the green cave of the trees. I can smell the spicy geraniums marching up the front walk. I giggle.

"It's so quiet I can hear a squirrel hiccup," I hiss.

"We could sleep in the backyard. There is a sleeping bag hanging over the back fence."

"Nope, the weeds are too high."

So we talked about the war and inflation and training bras and tuition bills and Benny Goodman[46] and revolution and petunia beds.

Eventually a tousled figure in baby-doll pajamas cautiously opened the front door and asked foggily, "What are you doing out here making so much noise? Don't you know it's almost 2 o'clock in the morning?"

That Priest Is Right: Wine and a Nap Only Fit Lunch

July 26, 1970

In the extraordinary cookbook, "The Supper of the Lamb," Father Robert Capon insists that the only proper lunch should include a glass of wine and a nap.

This unique suggestion is enough to make him one of the top ten men on my list of favorites, right up there with Burt Bacharach[47] and Robert Graves[48].

The sidewalk cafe, omnipresent in Europe, is seldom successful in America because the native lunchers hereabouts are accustomed to eating a half-cooked hot dog and a lukewarm cup of coffee from a paper cup while they stand at a counter with a group of frenzied others who watch the large electric clock or the wall.

A long time ago a good friend, the mother then of five tiny children, vowed once her children were old enough to make a halfway decent peanut butter and jelly sandwich, she would never eat lunch with them again.

Henceforth, true to her word, she took her lunch on a tray on the porch or stretched out on the bed.

At the time I thought she was particularly callous, but after years and years of sitting through lunch with the children, dodging strained applesauce, mopping up milk and listening to arguments, I began to think she was incredibly smart.

"Let's talk about the new flowers we saw on our walk this morning," I would say, wiping a dab of applesauce from my left temple where our youngest invariably aimed with relentless accuracy.

"Naw," they would reply, "let's talk about the dead snake with all his insides spilled out."

So much for conversation. For the next several years my lunchtime conversation was limited to "Shut the refrigerator door" and "Five minutes to naptime."

Just about the time our youngest got to kindergarten age and I began to think wantonly of egg salad sandwiches for lunch and the unopened books always just out of reach, the Baron began to come home for lunch.

"I married you for better or for worse, but not for lunch," I smiled bitterly.

"Hah, hah, pretty good," he said. "I'll take a club sandwich on rye with some iced tea and a piece of that pie from last night."

Somehow during all those months he never could adjust to walking into a house full of laundry to be folded, dishes to be dried and boxes of dry cereal marching across the coffee table.

"Listen," I would say, huffing and puffing as I hauled the vacuum cleaner out of his way, "if you come home at 11:30 in the morning, you can't expect The Four Seasons or Caesar's Palace."

"No," he would answer dryly, "but I didn't expect the Reconstruction Era right here either." Then both of us would eat our peanut butter and jelly sandwiches in silence and I would think how nice it would be if we still had a baby to throw applesauce at his unappreciative father.

Then the smallest would come in from kindergarten, and she always insisted on breakfast at lunchtime.

At 4 o'clock it was panic time with the dry cereal boxes still marching across the coffee table and the vacuum cleaner leering merrily at us from beneath the dining room table. I was certain the coffee pot was not unplugged for 27 months. (And it never broke! Whereas the vacuum cleaner broke every three months like clockwork. Maybe it was psychosomatic.

When I would go out to luncheons with other young mothers a piece of toast with chicken-a-la-king on top and a pretty sprig of parsley brought tears to my eyes, ice water in a crystal glass and a linen napkins made me tremble. When they gave me the menu for dessert and there was something besides animal crackers I was apt to stutter.

Several times I even had a martini for lunch and went home convinced a great segment of my life had simply been obliterated while I spent the years and hours between 11 and 1 mopping up milk and scraping dried jelly off the captain's chairs.

This afternoon I had a glass of wine and a nap with lunch, composing all the while a psalm of praise to this witty and wise Episcopalian priest whose books you must read. Then I fell asleep for forty-five minutes. I dreamed I was in the Chock Full of Nuts on 42nd Street in New York and all the girls on the softball team were lined up waiting for me to pop hot dogs into their open mouths while the milk kept pouring from pitcher on the counter and I could never catch it in the glasses.

All the children were gone—to summer jobs, to picnics, to softball practice. A squirrel hopped on the porch tentatively holding his front paws before him, his head cocked nervously or the alert.

"Would you like to 'stay for lunch?" I asked hospitably. It was a trifle late in the afternoon, but we polished off half-a-bag of peanuts between the two of us.

Pigtails, Braces Recalled as the Graduates March

June 21, 1970

Like most other solemn occasions, it began on a note of panic.

With only 15 minutes left to get to the high school auditorium for our son's graduation ceremony, we waited on the front porch while, unknown to her mother, a 12-year-old sister was entering the primary stages of hysteria as she hunted for her sandals.

"What's going on?" I asked mildly. Then asked the same question thirty seconds later.

"I won't say anything," puffed hubby through a cloud of cigar smoke. "You'll only get excited."

Two minutes later we repeated our lines like characters in a second-rate production. "I am excited now," I declared. "She can't find her shoes, that's all," he replied. "Let her go in her sneakers. No one will notice."

"Is that all?" I screeched. "They're under the car seat with the bag of old tennis balls and the checkers!"

Thus we proceeded at perilous speed to the high school while Miss Missing Sandals finished her wardrobe, and I wondered idly if anyone would remind the seniors to comb their hair before they had the group picture taken.

A warm humid evening with the mixture of after-shave lotion and heavy perfumes lingering over the auditorium. Giant yellow chrysanthemums banking the stage. Familiar creaking and rustling of auditorium seats and folding chairs as parents and friends chattered nervously. Anticipation softened mildly with relief.

Then the rush of unexpected emotion as the brass choir began and the young girls with long hair to their waist and solemn long white robes and caps began to file in. Interspersed with them came the boys, suddenly tall and formal in their burgundy robes and occasionally daring glimpses of beards and muttonchops and mustaches.

Wasn't it only yesterday they were all marching off to first grade with their new lunch box with the red vacuum bottle inside? I looked away for only a moment and they all glided as smooth as birds through the autumn air right through adolescence into adulthood.

I saw faces that belonged to those who played hopscotch and waded in the pools of water after rain. Smiles that had wreathed braces. Long hair that had been in pigtails with satin bows.

Little leaguers became men while I looked away for a moment and they all grew gracefully through the tumultuous sixties into this forward-looking class of 1970.

By then I could see no more and groped blindly for my handkerchief. I had a sudden quixotic wish to lean over the balcony railing and hold fast to the giant hands of the large old school clock on the wall.

I remember holding him on my lap while we read 'The Little Engine That Could." I remember his father holding him high over the crowd while countless parades passed by. I remember parting his hair in the morning and writing funny notes to put in his lunch.

And now he's reading college catalogues and motorcycle racing digests. And now he dwarfs his father's stature. And now I could not reach the part in his hair if he would ever let me touch that hair so sacred to his generation.

A somewhat skitterish middle-aged group, we drew our breath in sharply at the calm and well-thought-out program. This was the spring of discontent, of student strikes and fire-bombing, of defiance and distrust. We were prepared for anything.

Except for such beauty and clarity.

The pastor who had earlier chaperoned them on a realistic week-end to Greenwich Village and Harlem, spoke of the beauty and joy of their lives intertwining. They listened with affirmation and detachment.

A member of their class urged them to avoid the entrapments of self-drawn boundaries. Leave your shells, become vulnerable, she directed them almost kindly. Her words were clearly vulnerable, clearly able to yield to the wind.

The choir sang with controlled exuberance a word poem enumerating 'The Manner of the World Nowadays." It spoke of violence and distrust, uneasiness and unplanned miseries.

Then in a very calm and measured voice one young male graduate informed us the song had been written in the 15th century.

That later became known as the 'Renaissance,'" he added. And we went out in groups of three and four into the clear starlit night.

Canoe 'Kick' Weathered but Gliding on Horizon

July 12, 1970

Dear Ann, Abby, Dr. Reuben[49], and others!

After 19 years of sharing the same sandy summer beach apartment, the children's arguments and the salty stews, the Baron has informed me we are incompatible.

Another woman? A new career in Europe? Too much salt in the stew? No, a canoe.

I quite calmly announced that I had no intention of spending our two-week vacation shooting rapids in a canoe or carrying my end of it up some rocky cliff.

He was aghast. "But you're always so agreeable," he wailed.

"Of course," I replied. "Try another approach, say twilight at Rome or the view from a safe, clean, modern hotel in Maine."

He was aloof. "It is obvious we are not compatible and never have been."

"You never asked me to spend two weeks in a canoe before."

"You used to like to canoe," he reflected petulantly.

"That was before we were married, and we weren't doing much canoeing. And you thought we were pretty compatible then!" I finished triumphantly.

"Are Mommy and Daddy having a fight," asked our 13-year-old avidly.

"No," answered her bored sister. "Mom doesn't want to spend our vacation in a canoe, and Dad says they're incompatible now."

"Are they getting a divorce?" she asked eagerly. This kid teethed on "Peyton Place" and "Divorce Court." She thinks our life is terribly prosaic.

"NO!" shouted the Baron. "We're getting a canoe!"

Both girls dissolved into tears and headed for their room. "This whole family is, is ..." sputtered the Baron, his face red.

"Incompatible?" I asked, turning out the lights.

The following day the Baron, using the soft sell approach, pictured a rosy family group around the campfire at day's end, eating the day's catch, the smell of frying fish wafting over the pine trees, the tent and the overturned canoe.

"You haven't eaten fish in 19 years," I reminded him.

"Do we have to carry the tent in the canoe?" sobbed the girls, whose idea of roughing it is going away for the weekend without a hair dryer.

This entire crisis started one very quiet summer evening when we invited new neighbors in for a drink. (This should be a lesson to all of you to watch who you invite for a casual drink and conversation!)

They are physical fitness buffs and dedicated canoe vacationers. Canoeophiles?

They both had a glass of tomato juice with a dash of lemon and instantly launched into a glowing tribute to the joys of canoe vacations. (I later discovered they gave each other matching jogging outfits for their anniversary and wouldn't think of eating anything without a liberal sprinkling of wheat germ.) They found an instant disciple in the Baron.

Having just read James Dickey's[50] brilliant spine-chilling book about a canoe trip involving assault, murder and mayhem—"Deliverance,"—I was somewhat disqualified as a disciple.

Later that week an old friend recalled wryly how his daughter recovered from all the moody tantrums of adolescence at a canoe trip in Canada where she was allowed to notch her canoe paddle after fifty miles of paddling.

I admitted I would much prefer to notch my beach chair after ten days in the sun or my bicycle handlebars or the dashboard of the car. Anything except a canoe paddle.

Canoe aficionados, as sailboat enthusiasts and bowling converts, are evangelistic about their enthusiasms. They want the whole world with them.

"You're entitled, you're entitled," I tended to say philosophically, retiring to my rock garden when things were going badly and I found the rocks growing so pleasantly with no backtalk.

All this took place several weeks ago. We have been through the catalogs, the price lists, the stores, the second-hand advertisements, and we are now in a debriefing cycle. Fortunately the canoe friends have left for the West. The lease is still on for the sandy beach apartment. The Baron has stopped painting word pictures ever since the night I fried fish and did not make him his customary chopped sirloin steak.

He just called to tell me he is bringing home his new friend at the office along with his wife. Guess what, he asked me, happy as a kid, they actually own a glider plane and they know everything there is to know about gliding! What do I do now?

Collect Call from College
Brings Irrelevant 'News'

August 2, 1970

It was, naturally, a collect call.

"Will you accept the charges, madam?" asked the pleasantly anonymous voice. "Of course, I will!" I answered impatiently. I have been picking up after that boy for 17 years, and his room has been uneasily neat and clean for two days. Let me talk to him!

He refused to be driven to freshman orientation. He wanted to arrive by public transit systems, anonymous, unknown, alike. He refused to take a suit, acceded to a necktie, was chagrined by the raincoat pressed upon him at the last minute. I knew he would spend the two days in jeans and sneakers, and he did.

So he left in the cool quiet dawn with all the neighbors he has known since kindergarten still sleeping in their air-conditioned bedrooms on this quiet suburban street. He carried the suitcase his father carried to Germany, and he was pleasantly tolerant of a parent's last-minute instructions.

Wow, I thought over morning coffee, where did the last ten years go? It was only a moment ago he was leaving, slamming the door, for a weekend camping trip, and now he's leaving for four years of college, or almost. I became the superb caricature, worrying over clean socks, wondering if the food service would be good, reminding him to take his night brace.

It was necessary to be busy with meaningless details.

"Do you have money?" "Do you have the tuition check?" "Do you know what time the bus leaves?"

"Yes, yes, yes," he answered patiently, waiting for his father to finish dressing. His father was to drive him downtown through the sleeping suburbs to the bus station. It was an amicable agreement of sorts.

And so he called. "I'm taking astronomy and philosophy," he said easily.

"Do you have a room?" I practically shouted. "How is the food?" The heavens he may chart, Kierkegaard he may study, but first a mother should know that the sheets are clean and the meat is chewable.

"Mom," he explained patiently, "this is costing you money." "Really, everything is fine. I played billiards with a guy from Brooklyn last night and there is a barn right outside the dorm window." I sought hastily for relevance. Finding none, I went back to the forty questions gambit.

"Look, I'll be home this evening, and I'll tell you all about it. Okay?"

"Okay," I answered, already planning the chili he never tires of. "Listen," warned his father. "We can't have this collect calling all year long every other day, every other time you two want to talk." I bristled. "How else is a mother to know?" I had a distinct sharp feeling that the sanity and health of many middle-age marriages must rest on this tender subject of collect calls from the peripatetic offspring.

He was late coming home, carrying his heavy suitcase with its unused raincoat, unused necktie and unused white linen handkerchiefs.

I wanted to walk around the city and just think," he explained reasonably. He was not sure he had a room; he might have to live in temporary quarters for several weeks until the dorm situation was straightened out. Everything was organized, everyone was pleasant, and he thought he would have to get a bike to make it to every class.

Yes, yes, of course, a bike, a rocket ship, whatever is necessary. He kept coming back to the dorm with its country smells of cows and horses, a fascinating anachronism in this sprawling urban college where one will forever be carried on the records by a Social Security number.

There had been a lecture on ecology. There had been a lecture on drugs and the consequences of a "bust." I thought, just a breath away, a century before when during my own first evening at college I was shocked to discover a roommate who had to go to the "smoker" for a cigarette before bed so she could sleep.

I think I will join the American Mercenary Society, he mentioned, grinning at my astonishment. "Mom, it's not a radical group. It's a historical society. They re-enact battles."

I had to digest that for awhile, a group that actually looks into the Battle of Hastings in a decade when every major campus on country has been the scene of bitter battles of their own! It had, after digestion, an oddly comforting quality.

"I'm taking piano lessons," he explained off-handedly. Perhaps, I suddenly felt, it is the sudden surprises of moments like this that make all the hours of conflict worthwhile in this back-breaking business of raising kids.

"Hey, welcome home, big college man," quipped his sister, who strolled in casually, laying her tennis racquet on the table. "Meet any neat girls down there?"

I reached out to touch the minutes floating by but they just kept on disappearing effortlessly into the horizon, and I had no resort but to go into the kitchen and turn on the fire under the pot of chili, something women have been doing since the Battle of Hastings.

A Night out for Daughter
Keeps Mother on the Run

1970

Erich Remarque[51] convinced me I wanted to be a race driver.

My 15-year-old daughter convinced me otherwise.

Ah, to be 15 now that summer is here, the skies are blues, with nothing to do. And Mom to take us swimming, picnicking, shopping and dancing.

First comes the build-up. After which I break down.

"Mom, there is a dip and dance Friday night, and everyone is wearing bell-bottoms, and you know I have really been helping a lot this summer and I haven't really asked for a thing since my Easter shoes."

"The sandals and the dress and the two pairs of shorts don't count?" I asked mildly.

Her face fell. "Oh (little "o"), I forgot."

Then I "gave in."

We spent Thursday shopping. Rather I spent Thursday on the freeways, beltways and shopping center parking lots hunting for parking spaces. She spent her time in the air-conditioned bell-bottom boutiques with clever names like Dante's Fifth Level and The Dropout Scene.

"Do you mind telling me," I asked, "If it's a swimming party, why you wear bell-bottoms?" She was extremely pained by my foolish questions.

Friday was spent washing and brushing hair and telephoning friends. She graciously vacuumed and cleaned her room and even volunteered to make a hamburger lunch for the crowd of gathering natives around 11:30 a.m.

That night, after a full day of preparing for the dip and dance, the girls in a giggling gaggle, left the house for the pool, looking for all the world like faded gypsies bound for a life in exile, draped in their fringe and beards and tie-dyed shirts and faded bell-bottoms and shining noses.

At 11 p.m. I slipped a raincoat over my pajamas and left in the family car for the swimming pool to pick up the gypsies.

The parking lot was the scene of a great noisy thrashing of gears and screeching of tires as the young crowd maneuvered for space in line to make the long climb up the hill to the main road. (I was only happy that there were no fathers about to witness this great grinding commotion of family cars.)

My traveling companion, a sedate cocker spaniel, tried to climb inside my raincoat as she trembled in fear. Finally, I had to leave the confines of the car to seek my very own gypsy from among one hundred identical bell-bottomed, fringed 15- and 16-year-olds.

There was a great screeching of tires and generous scattering of gravel as a new sports car just missed running over my very favorite left foot.

I glared in the manner of an irate mother, quite happy at last to give in to the role.

"Isn't he cute? That's Freeway Freddie."

I was astonished. "Isn't he the acolyte at the early service on Sunday?"

"Yah, that's right. Except he's growing a mustache this summer." Fine. Couldn't be more pleased. Now to try the left foot again.

As we pulled into the driveway the gypsy set said casually, "Hey, let's walk down to the sub shop and get a pizza." Great hurrahs.

I settled more definitely into my role of irate mother. "You are not, repeat, not walking to the sub shop at this hour of the night." I had visions of Freeway Freddie wheeling about the supermarket parking lot and glanced apprehensively at my daughter's lean brown bare feet.

While I was waiting in the car in front of the sub shop, I noticed a very swinging supper club had opened at the other end of the shopping center. Sounds of hard rock music wafted through the pleasantly cool, summer air, and I began to relax thinking of how nice to be 15 and free as a bird in the summertime.

A very tall elegant gentleman attired in purple bell-bottoms and sporting a long handlebar mustache leered through my windshield as he parked his car and ambled to the supper club. My traveling companion snarled inhospitably. I smiled defensively. Hasn't he ever seen a slightly tired housewife just meditating at midnight in her pajamas and pink raincoat with her faithful and trusted dog companion? Suddenly I was annoyed.

Three pizzas later, the gypsies arrived pleasantly polite and bearing a surprise: a vanilla milkshake for me and half a chocolate milkshake for the pooch. We drove home with the smell of chlorine from the pool and oregano from the pizza filling our heads and the cicadas chirping merrily away in the leafy treetops. There were hushed and giggled goodnights on the porch.

In the living room Papa Bear was just awaking after a long evening's nap before the ball game on television. "Gee, it's nice to relax. Want to walk down and get a pizza before we turn in?"

"Have you ever heard of Freeway Freddie?" I asked, pushing him back on the sofa and producing before his startled eyes a large still-warm piece of cheese pizza.

The gypsy retired, giggling, to the upstairs telephone.

Going to the Seashore Can Be Quite an Ordeal

August 9, 1970

Going to the beach in the last days of summer is taking along five blankets and forgetting the suntan lotion.

Is ironing for three days and then folding it all up in small pieces in suitcases.

Is making two gallons of applesauce to take along and having it eaten while you are out buying more groceries.

Is buying everyone more underwear and socks and shorts to take along, trying not to admit that you know they won't wear it.

Leaving for the beach is—

Having your husband tell you he wants to leave at 6 because he knows you will be late and he really only wants to leave at 7.

Knowing you won't really leave until 9.

Carrying all those impossible bags and bundles and suitcases to the car while he is upstairs shaving because you can't face the music.

Trying not to listen to the screams when he sees all the bag and boxes and bundles.

Finding a place for everything in the car except the handlebars to two bikes and your youngest child.

Convincing your other children that it is more important to you to take along the youngest child than the two handlebars.

Driving two blocks to the gas station in silence because no one is on speaking terms after the car has been loaded under conditions resembling a Chinese blockade.

Listening to the gas station attendant's jokes about what happens to overloaded cars and wondering how to break the news to your husband that the ice chest with all the food inside is back home on the kitchen counter.

Driving to the beach is—

Being certain your husband is never once going to use the golf clubs, the tennis racquet and the fishing rods all week.

Being certain that the girls will not use the hair dryer, the electric curlers and the giant pink curlers once a week.

Being honest and admitting that you are really not going to read even one of those seven thick books on the American theater that are propping up someone's feet in the back seat.

Being a little nervous because you haven't been certain, really certain in 19 years of beach vacations that you pulled out the plug to the coffee pot before you left home.

Stopping along the way to the beach we—

Walk the dog, buy some fresh produce, drink too much coffee, walk the dog some more and, of course, spend many long minutes in lines waiting to cross bridges and enter toll roads and leave toll roads.

Along the way we plan mutiny, murder, divorce, separation as the temperature soars near 100 degrees. No one can remember for 120 miles what we did with Daddy's pen and American Express checks back at the gas station. A cheerful martyr he, Daddy, had private malevolent thoughts of his own.

Arriving at the beach after 51 weeks of anticipation is—

Discovering the temperature already has dropped 20 degrees, and being relieved that you did pull out the plug coffee pot because one of the girls has been holding it on her lap for the past four hours.

Hearing the measured lapping of waves and seeing the same familiar lifeguard's face at the sandy edge of a marvelous stretch of blue water.

Watching the children unpack in five minutes flat, take possession of their rooms, demolish lunch and leave for the great surf beyond with scarcely a ripple of confusion.

Smelling the fresh salt breeze and knowing your hair won't be the same for a month and not really caring a tinker's dam.

Being proud of yourself because you remembered to bring the electric cord to the electric frying pan until your husband asks you quite seriously why you didn't bring the electric toothbrush.

Leaving the beach after too short a time, we—

Wash tiny white and pink stones and lovely fluted shells and carry them home safely in the medicine chest.

Walk down to the early foggy beach to splash our toes in the water one last time and face the wind and watch the swoop of sea gulls across the sky.

Wait for the girls to say good-bye to all the tanned and smiling young boys up and down the boardwalk.

Wave to the same friendly lifeguard, and turn inland, strangely quiet, strangely a little sad, wondering as we have done every year, why the best of times always go the fastest.

On the way home we keep busy designing furniture verbally for the mythical beach house we will buy some day when our mythical "ship" comes in. And we take turns holding the coffee pot and the two sets of handlebars.

'Modern' College Mother Permissive—Up to a Point

August 30, 1970

"I'm dying to tell him not to go out in the winter without a hat, but I don't say a thing!"

Her long brown hair flopping emphatically, the mother from Brooklyn continues: "Listen, a thousand don'ts I've got in my mind when they leave home! Will they remember a thousand? Of course not! So I just say 'Have a good time kids' and then by myself I pray for the thousand don'ts."

It was the morning session of a daylong seminar for the parents of entering freshmen, and the parents, shy and nervous at first, were now competing anxiously for the use of the microphone to voice their theories.

The lady from Brooklyn got a fine round of applause. A small kindly man with white hair spoke softly: "I feel very old today. This is the fourth daughter I've sent away from home, and all I can tell you folks is that theory which works best on Monday will not necessarily work on Tuesday." Again, applause.

This was, after all, the generation of parents who didn't let a fevered night go by without checking Dr. Spock, who pressed early and emphatically for the uses of Vitamin C, fresh air and a college education. Suddenly the kids were going to be living away from home where they might not bother to get up for breakfast and where their sole contact with Dr. Spock might be at an anti-war rally which

257

would be on the 6 o'clock news, and no one wanted to see the kids on the 6 o'clock news, please!

A tired man with a half-smile carefully broke his luncheon roll into small pieces. "I've got three in college this year, and me? I sell neckties and shirts. Do you know how many neckties I've got to sell to put three kids through 24 weeks of college a year?" He shook his head ruefully, and accepted the sympathetic nods of his luncheon companions.

Parents were told where their offspring could go for books, if they caught cold, if they needed money and if they just wanted to talk to someone about their unhappy romances.

Student actors, enjoying the reversal of roles with delicious wickedness, did a bit of impromptu dialogue projecting the parents' worst clichés. At last a parent could stand no more of the satire, interrupted the dialogue; then another, and another. Instant sensitivity training session. Encounter group when no one had been told it would be. Bared hang-ups.

A timid voice from the back: "Could I please just ask where my son can get his sheets washed and ironed?" Laughter melted tensions, and the shy young mother in brown blushed prettily.

I came home chanting, "You can't tell him not to go without a hat in the winter." I felt enlightened, liberated, quite the modern college mother. The kids were astonished.

"Mom, we're going to the quarry swimming!"

"Have fun, darling!" I waved gaily. So I didn't tell them to watch out for the snakes and the deep water and the rocks. So I just took a few aspirin while they were gone!

"Mom, we're going out for ice cream cones with Johnny!"

"Have a good time, sweeties!" I wave happily. Do I remind them that Johnny has only been driving his father's car for six weeks and they should fasten their seat belts and lock their doors and be in before dark. Of course not! I have two martinis.

"Mom, we're going to the rock concert!"

"Enjoy the music!" I shout. Do I warn them about riots and rocks and dope addicts and over-priced seats and keeping all their money in one place and getting home by midnight? Who me? I read four chapters of a book, don't remember a word I've read, watch Johnny Carson[52], recognize no one on the show and sneak upstairs when I hear the car crunch on the gravel of the driveway at 11:55 p.m.

"Mom, some of the fellows are buying a Chinese junk and splitting for Morocco in September, and I'm going along."

"Have a nice … WHAT? Morocco, Schmorroco! You're doing no such thing. College we pay for. Chinese junks, no. You've been oriented, we've been oriented, but you're carrying this Orient business too darn far. Don't you start pulling that stuff with me! Don't come around here with those smarty-pants ideas. What? What are you smiling about?"

"Gee, Mom, we were starting to worry about you. It's nice to hear you raving again!"

Like the man said, what works on Monday won't necessarily work on Tuesday!

Little Suzy Yamaha Turns
This Young Man's Fancy

September 20, 1970

It all began with Bronson.

Bronson, played effortlessly by actor Michael Parks[53], became Wednesday's hero.

While our teens were struggling every Wednesday night all winter with a knotty geometry problem or another chapter of world history, Bronson in his knitted ski cap went tooling along the Big Sur on his motorcycle.

The teens went absolutely glassy-eyed. Here was adventure. Freedom. Grassy meadows and beautiful girls. Escape.

Henceforth, and this shall come as no news to high school teachers, geometry and world history came second in the lives of our children on Wednesday night.

Number One son took to wearing a little knitted ski cap all winter. I should have taken the hint. At least I should have noticed he no longer was spending money on milk shakes and movies.

"I'm going to buy a cycle, Mom."

"Mmn, that's nice," I nodded, stirring the chili. We all need our dreams. I buy beach houses. He buys cycles.

But there was a difference. He got the cycle.

He was to spend the summer working in the library, shelving books and being a general helper. I could not help but he delighted, remembering long cool afternoons discovering Henry James and Disraeli and Ezra Pound deep in the stacks of the same library. Perhaps in this cultured, serene environment he would discover another world not bordered by Woodstock and the draft.

Every day became a fresh new experience. I would say, "How did work go, dear?" and he would come out with something like, "Hey, like great! This new friend of mine in the library has a Chickasaw Toothsome and he knows a great second-hand cycle shop."

Like bird watchers and stamp collectors, the motorcycle-mad crowd found themselves among the Henry James and Disraeli and Ezra Pound, where they presumably discussed the merits of the Chickasaw Toothsome over the Wild Bonanza.

It was an entirely new language. One young fellow, a graduate of world history, was the proud owner of three fine motorcycles.

Then "Easy Rider" came along. I decided not to see it, hoping to preserve my somewhat shaky mental balance. Dennis Hopper[54] might be brilliant, according to glossy Hollywood mercantile standards, but I had heard him speak and he sounded like a young man who had trouble keeping his thoughts organized.

It became a summer when torn shoelaces were not replaced, when records were borrowed from the library instead of being purchased, a summer of no movies, few concerts and no new clothes. Paychecks went promptly into the bank.

One day, there it was sitting proudly in the back yard—a pretty, little, bright blue Yamaha.

Bronson II glowed with proprietary pride. He shined her, polished her, waxed and buffed her, stumbling over his broken shoelaces and getting grease on his father's best white shirt, which he happened to be wearing.

All the children under six in the neighborhood came to bask in her glory. Even I had to admit she was a tidy, efficient, little tigress. And could she purr. Especially at 11 p.m. when all those little kids were in bed asleep!

"Take the car, son," I pleaded. "Go ahead, take the car, enjoy yourself, drive to San Francisco for a few days."

It fell upon deaf ears. While his room remained in a state of urban renewal, and I sometimes had to remind him about his night brace, he took excellent care of little Suzy Yamaha, fretting over minor smudges and covering her gently with two layers of plastic sheeting to ward off night dampness.

Once more, he started coming home promptly when he said he would, and he spent Saturdays tinkering with oil and grease and tools.

Like the family pet who knows all the sounds of every family car in the neighborhood, I became attuned to the sounds of various motor-cycles so that I can identify it as he makes the final turn at the bottom of the hill.

He bought a shiny, new white motorcycle helmet and a pair of sur-plus aviator sun glasses. I bought him some new shoelaces. He looks more like Easy Rider than he does Bronson, but the dog still lovingly pounces on him when he comes in the door, so he can't loom too menacing.

For the first time in years and years, he is obliging about running down to the shopping center to pick up ice cream for dessert or stop-ping in town to see if the fall slacks in his size have been ordered.

Next week he leaves us all for University-land with its unsolved geometry problems and world history chapters. But we feel sure we'll see a lot of him on weekends. Little Yamaha is staying home with us until first semester grades come in.

Having Teen-Age Children
Is What Causes Middle Age

December 13, 1970

Middle age has got nothing to do with age.

What causes middle age with its much-publicized slumps and symptoms is having teen-age children. Look at it this way. When the children are younger, say in kindergarten or elementary school, mom and dad call the baby-sitter, stock up on TV dinners and go out to the little Italian restaurant for a quiet evening together. Right?

OK. The kids grow out of elementary school, but mom and dad no longer go out to the little Italian restaurant for a quiet evening together. Does it mean they're not getting along, that their life together has lost its little surprising romantic notions?

No, it simply means their children are no longer interested in a TV dinner, the Jackie Gleason show and ten games of checkers with the new baby sitter.

The last time the Baron and I had one of the intimate little tete-a-tetes was last spring when all three teen-agers had parties on the same night and we slipped out of the house and left the key in the milkbox.

We spend a lot of our Saturday nights lately on the parking lot of the high school. Too dark to read, too cold to sing. There are three hundred other cars on the parking lot waiting for the basketball game, the variety show or the auction to be finished. Meanwhile back home we miss the climax of the Saturday night movie and end up with a half-a-dozen kids in the kitchen popping corn.

Well, darling, I say philosophically looking for butter the next morning (there never is any butter Sunday morning), you always said you wanted to know where they were. Better they should be in the kitchen melting butter.

Saturday night dinner used to be at six o'clock. Now it is getting to be short order service until ten because (1) basketball practice isn't over that early (2) there was a "dreamy" guy on duty at the local library desk (3) no one had a dime to call home.

All the children have dimes sewn in the linings of their coats (remember the mittens on strings?). "If you're gonna be late, CALL!" I shout after departing cars, motorcycles, bicycles, etc. I am the bane of their existence, and our telephone is like the central switchboard of the Beverly Hilton Hotel.

Now suppose one child has a date, and there are two at home. You get to go out, right, because presumably the two at home have passed that point in life where they put ants in one another's ice cream? Wrong. You can't go out, because SOMEONE might call up with an extra ticket or a blind date, and then where would they be? So you all play Monopoly and popcorn and talk about new facials.

Suppose TWO go out, and only one is left at home. Just because the one at home is baby-sitting babies now for two years and is capable of running a logging camp single-handed, do you go off to dinner and leave her at home with a Mrs. Swanson's chicken pie? No, of course not!

You all go down to McDonald's for hamburgers and milkshakes, and she sits crouched down in the back seat so no one in her class will see that she is out with her parents on a Saturday night!

I look at all my young friends with small babies going blithely off to the theater and dinner after having tucked in the babies at 6 p.m. And I listen to the roar of the approaching motorcycles with trepidation in my heart knowing full well there are only two apple pies in the freezer, and the Baron and I haven't been alone in three years.

The last time we went to the theater we forgot the door key and woke the children with our giggling at 1 a.m. From the expressions of their faces I was sure someone on the sermonette had said, "It's 1 a.m. Do YOU know where YOUR parents are?"

Sunday morning while I was waiting in line to get in the bathroom (don't laugh, I've read almost all of Proust that way this year), the Baron asked me out to dinner.

"I can't go; I've got basketball scrimmage."

"I can't go either. I've got a term paper due."

"I wasn't talking to you," said the Baron. "I was asking your mother."

I went all to pieces. "What will people think? Seeing the two of us together alone? At dinner? Without the children? Will they suspect anything? What will the children eat?"

The question is, can a 15-year-old and a 13-year-old and an 8-year-old find happiness on a Sunday afternoon with three frozen TV dinners and the third re-run of a Barbara Stanwyck movie?

I'm going to lock myself in the bathroom with the hair dryer and refuse to think about the whole thing. What's this? Someone is sliding a dime under the door. "Mom? MOM! If you're late, CALL!"

With Her for a Customer
He Can Skip Group
Therapy

March 28, 1971

Encounter group therapy probably does well by people like systems analysts, computer programmers and elevator operators.

People like plumbers, electricians, washer repairmen and upholsterers don't need encounter therapy to build up their self-confidence and self-esteem. They have people like me falling over themselves to love them for what they are every day of the week.

My friend the psychiatrist I can call on the spur of the moment to ask about a new book I just heard of.

My washer repairman I hesitate to call on his lunch hour even though the basement floor is six inches deep in soapsuds. After all, it might aggravate him.

My doctor I can call Sunday to ask about the funny rash the kids have had since Friday night but I am just starting to worry about it.

My electrician I would not think of calling Sunday for fear of antagonizing him forever. We can use candles. Why risk it?

When the Baron's reclining chair had been refused by three major charities, I began to nose around for the names of good upholstering experts. I discovered friends to be very sneaky people. They will tell you what's wrong with our lawn, how to raise your kids and where to get off. They will tell you the name of their doctor, dentist or taxman.

They refuse, however, to give up the names of electricians, plumbers or upholsterers.

Finally one night after a sumptuous beef stroganoff dinner and some fine rose wine, my next-door neighbor divulged the name of her upholsterer in a crying jag over the fourth glass of wine.

That Monday I gave him a call. I was sure he wasn't listening. Perhaps he was playing chess by mail. Perhaps he was taking care of an ingrown toenail. Reading a murder novel. He didn't say word one for quite a long time.

I imagined I was babbling.

"Stop babbling," he said briefly. Then he told me he would come to the house to look over the "job" Thursday evening. I spent most of Thursday worrying whether to serve coffee and rolls or beer and cheese.

He arrived promptly Thursday evening and sat rather distantly in the most uncomfortable chair in the room as he surveyed us and our possessions.

We had to lock the dog in the bedroom as she threatened to overpower him with kisses and tail wagging. I got the impression the only interest he would have in dogs would be as bookends or ornaments for the feet of chairs.

We skirted politics, economics, Wall Street and what was playing at the local cinema.

I curbed my usual outspoken opinions so he wouldn't get up and disappear in a puff of smoke.

"That's one heck of a looking chair you've got there," he said quite loudly.

"Oh yes! Yes, indeed, that surely is!" I echo inanely. We might have been discussing the traits of a particularly naughty child, or the escapades of a profiteer. All my compassion and tenderness and pity for the moth-eaten reclining chair just disappeared. I stared at it venomously for several seconds. A few fragments of dried foam rubber drifted down on the rug.

"I thought orange?" I said hopefully.

"Blue," he said.

"Yes, I've always loved blue," I smiled.

"How much will it cost?" asked the Baron.

"Darling," I giggled. "One just doesn't come right out and ask. There are variables."

"What do you mean? When you were pregnant I asked the doctor how much it costs to have a baby! Why shouldn't I ask how much it costs to have my own god darned chair done over!"

Our friend the upholsterer was charmed. He laughed uproariously and had a beer and some rolls. Told us about his shop. Stressed blue. Pointed out my lack of color sense. Suggested an ottoman.

I will be happy to tell you anything about the new fabric for our chair. Anything about blue. Anything about what is wrong with economics, politics or the local tennis courts.

Just don't ask for the name of my upholsterer.

Dad Swings to Mod Music, Chants "Om" While on Head

June 20, 1971

The Baron's friend, Harold Hondasruff, came over to watch the baseball game and have a beer. He was wearing lavender striped bells, a floral patterned shirt and a three-inch wide suede belt with the peace symbol buckle.

"Gosh, Harold, for a minute I thought you were one of the kids who hang around here Friday night waiting for the pizza to finish."

I told Harold he could hold our son's guitar while he watched the baseball game if it would make him feel more comfortable.

"The kids got the outfit for me," Harold explained sheepishly. "Say they want a dad who's up-to-date. All I know is I can't lean over to weed the garden in these pants."

"You even make Rock Hudson look dated. Why don't you grow a goatee and get some shades?" I offered.

Harold slunk lower in the overstuffed chair and meditated over his beer. "I think I'm having a delayed identity crisis."

"Will you shut up and watch the ballgame!" said the Baron.

"Remember when fathers all wore white shirts and black ties and went to work with briefcases and bowled with the boys once a week?" Harold commented sadly.

"Yah. So?"

"Well, everyone in my department wears striped shirts, has a mustache, goes to the Organic Juice Bar for lunch and three of the guys on my bowling team have quit to take yoga."

"See, that's what happens when you let your kids quit Little League."

"I don't know," Harold said. "My daughter calls me Daddy-O, my son who never cared for history is talking about the revolution and my wife buys me incense for our anniversary. She won't even let me eat white bread anymore."

"So? What are you a father or a mod creation designed by your family? Put your foot down. Wear an old tee shirt with holes under the arm. Listen to Tony Bennett and Frank Sinatra. Eat chocolate sundaes. It's YOUR house."

"I dunno," said Harold. "I can't even use the phone anymore. Someone is always on the upstairs extension chanting "Om!"

Harold left in a haze of marjoram incense, and I forgot about him until the kids started talking about Father's Day.

"We're getting dad the latest Bee Gee's[55] album," exclaimed one of the girls enthusiastically, twirling her hair over the ironing board.

"It sounds like an exterminating company. I don't know if your dad digs the Bee Gee's. What about some Peggy Lee[56]?"

"Was she that pilot whose plane was lost in the Pacific?"

"I refused to be led any further into the gap. "Why don't you get your father a nice shirt? He needs shirts."

"Groovy! I saw this tie-dyed mauve and magenta with green silk embroidery."

"I'm sure the boys at the bowling alley would just love THAT."

"Mom, you could get dad a belt. I saw this really neat one at the new boutique with a peace sign on the buckle."

I glanced at the Baron sitting peacefully before the chessboard in his undershirt with the faded college seal still clinging to one pocket and the pair of golf shorts that are held together with masking tape and imagination.

"Do you really WANT a mod Dad?"

"Everyone's wearing mod clothes, Mom. Why not let him live it up. Release the inner energies. Give that aging blood a jolt. Liberate the positive ions."

(This comes from a child who has difficulty remembering if her mother sent her to the store for half-a-dozen eggs and a loaf of bread or half-a-dozen loaves of bread and a chicken.)

Last night I noticed fuzz on the Baron's upper lip. "Are you growing a mustache?" I shrieked.

"No, I'm not," he replied defensively. "I just shaved a little sloppily." But he touched his upper lip quite gently.

And last night, I'm really not sure, but I thought he was in his workshop repairing a light fixture and when I went to the door he and Harold were standing on their heads chanting "Om!"

I closed the door gently and went upstairs. Only next year for Mother's Day I want a hot pants dress instead of a Betty Crocker cookbook!

It Takes Mild Hurricane to Make One Like Camping

August 29, 1971

It took the tail end of a hurricane to make me admit I might be wrong.

The place was the wrist-like portion of that mighty flexed arm, Cape Cod. Time: midnight. Dark, dark midnight.

All the Starkly Modern Motel people were tucked into their beds, watching the late show while the "No Vacancy" signs blinked on and off all over New England. Hardy campers were sound asleep or playing bridge by the light of their Coleman lanterns.

We were about to become campers, instant campers, thanks to the foresight of the Baron who had borrowed a tent and sleeping bags from a group of believers. I, the only non-believer in the group, huddled in the car in my inappropriate drip-dry cotton dress and new white shoes, hardly the proper dress for a New England storm.

A short time later we were all tucked into our sleeping bags while the lantern slowly faded and the wind outside sang to the cluster of tents at the base of a dune covered with scrub pine.

We awoke in the night as rain beat down and the wind commenced a teasing tattoo against the sturdy little walls of the tent. "We'll float away," I said, sitting up to wait for doom. "Ung" sang the foghorn. Once more sleep returned.

I awoke at dawn to absolute stillness, a fresh damp mist rising through our tent windows. Everyone was snuggled deep into their sleeping bags, but two bright brown eyes watched beside me. My 13-year-old adventurer was all ready to move out.

Stealthily we donned our warm slacks and sweaters, zipped open the tent and stepped out into an incredible landscape. Clambering up into the dunes, covered with brilliant green scrub pine, we came to the top of the hill where the lighthouse was just a hop and skip away.

A spider web glistened with morning dew, caught lightly along the tracery of cranberry branches. We stopped to admire it and to watch the mist swirling away across the horizon. It could have been Belgium or England. It could have been the 17th century or the 21st century. We were transfixed by the sense of timelessness.

Racing back to the tent and shivering with cold and excitement we frantically ordered everyone to come and see the sights. The veteran campers around us smiled patiently as we babbled. They made coffee and started breakfast while we insisted on playing Columbus.

That night we met our neighbors along the dunes: teenagers from Montreal, schoolteachers from Philadelphia, a family from New York. Everyone clustered at the cliffs to watch the sun go down over the now becalmed sea. There were discoveries of lovely shaped stones, a shell fragment, a rose hips bush and a cloud that looked like a lion.

Then it was back to the tourist trail and the Starkly Modern Hotels. I admired the glistening bathtub, the colored television, the wine list, the room service number.

One of the children climbed grumpily out of the bed and curled up inside a sleeping bag on the floor. I was aware of the air conditioning humming incessantly, of muted television late movie sounds, high heels clicking along the cement sidewalk.

It was almost 10 until we awakened. I looked out the picture window onto the freeway before. It could have been Connecticut, Michigan, Florida. A freeway is a freeway.

"I hate to admit it," I sighed. Everyone looked up expectantly, dramatically. "But I miss the tent."

There was, of course, wild rejoicing among the troops.

So for those of you who demand revenge, I'll be eating my words of a few weeks back spoken in haste about the discomforts of camping. Words of a novice, of a nebbish. Time? Oh, say next August. Place? How about Nova Scotia? They say the scenery is tremendous. My tent will be the one with "I believe" sign painted just over the red geranium window box.

Can a Clock Hater Find Happiness with Clock Nut?

August 22, 1971

The question is: Can a woman who refuses to wear a watch find happiness with a husband who is bananas over clocks?

If the Baron had his way, there would be a clock in every corner and one on every shelf.

If I had my way, there would be no clocks since they only serve as reminders that it is time for the school bus, the dentist appointment and the mortgage payment.

Three years ago he began to build a grandmother's clock. From scratch. In the meantime the living room ceiling developed a crack rivaling the Grand Canyon and the back porch began to flake away.

Every time I mentioned this to him, he bought out the college sweater I was supposed to mend when our oldest child was still in training pants.

When the monsoon season began and everything in the basement began to float, we all assembled to help save the clock.

Blankets sank, jars of strawberry jam floated by, but we held the clock high and dry.

"I'll be so darn glad when this is finished," I huffed and puffed. (A clock that size weighs as much as a St. Bernard and is considerably less lovable.)

"Clock-makers develop a language all their own. It's called Clock-onese. Weights, pendulums, whatchamacallits, winged axles, crossed side-ribs and a lot of other things.

"You should be put away in a clock tower somewhere 'till you cool off," I snarled.

He smiled blissfully.

The doors to the clock (and why does a simple clock have to have as many doors as our house?) were assembled in 17 different operations, which meant that every bed or table in the house had two pieces of molding attached to a clamp on it.

The glass arrived, and since the clock wasn't yet ready for the glass, that had to be moved from one precarious perch to another. I still consider it one of nature's modern miracles that a pane of glass has existed for two years in a basement filled with teen-aged elbows, electronic equipment and assorted stray animals.

This week the "works" arrived.

The "works" consist of the pendulums, the actual face (our daughter moaned, "Roman numerals, AGAIN! Daddy, why can't we ever have a clock with American numerals?"), the weights and assorted other pretties.

On the box were symphonic instructions written in high German that could only be read by a 15th-century monk. We just laid all the pieces on the rug and admired them for twenty minutes or so.

"Where are we going to put it when it's finished?" I asked casually surveying the 13 tennis sneakers under the coffee table.

"In the center of the room," declared the Baron.

"In the center of the room! NO ONE has a clock, a grandmother's clock in the middle of their living room!"

"Well, we are," he said, polishing a bit of gold leaf with his shirt sleeve.

It was then and there that I decided to build a harpsichord.

I've received brochures from half-a-dozen harpsichord kit manufacturers (sort of like a do-it-yourself car—fun, but insane) and invitations from Maine, New York and Richmond to visit harpsichord builders.

I'm learning to speak harpsichordese. Which is a lot like clock-onese but more fun than car poolese.

"Where are we going to put a harpsichord?" screeched the Baron.

"In the kitchen," I said calmly, taking the door off the hinges.

"You never wanted a dishwasher because the kitchen is too small."

"It won't be. Not after the geodesic dome is finished."

"Geodesic dome?"

"The one we'll use as the kitchen, then this kitchen can be turned into the music room, I said, removing the quarter-round from the wall around the refrigerator.

"How long?" asked the love-of-my-life with a gleam in his eye that really didn't signify passion.

"Oh, not for a while, because I have to go to the university for my seminar in geodesic building, and I have to learn to speak Buckminster Fullerese of course. It may take a while."

If you see a tall, friendly man hitch-hiking across the turnpike with a grandmother's clock strapped to his knapsack, be kind to him. He has a terrific sense of humor.

Daughters Can Be
Difficult—Timing Always
Different

November 7, 1971

Actually the father who married off four of his daughters in one ceremony was smarter than anyone gave him credit for.

It is difficult imagining our daughters getting ready for anything to be done in the same ceremony. They can't even arrange to wash their hair on the same night.

All the children went through measles, chicken pox and mumps sequentially. Just when I would be coming up for air after three or four nights of rocking a feverish child all night, the second one would complain of spots on her tummy, and so on, and so on.

I was past 30 until I could get to sleep without first rocking a child to sleep.

It has been the same with dental work. I've married off two dentist's receptionists and three hygienists while the children have been getting their teeth straightened. I have read every issue of Sports Illustrated in the waiting room since 1967, and I still haven't talked the dentist into subscribing to Good Housekeeping.

When the kids were babies, none of them took a nap at the same hour. I saw other babies' mother taking bubble baths and reading long novels while their children slept away the afternoon. I always had one in the crib fussing himself to sleep and another in the kitchen ready to whip up another handy-dandy batch of home glue for play-time after his nap.

To this day none of them keeps any semblance of a metabolic rhythm (a scientific term invented by scientists who are busy in the laboratory while their wives sit up with cranky kids who don't know why they are cranky.)

One of the girls likes to talk until 3 a.m. Naturally she's a zombie until noon the next day. Her sister wakes up bright as a penny and grows increasingly talkative from 7 a.m. onward. "Are you listening, Mom" they keep prodding. Listening? I'm always listening!

One of the girls is always ready for concerts and trips half-an-hour ahead of time. Of course once we've started she discovers she has no Kleenex. She's wearing socks that don't match. Her hem is coming out.

The other lass is still combing her hair in the car, and fastening her buckles and buttons in the parking lot. The school bus driver calls her by her first name and her homeroom teacher never takes attendance until after the bell rings.

Monday night one of the girls went to gymnastics class. Tuesday night her sister had to have an allergy shot. Wednesday the first girl had to be driven to the library to research a report. Her sister, the following night, had to be taken to the doctor to have an ankle x-rayed.

Friday night I headed for the car with my dinner plate. "What are you doing?" yelled the Baron.

"I feel more at home behind the wheel."

Being over 30, somewhat rundown from lack of sleep and listening all the time, I tend to get forgetful. "Mom, I have to have three dollars for an activity ticket by Friday."

"What? You just bought one last week!"

Her sister pipes up: "That was me, Mom!"

One week I do nothing but go to PTA meetings night after night. Sometimes it is an act of terror. Once I was named to a program committee and I lost four months of my life while stuffing envelopes for a fund-raising drive.

Saturdays I am led from boutique to boutique while they try on an endless chain of strange clothes. I grow so accustomed to flashing black lights, sonic boom rock music and aluminum ceilings glaring at me, that I wander into a sedate men's shop by mistake and spend five dollars on a tie the Baron will absolutely hate.

Saturday night I drive six 14-year-olds to the skating rink, and they ask to be let out of the car a block early so no one knows a mother brought them to the rink. The car is full of giggles and bright talk and garbled directions to Wanda's house. I get home just in time to make hot chocolate for the basketball crowd.

Sunday morning in church I blatantly daydream while I listen to a sermon on the orderly life. "What were you thinking of?" prods the Baron.

"I was wondering what it would be like with all the girls going up the aisle one at a time."

Big Brother Far Away, But Confusion Is 'Normal'

1971

Now that we are one less (Big Brother is away at college) it should be so much easier. Why isn't it?

Well, for one thing Big Brother comes home every weekend for apple pie, ice cream and a quiet place to sleep. (He's rooming with a bongo drum aficionado.)

That means we spend Thursday evening getting ready for the onslaught of young male appetites for home cooked food. Then we spend Sunday night getting him off to the bus station.

He would far rather hitchhike. I am sure that 80 percent of the younger population of our nation must be literally "on the road" most of the time. They are fascinated by the fast friendships they form, the insights they make in a short time. ("He knew I was a Taurus, and we hadn't spoken more than ten minutes.")

In his drawer lies a beautiful cable-knit-cardigan in gold tweed that makes autumn pale in comparison. He prefers the heavy denim work jacket, vogue for freshmen at the university this year. I have stopped trying to figure it all out. After all, I come from the dark ages when people wore crew cuts and saddle shoes.

Now that we are one less, things could be quieter, more organized, right? Wrong.

The girls have set up a protectorate in the bathroom and are embarked on the longest crash beauty program in history.

"She has been in that shower three hours. Her skin will peel off. Will you get her out of there?"

It is the anguished cry of a father who has gone too many places this month shaveless and showerless. He has developed a neurotic symptom of sitting on the edge of our bed and pretending to read a magazine while he waits for an opportune moment to dash down the hallway and get in the shower first. We trained our girls to eat healthy, drink lots of fresh orange juice and exercise, and they beat him every time. The last thing he sees as he scratches his stubbly beard is a sweet young face swathed in Noxema peeking demurely out from behind the bathroom door. "Only be a minute, Dad."

"I could take a room at the Y and check in every morning just to shower and shave."

"We could move to that new house with the fireplace and the three full bathrooms," I smile invitingly.

"And the giant-sized mortgage," he groans, going back to the edge of the bed and the waiting game.

I personally have no problem at all since I've stopped worrying about split ends and blackheads and find three o'clock in the morning the perfect time for a long soak in the bathtub with the newest book club novel.

Meanwhile, someone keeps putting empty ice cube trays back in the refrigerator. I leave large signs in red letters posted to the refrigerator door. I sob, I cry, I shout, I threaten. The empty ice cube trays are still in the refrigerator every morning.

Everyone in the house insists it can't be he or she. I am even getting suspicious of the paperboy and the milkman. Who is this strange tormentor who keeps my ice cube trays empty?

"Detach yourself, remain philosophic," calms the Baron, flicking his cigar ashes into the nearest pot of ivy. If I really thought he was serious about this detachment, I wouldn't have put away the phone bill before he could see all those collect calls from Big Brother.

"How do we get so involved?" he moans, picking up seven giggling teen-agers after a dance at the high school.

"How do we get so involved?" I echo, driving across town to tow son and motorcycle home and then putting his dinner in the oven because it is essential he talk to his girl for three hours right that minute.

Meanwhile, the 14 year-old dowager dog of the household has gone bananas over a young terrier down the street and gets up in the middle of the night to bark at the back door, demanding to be let out and go bark at the back door of the terrier people. (How else do you think I manage to get awake in time to have the bathroom all to myself at 3 a.m.?)

"How do we get so involved?" A young beautiful bride-to-be was describing to me how it would be in the evening when she would greet her husband at the door with a loving kiss (instead of a broken axle) and a tall drink (instead of a broken washer) and the long, deep reflective talks they would have over dinner. (Not about taxes, report cards or the car payments.)

It was really funny. I just sat there and listened in a state of euphoria, then I got up and took the Baron's golf shoes off the mantel and went upstairs to gather up the 499 dirty towels in the bathroom.

Mother Was Inventive in Dealing with 'Gibberish'

1971

William Buckley[57] writes of his father shipping half the family off to English boarding schools when he had become convinced none of his children could speak an intelligible word.

I sympathize wholly, but having had neither the resources nor the time for such measures, I've had to invent a few over the years.

I became an absolute expert at gibberish when our first-born was only five months old and muttering his first gibberish sounds. Some mothers become gibberish experts even earlier. Families gather for holidays; the baby reaches for the bowl of mashed potatoes and says, "Ketchemapapum," and mother translates instantly (just like at the United Nations): "Charlie wants butter on his potatoes. Isn't he darling?"

But Charlie eventually has to put on his galoshes and go out into the cold world of kindergartens and kindergarten teachers. While being immensely skilled at gibberish, kindergarten teachers would prefer Charlie say something besides "Ketchemapapum." Charlie gets annoyed because Mama isn't there all the time to translate.

My own little Charlie, I became convinced, would never speak anything but gibberish. I even tried papering the roof of his mouth with peanut butter to make his tongue do more work. But the doctor told us not to worry and sure enough by age 16 he was talking non-stop. He once talked on the telephone for eighty minutes and learned to call collect from any major city on the Eastern seaboard.

Our second-born developed the habit of beginning every sentence with "Ahhh" like an old cello tuning up for practice. We could wait forever, hinged on that eternal "ahhh," but she often forgot what she was going to say or became so immersed in the flexibility of her "ahhh" that she began a little humming sound and wandered off to the sandbox to play.

One summer when she was about 9 or 10, I gave her a Mason jar filled with pennies. Each time she said the "ahhh" before speaking, she had to return a penny to Mom. Pennies flew back and forth all summer but by August she had stopped saying "Ahhhh."

She then connected all her sentences with "and-ah" so that her entire conversation became one long narrative. People were afraid to interrupt, to interject, to leave her side. Forever suspended on the slender thread of "and-ah" they waited for the next sentence to come struggling or spurting forth. Dinner conversations became crackly with tension, because, after all, one does just not ask for the salt during a particularly portentous "and-ah."

She was obviously past the Mason-jar-full-of-pennies routine and I had even stopped reading the "How to Get Along" books.

What we finally discovered was how carefully people listen when they have stopped listening for a while. Her antennae screening the kitchen, she could tell instantly whether I was truly thinking about the new biology teacher or if I was secretly composing a note to my congressman in the recesses of my mind.

By age 16 she, too, was talking non-stop and was an expert on long whispered conversations at midnight on the patio. Sixteen-year-olds who gather in coveys tend to giggle, and I eyed the Mason jar full of pennies enviously, but rejected it.

With two older non-stop talkers it was inevitable of course that the third child should be quiet. When she talked it had to count. I think she spoke her first full sentence at age one when she said "Stop bashing me on the head with that rock and give me back my bottle," to one of her siblings. From thence on she spoke in regulated paragraphs. But she seldom spoke.

Before she could reach for a toy or a helping of food there was an older brother or sister there to reach for her or to speak for her. Like other children who come on last in the family, she learned to play chess while the other children were still figuring out right side from left side.

Now all three get together and, hard as I try not to think about it, sometimes it begins to sound like gibberish. William Buckley calls it "Kidspeak" which is perhaps more appropriate. It's "what's happening."

I have a friend who is immensely proud she can identify the calls of more than 20 birds. I would be proud, too, but lately everyone has been talking at once and I can't even hear myself think. And I have developed this annoying habit of starting every sentence with "Ahhhh." I hope it goes away soon!

Contract Might Prevent Marriage's Great Debates

December 5, 1971

I can't understand all the commotion over the alleged marriage contract between Jackie and Ari Onassis[58].

Frankly I wouldn't even consider getting married again without a contract of sorts.

We wasted so much time before deciding on irrational things like what to call the children (they never come when you call them anyway!) and where we would spend out honeymoon and whether I would ever wear curlers to bed.

None of the really important things were decided.

Such as who is going to write the monthly checks.

Such as who is going to turn off the alarm.

Such as why my dry cleaning costs more than his.

Such as whose family we should go to on holidays.

Oh, yes, we discussed all the heavenly big things like where we would build a house, where we would take our vacations and where we would send our children to college.

Those are the kind of useless decisions we all make while we're still trying to save money for the down payment for the house, for the trip to Spain and for the kids' tuition.

We never discussed who should go out for milk at midnight.

Not once did we talk about who should get dibs on the bathroom in the morning. (In every contract there should be a special clause for things like putting the top back on the toothpaste tube and wiping down the tile after showers.)

We never once had a sane conversation about the merits of Sunday afternoon football, and I can't think of a second more important subject in any marriage. (With apologies to Dr. Reuben)

Someone once suggested that every engaged couple should have to spend at least one weekend cooped up in the house with four children in varying stages of the flu. Something like basic training.

I suggest further basic training. Throw in a few stopped up drains. A few overdue charge accounts. A quarrelsome neighbor. A leaky ceiling. Brief vignettes of life, the nitty-gritty!

We decided on the children's names before they were even in the bassinette but to this day we can't compromise on a solution to their allowance problems.

"Well, when I was a kid," begins every exploratory talk on allowances, dating, pet peeves, dirty rooms and teenage fads.

The biggest decision of all would have to be who would have to answer the telephone when none of the children is home. Who knows how many marriages this day would still be workable if this decision had been made before irrevocable damage was done on a Saturday evening between 5 and 7 when the telephone rings 350 times?

The marriage contract could cover all the annoying habits like eating pretzels in bed and cracking knuckles while watching the tube.

It could cover grocery shopping, changing snow tires, writing letters and going to the PTA.

When the Baron bought his first car, he signed a contract with what seemed like a million words in fine print on the back.

When he bought his first house he signed a contract that took three hours for the officers of the bank to sit around a large table to explain to him and to me.

When he signed the "contract" for me he never knew that I couldn't cook, didn't know how to drive and ate pretzels in bed. Grounds for aggravation!

He always has to shop for the Christmas tree because I hate to.

I always have to shop for the family gifts because he hates to.

I turn the radio down. He turns it up. I close the window and he opens it. I turn down the air conditioner and he turns it up. He likes Westerns; and I fall asleep in them. But we both love raking leaves in the autumn.

If we had a contract it would cover things like whether to buy 60 watt or 100 watt light bulbs. Overdue library books. At what point a child's fever is cause for alarm—101 degrees or 104 degrees. Who walks the dog on cold nights. Who tells the kids they can't watch the late show.

The more I think about it, the more amazed I am at all the busy married couples in my own neighborhood getting to the supermarket, picking up their kids at the bowling alley, leaving for sailing trips together.

Most of the world I know is existing without the much touted "contract." I keep wondering who reminds Ari when it's time to take the yacht in to have the motor tuned up or whatever it is they do with yachts. As for us, we're still arguing about whose turn it is to take the car to the garage for snow tires.

Mother Has Trouble 'Understanding' Son Who Hides Million-Dollar Smile

January 18, 1972

I like to think about all the other families in America with those million-dollar smiles.

Every family on our block has at least one child in braces.

The second-grade group picture had rows of smiling gaps where baby teeth were missing.

The eighth-grade group picture looks like a convention of Peruvian tin magnates.

Our son has one of those million-dollar smiles. We coaxed, threatened and cajoled him to wear a night brace. The dentist twisted, tightened, grimaced and got a receding hairline while the million-dollar smile was being fixed.

Finally the braces were removed. Now he won't smile.

"Cmon, baby-cakes, give us a big smile!"

He groans. "Mom, I'm 19. I don't feel like smiling!"

"What has that got to do with it?" I plead.

"You'd never understand."

I don't.

Our second-born was eager to get on with straightening the smile. Unfortunately it was before Ali McGraw[59] made the crooked smile and unhappy love affair popular. Oh well, she can still have the unhappy love affair.

The dentist's hair was turning white. His fees were rising. The parking lot was more crowded. Only the issues of the same magazines were still in the waiting room, and the paneling was starting to look seedy.

We once had a call from the school nurse informing us our son had his sweater caught in his braces (don't ask) and should she cut the sweater or bend the braces? "Cut the sweater!" we yelled.

Last week our second-born came home in tears. "The most awful thing happened," she moaned. She had stopped lisping. (Everyone lisps the first week in braces. Or gets very quiet.)

It seems a friend had given her a lollipop with a caramel center. The caramel center became affixed to the inside of her braces and would not come loose.

"Here I was in my new sweater and new boots, walking around the high school, with a lollipop stuck to the roof of my mouth. I almost died!"

"Why didn't you pull?"

"I did, and the whole thing came out." (Hers are removable.)

She promised she never would set foot in the high school again or look another friend in the face. I suggested she might do better simply to give up lollipops. The next morning she left the same time on the school bus. I guessed the crisis had passed.

We once had to tear up a neighbor's hedge while we hunted for a temporary orthodontic device called a "retainer." It doesn't do a thing for retaining family harmony.

We once had to re-do 400 miles of turnpike travel.

That was the time the retainer was left in a Howard Johnson restaurant during a busy lunch hour.

What amazed me was the waitress wasn't even surprised to see us come traipsing back in. Of course we had to pick out our own retainer. Seems some other people had to come back all the way from Maine.

"Smile, sweetheart," I say.

"Yeah, smile, Miss American-Pie," says the Baron as he signs another check.

Then there are all the appointments. With the appointments come the arrangements for the car pool you can't make and the excuse note they are going to need to get back into classes.

"If you had been meant to get out of class every two weeks to have your braces tightened, the school board would have given you a dentist instead of a career counselor," I say, frantically hunting for a blank piece of paper on which to write an excuse. The bus driver is outside honking his horn. He has no patience. All of his children have straight teeth.

"I am not wearing braces when I am married," says Miss American-Pie.

"You don't have time to get married this week. You have four book reports due. You told me so yourself."

"But I'll never get these braces off. I'll be wearing them the rest of my life," she sobs. This is Sarah Bernhardt Day at the farm.

"Oh no you won't," says the Baron. "I won't pay for them forever. You will have straight teeth within two years. We were promised!" What a believer.

"Smile, careful now, smile," says the family photographer. But no one was smiling that day. There was a feud about whose turn it is to feed the bird or take out the trash or watch for the first star.

"We don't feel like smiling," I tell the photographer.

"I don't understand," he says.

"You wouldn't," I tell him, looking at his straight teeny teeth.

Parental 'Peculiarities' Push Dress Code into Background

January 23, 1972

It was a meeting on dress codes.

Harry spoke first. "Well, it's this thing with my Dad. A real drag. He won't wear anything but white shirts, Monday, Tuesday, Wednesday, Thursday, Friday. No way to get him to break the chain."

Harry was wearing his seven-year-old jeans and his Woodstock tee shirt.

Marcia agreed with Harry. "I know exactly what you mean," she said as she braided and rebraided the fringe on her vest and coat and shoes. "My Dad wears colored shirts now, but his suits are all one color. That's gray." She rolled her eyes skyward.

Sam nonchalantly loosened the belt of his safari shirt with the ski emblems and scratched some imaginary dust from a pair of sneakers held together with three blue rubber bands. "My mother still wears an apron to cook in. With flowers on the pocket, for crying out loud. She heard the Beatles broke up and went out and bought some bug spray."

"I don't understand it," sighed Casey, squinting into the light. Casey hasn't parted her hair since 1968.

"I can't say that I agree with you guys," Tad argued. "My dad thinks he is the NBC peacock. You have to wear a radiation badge when you check out his new ties."

Tad was wearing his father's World War II Army overcoat with all but two buttons missing. His jeans were held up with a rope.

"The trouble is you can't talk to them about it," Sue complained. "I tried to tell my mother something about the terrible way she's wearing her hair, and she pouted for three days." Sue patted her own frizzed-out 1920 hair-do and made an imaginary pout with her Clara Bow[60] red lips.

"Yeah, it's sad, the minute you try to help them, they get all defensive, I wanted to persuade my mother to buy this really neat pair of red crinkle boots, and she told me to stay out of her life and let her buy any pair of loafers she wanted. Boy, is she touchy." Carolee adjusted the dragging strap of her summer beach sandal and inspected one peeling toenail.

"They'll just have to learn on their own."

"Yeah, it's really no use trying to help them when they aren't willing to help themselves."

"All you have to do is mention clothes to my mother, and she just goes all to pieces. My aunt sent me a hand-smocked dress when I was six, and Mom still thinks she should keep it hanging in the closet."

Johnnie arrived at the meeting late. He was wearing the Marine fatigue jacket rescued from a Louisiana swamp by an old friend. "Sorry, fellows," he muttered. "We had a problem at home. My Dad was going to a business meeting in Los Angeles, and he couldn't find his blue and gold striped tie. Really funny about that tie. Won't go anywhere without it." He shook his head sadly.

"Have you tried professional help?"

"Yeah," Johnnie said. "Last week I took him down to the Total Wipeout Boutique and made him try on every darn tie in the place. Didn't do any good. He doesn't want my advice."

"All we can do is guide them in the right direction and hope they may someday learn these things for themselves."

"Yeah, I suppose so," said Harry, stroking his bright red beard and walrus mustache. "My father's really paranoid about his shaving things. A regular ritual. All that. He gets some kind of kick out of punishing himself with that blade every morning. My mother patches him up with pieces of wet paper towels so he doesn't bleed on his white shirt."

A groan arose from the audience. Fortune Cookie arrived just then. Fortune Cookie runs a kindergarten on Saturdays for busy mothers and in return gets to clean their attic trunks. She was wearing a feathered boa with most of the feathers missing, a purple velvet slouch hat, and a jersey dress that must have known Carole Lombard[61].

"I'm so worried about my Mom," admitted Fortune, who has been known to try to organize a group therapy session on the jitney bus service into town, which only takes 10 minutes.

"She's started wearing white gloves again. All the time." A gasp went up. "Let us help. Maybe we can organize a neighborhood group. We could take turns staying with her."

"I really thought she was going to be all right after our long talk. She even took up the hem in three skirts one evening last week. Then yesterday the white gloves."

Just then the school principal stuck his head in the door. "Sorry to break up the dress code meeting, kids, but we need the room now."

'Lapsed Housewife' Is Ready to Tell It All in a Book

January 30, 1972

I'm thinking about writing a book.

I want to call it something like "Confessions of a Lapsed House-wife." Or "Worn-Out Wife" by D. Maybe "Memoirs of a Mean Mother."

Too bad "Diary of a Mad Housewife" was already used.

But nevertheless I think it's time everyone climbs on the band-wagon and gets out a book.

I plan to confess about the basket of darning I threw away in 1957.

I shall even admit to leaving the warm marital bed (inhabited by three children with flu and a dog with bad breath) to write a fan letter to Paul Newman.

Nothing will be spared. Dropping out of Arthur Murray's ten easy lessons. Dropping out of bridge in ten easy lessons. Dropping out of gourmet cooking in six easy lessons.

I will describe my experience while falling asleep during a group therapy session while everyone was shouting.

I will describe the terrifying amnesia I underwent during football season when my husband came to dinner only twice in three months.

There will be the glorious description of our thrilling two-week vacation in End-of-the World when the cruise director jumped ship and no one noticed.

There will be descriptions of the freeway at five o'clock on a snowy afternoon. The neighborhood kiddie car-pool in a flu epidemic. The parking lot of the senior high school with 37 student drivers turned loose at once.

I insist upon telling it all.

Roaming the aisles of the supermarket looking for a cheaper peanut butter. Parking illegally in the loading area of the supermarket. Winking at the produce clerk while he weighs the romaine lettuce.

There was the time I bought a dozen bottles of clam juice to get enough trading stamps for the grill.

No one in our house drinks clam juice. No one in our neighborhood thought red-tissue-wrapped bottles of clam juice appropriate during the holidays. No one in our house has a sense of humor.

I will tell you about the half-cup of green fuzzy things in the back of the refrigerator.

There was the time I ironed the Little League uniform and affixed the numbers "86" permanently to the ironing board.

I will reprint my famous, "Please excuse my child from school" notes that won a prize in the "Tall Story" competition in Minnesota.

I will publish all the scathing notes to the children pasted on the doors of their bedrooms.

I will not, repeat, will not permit those bedrooms to be photographed.

If pressed, I will publish my famous recipe for elastic spaghetti, which is now under attack by Ralph Nader.

Let me tell you about my forty-nine handy little excuses for not getting to the dentist.

Let me tell you about burning the chili, burning the pudding, burning the carburetor.

This book will be a detailed candid look at just what is wrong with kitchens today: No one in them when you need help and everyone in them when you are trying to sneak the last chocolate éclair.

It will examine in detail the failings of modern American marriage: Too much football, too much ironing, too many car pools, too many PTA meetings.

It will give you the inside dope on how to soak burned pots, how to avoid being named program chairman of your club, and how to take care of live alligators in a basement laundry tub.

We will deal with Lazarus the garter snake who lived in a pillow-case, and Jasmine Sweet, the tomcat with the unfortunate name, who thinks he lives in our four-year-old Ford.

I will never disclose, no matter how severely pressed, the location of the five baskets of ironing that disappeared from my life forever during Christmas week 1970. A woman is entitled to some discretion.

When the book is published, I guess I'll just back up the car in the driveway over the mound of topsoil I never did finish distributing, I'll head West for Hollywood, and maybe if the kids are good, I'll send them the address!

Mother of Athlete Is Forced to Put up with Bumps, Too

February 6, 1972

My friend Maude Mothermost was confiding to me her concern over her child, who spends all day reading in his room. "I wish he would go out and play some baseball or picket the school or do something!"

"Listen," I told Maude, "be glad he's so happy. All you have to do is drive him to the library and replace the light bulb in his reading light, right?"

"Well, actually, he eats a lot while he reads."

"So did Shakespeare. So did Updike. So did Saul Bellow. Relax." I told Maude. I explained that from my vast experience as the mother of an athlete and also my vast experience as the mother of a reader, the latter is infinitely easier.

When the athlete loses it's the mother who cries. When the athlete gets bawled out by the umpire, it's the mother who screams at the ump.

When our son graduated from Little League to girls, I breathed a sigh of relief. It didn't last long. Our elder daughter, destined for pink roses and frilly slips, or so I thought, fell in love with the school gym.

Then she fell in love with the basketball coach. The love for the coach faded, but the love of basketball remained.

After a few years' respite between Little League and Girls Basketball, I took to the bleachers again. I learned how to climb over piles of shouting kids straight to the top where one empty seat remains. I learned to scream myself horse at referees.

The first thing about being the mother of an athlete is learning that dinner will never again be on time. Games are scheduled by people who never eat dinner. There is some mysterious mechanism in effect. During dinner hour any night in the season, the mother of the athlete is either in the bleachers, driving the team through fog on the expressway or taking someone to the hospital for diagnostic X rays.

The season is a nebulous thing anyway. It lasts from about the first day of school until about two weeks after school when the teams are still having picnics to celebrate the "end of the season."

The athlete, of course, must be kept in prime condition. This means steak and potatoes and orange juice. By the ton.

The next big thing the mother of the athlete has to be concerned with is her athlete's uniform. While the rest of his room is in complete shambles, about to be condemned by city authorities, the uniform rests in resplendent unwrinkled beauty on a hanger on the back of the door.

Last week my daughter the athlete needed special socks. She pressed every pleat in her uniform with loving care (while the dozen unironed blouses just sat around getting dusty.)

We spend hours just washing and drying athletic socks. Big business.

The athlete is never around when you need someone to go to the store or put up the awnings.

The athlete is always "in training." This means he eats a lot, sleeps a lot and is never home when you need him.

They accumulate trophies. Big trophies. Little trophies. There is no more room even to put the piles of wooly athletic socks. (Ask Mrs. Namath. Ask Mrs. Unitas. Ask me!)

Parents who play bridge together and go out to celebrate one another's birthdays suddenly stop talking to one another in the middle of a crucial game. And all because the wife's sister-in-law, the one who is the referee, made a bum call. Parents of athletes are great at school board meetings and ecology groups. They've had basic training in counter-attack and infiltration. They are also, by training, enormously patient. (Just ask any parent of an athlete who has been eating his evening meal at 8:30 p.m. for the past four years!)

The girls on our basketball team had a dance last fall. They stayed in the gym late putting up decorations and making paper flowers. Then they had scrimmage for an hour. A group stopped by the house on their way to the dance, and I never saw a lovelier group of sophisticated young ladies, so graceful in their long dresses and up-swept hairdos. Then someone mentioned the score of a professional basketball game the previous evening.

Instantly every girl in the room was shouting her two cents worth. I went around slowly and lifted the skirts ankle-high on each girl's dress. "Just checking kids. Didn't you leave your uniforms at home? This is a dance night, remember?"

They giggled, but someone in that group had a referee's whistle in her evening bag and we heard it shrilly across the lawn as they left for the gym. The gym is our daughter's life.

Parents Constantly Amazed
by the 'Gypsy Generation'

February 27, 1972

Don't kids ever stay home anymore? We are the parents of a generation of gypsies.

A great many parents of teen-agers in our neighborhood are down at the airport picking one up, seeing one off. If not there, then the bus station. Or the cloverleaf of some obscure junction of the Interstate highway system where junior suddenly decided to give up hitchhiking.

"I think I'll go to Denver," declared my 10-year-old gypsy.

"Really, before dinner?" When he was much younger, he always managed to run away from home AFTER meals.

"Maybe California."

"Do you have enough clean underwear?"

That week Neighborhood Nomad Numero Uno came home. Willie the Wanderer was home from the Western commune minus his mustache and looking indestructible. Max showed up after seven weeks in London, still wearing the same pea jacket and with the same scuffed loafers I have seen him in since sixth grade. Gaunt and thoughtful Bill stopped by with plans for a homemade camper he's taking to Alaska.

"What is this? The Traveller's Aid Society?" The Baron stepped over three lanky bodies on the living room rug exploring maps.

"I hear the food isn't so hot in Argentina."

"My sister Cindy ran into Crazy Jane last week in Cairo."

"Have you ever seen Minneapolis at night in a blizzard?"

I told the Baron we should have cancelled our subscription to National Geographic.

Then I figured out a theory stemming from car pool attraction. Where do kids spend a large part of their growing years? In car pools! They seem to be unable to break the pattern of staying on the move.

The theory fell through. "I always got car sick, don't you remember?" said the 19-year-old?

On Monday he went shopping for a waterproofing compound for his boots. This took all afternoon.

On Tuesday he waterproofed the boots. "Snow gets really high in Colorado," he told me seriously while eating his third snack for the evening.

Wednesday he shopped for long underwear. "Did you buy any?" I asked.

"No, I wasn't sure about the fiber content. I'll go back tomorrow." He switched on the television and worked on the boots some more.

Thursday he looked at overcoats in the Army surplus store. "Maybe you could go South?" I offered. "It would be warm, and you could travel lighter."

He told me he could buy a World War II full-length Army overcoat for $11. But he wanted to think it over.

Friday I suggested he buy some heavy wool socks. "Why? I can only wear one pair at a time."

Saturday he slept late.

"I'm going grocery shopping. Will you be here for dinner tomorrow?" I asked.

"Sure. The whole week is gone now. I'll probably leave Monday."

I kept telling myself I was a calm mother. Then I brought a carton or cigarettes, and I don't smoke. I drove to the shopping center, left the car there and walked home.

"You're nervous."

"Don't be silly. The kids have to leave home sometime."

Monday came. He asked to borrow the car to go to a ski shop and price parkas. "I probably won't leave until after the Olympics. Max might meet this friend of his in Naples, and he asked me to go along."

"I'll put another hamburger on," I replied meekly.

These kids amble off to Asia as casually as I go to the grocery store. They are halfway across the world with a knapsack while we are still in the shop deciding on initials for our luggage.

Our 14-year-old was in the kitchen fixing a bag lunch, cutting up oranges and wrapping cookies in foil.

"Mom, I'm leaving!" she called to me.

"Please, darling, you're so young. We have things to talk about, songs to listen to, snowmen to build, clouds to watch. Please honey, don't do this to your mother," I pleaded.

"My gosh, Mom, I'm just going to the 'Y' to swim. Watsa matter? Are you feeling blue or something?"

I smiled gently and bent over to pick up the stack of maps off the living room rug.

Liz Makes Cover of Life;
Life Just Passes for Mother

March 5, 1972

Elizabeth Taylor turned 40 and had her picture on the cover of Life.

I turned 40, and my dentist called to warn me about letting those six-month appointments lapse.

Richard Burton bought Liz a jewel big enough to choke a cat (he was thinking about buying her Bucharest, but someone else got there first). The Baron gave me a paintbrush and told me the paint on the windowsills is peeling again.

The hairdresser asked me if life had begun yet. Then he laughed and choked on the hair spray mist he walks around in all day.

My son started opening doors for me, running ahead to do it. (Well, 40 does have its rewards at that!)

Actually I've been lying about my age for so long, even I don't believe my own birthdays anymore.

My doctor calls and says its time for a yearly check-up. "Are you kidding?" I laugh. "I was just in to see you last week. When the baby was teething. I remember it distinctly."

He reminds me the baby is going to high school next year.

"My, how the time flies when you are having fun," I reply, moving two dogs and 25 socks that don't match off the telephone chair.

(By the way, a local hippie told me what happens to all socks. Put 25 in the dryer; only 24 come out. Right? Put 14 in the dryer; only 13 emerge. They all go to the Big Sock Heaven in the Sky!)

I got three notices for reduced rates on wrinkle creams from three separate department stores. Wrinkles are expensive I learned.

I read Elizabeth Taylor never uses anything but soap and water and never wears make up. I checked the cover of Life. "What are you doing?" asked the Baron. "I'm measuring eyelashes. Get out of my way."

"Why don't you buy me something exciting like the Hope Diamond or Minneapolis or the St. Lawrence Seaway?" I smiled (uses less wrinkles.)

"I was thinking of something with more class like a new battery for the car or two tickets to the hockey game," the Barons said.

(That man is all heart, I swear.)

My neighbor Sadie called to invite me to the Thursday afternoon square dance. Who ever heard of a square dance on Thursday afternoons I asked.

The senior citizens group, she told me.

One morning the sun came out and glinted on the new paint on the windowsills. I saw 10 or 20 new gray hairs right in the middle of my head.

That morning I turned down Sara Lee coffee cake. Then I went back to bed with the dog.

"Mom, mom," said the kids. "Please get up."

"Why, did your allowance run out? Do you need a ride to school? Is the peanut butter jar empty?"

"C'mon, mom, don't be that way. Get up, please get up."

"Why should I? Give me one good reason."

"Because. The kids are coming over and you're the only one who can show us how to Charleston!"

So there I was on a bright Friday morning doing the Charleston in my own living room with a bunch of longhaired kids who wouldn't know Rudy Vallee or Frank Sinatra if they fell over them.

That night I washed my face in soap and water and measured my eyelashes.

I called my hairdresser and made an appointment for a haircut. "Only 20 gray ones I told him. Do you have to charge me for the whole head?"

The Baron came home with a large package in his hands, wrapped in gold paper with a pink bow.

It's a heating pad, he grinned. You know how your shoulder acts up after those Thursday square dance sessions.

Somehow I never thought life really began just sitting around on Saturday night with the heating pad on our shoulder and worrying about the kids getting home on time.

Oh well, I just tell myself. I wouldn't want it even if he could buy Bucharest!

Female Slumber Parties: Tons of Food, Bras in the Freezer

April 16, 1972

"I can always tell when spring vacation starts," commented one of the neighborhood fathers. "The living room is always full of a dozen girls in sleeping bags."

"When they were little girls and spring arrived, they all used to go roller skating. Now they have slumber party marathons and eat hundreds of pancakes every morning." He sighed the sigh of an ex-patriate father, doomed for the next three years to watching re-runs of Peyton Place and standing in line to get into his own bathroom.

The prime idea of a slumber party is, of course, never to sleep. To sleep is to leave one's self open to danger. One's bra can be frozen in the family freezer. One can find cold cream in one's hair, jellybeans in the sleeping bag, little brother's pet mouse in the bag of curlers.

Just to see my girls leave for a slumber party stuns me.

This girl, this young slip of a thing, who this morning could not manage to get two tennis shoes on her own two feet, is now equipped for a safari.

Curlers, records, sleeping bag, hair dryer, shampoo, cards, Scrabble and bags of fruit are arranged in tidy piles to be picked up and delivered to the house of the hostess.

"I need a new sleeping bag," moaned one of our girls to the Baron.

What's wrong with your brother's? We paid a fortune for it, and he only slept outside half-a-dozen times in it!"

"It smells like wood smoke, and besides I saw this darling one with lavender violins embroidered all over it."

"You know you're not going to sleep anyway. Why don't you take an old Army blanket out of the attic."

Then comes the anguished wail. "But, Daddy!"

If you are fortunate enough to have a large galaxy of teenage girls in your neighborhood, it means you only have to have about two slumber parties a year. First, you sit down and make a guest list. This is meaningless, but it keeps you busy while the girls are mixing up some herbal brew out of Hawaiian punch and ginger ale, which they will consume by the buckets.

Then you sort out the refrigerator and move the furniture to make room for more sleeping area. Both tasks are also meaningless, since the refrigerator will be full of bras and hairnets and athletic socks by morning, and the furniture will have assumed the "After-the-Revolution" posture.

Actually we always have found the girls to be rather peaceful during the nighttime hours. They know scads of card games with names like "Spit" and "Slap."

One day our 12-year-old came home from a slumber party an accomplished poker player with purple nail polish. Another time she came home knowing all the verses to "One Hundred Bottles of Beer." All slumber parties tend to be what educators call "enlightening experiences."

In the wee hours when the rosy blush of dawn appears, the kids like to go out and roll their little brother's red wagon down the hill or play "Laugh-In" cheerleader on the front lawn, cheering all the bewildered milkmen on their routes. They become riotously funny, enlarging upon their own wild improvisations.

Sleepy neighbors lean out of bedroom windows to watch the craziness.

Breakfast is straight out of an infantry mess hall with dozens of everything and frequent explosions of hilarity.

When the Baron rises for his shower, there are three girls in granny gowns putting up one another's hair in the hallway and one girl in the bathroom experimenting with eyeliner.

"How do you like this eye?" she says, standing on tippy-toe and staring him in one bloodshot eye.

His remarks are unintelligible. By the time he is on the freeway headed for daylight and work, the girls are nestled in corners of the living room, snoozing gently. The dog walks about, sniffing for jelly-beans, and inspecting all the sleeping bags. Even the ones with little lavender violins embroidered on them.

'Best of Year' Awards
Presented on Back Porch

April 23, 1972

Those coveted "Best of the Year" awards were handed out the other evening, with the Baron acting as master of ceremonies in his golf shirt with no buttons and the ripped pocket.

This year we held them on the back porch. The previous year we held them in the parking lot behind McDonald's but the crowds became unmanageable.

"Wags," the friendly neighborhood scavenger, was there with a three-week-old steak bone, and six kindergarten moppets who giggled a lot.

I wore my favorite wrap-around corduroy skirt, recently rejected by Goodwill Industries, adorned only with my favorite bent safety pin.

"Best Supporting Actress" of the year went to our youngest daughter who recently starred in a ninth-grade women's liberation documentary in the school counselor's office. She was on location in her laboratory where she is growing lima beans and marigolds and could not be reached for comment. It was rumored she was passing out women's lib pamphlets at the local YMCA.

"Best Foreign Film" went to the Baron's vacation snapshots of the grass outside Paul Revere's shrine in Boston. The nominees gallantly agreed to donate a portion of their earnings to the purchase of several new rolls of film.

"Best Direction" of the year went to our friendly neighbor, Archie Knowitall, who directed that wonderful segment last year when the rain-spouting fell during repairs by his brother-in-law. He will be remembered best for his previous direction of the Halloween party for senior citizens in which two 80-year-olds eloped. Archie was unavailable at the time, having decided to run a traffic survey down at the crossroads.

"Best Performance by a Female' went to Gramma who cried for the entire group performance of the fifth-grade school play, "Gulliver's Travels."

Gramma was in Vegas, and when telephoned with results of the nominations, cried for 20 minutes at $1.65 a minute.

"Best Performance by a Male" went to a newcomer: Ulysses T. Fringe. Ulysses, who starred as Little League pitcher in earlier years, is now remembered best for the night his muffler fell off at 3 a.m., after having been stalled in the mud at the lakefront with cousin Irene. Ulysses, with his omnipresent guitar and coterie of admirers, had only one thing to say: "The whole thing is good, really cool. I dig it, really dig it!"

"Best Cartoon" again was won by little Scribbly Sally, who last week did an entire hallway in her "A, B, C's" while her mother was on the telephone.

"Best Supporting Actor" of the year was awarded to our elder son, who managed to drive his mother's Volkswagen for 400 miles on half-a-tank of gas. He last starred in the Sunday school picnic where he consumes 14 deviled eggs at one sitting.

"Best Documentary" was won by Zack Hilton, who has seized that unforgettable moment on film when the Baron broke his tennis racquet on the backward fence in a moving portrayal of Marlon Brando.

Zack is remembered for his previous documentaries of the Christmas Office Party and the Skinny Dip Party at the country club.

Zack announced to his surprised audience that he planned to donate his films to the local branch of the library and retire to his fishing lodge and watch for balloons.

"Best Show of the Year" was a shoo-in once more this year. The stunning performance given by our elder daughter at her first formal when she had to be sewn into her gown 10 minutes after the finals of a basketball tournament. That was the sequence when the living room ceiling rained and the dog had a coronary. Great drama in a single evening's performance!

Immediately following the awards, we all retired to the kitchen to watch the ice cube trays melt.

Tee Time Creeps up on Us and Life's Not up to Par

April 30, 1972

The Baron sat at the dining room table drinking black coffee and nervously tapping the tabletop with his fingertips.

It was Saturday 5 a.m. and it was raining. Ordinarily I would not be caught alive at that hour of any morning (I'm not sure I would know if I were alive at that hour), but what do you do when your husband brings in three golf buddies who need black coffee and pancakes to soothe their jangled nerves.

"Call the weather bureau." offered one.

"No, call the State Police," said another.

"Oh, lord, why me?" asked the paranoiac in the group.

"More pancakes, anyone?" I asked as brightly as possible under what we used to call "stress" conditions.

A tousled head appeared at the doorway. "The dog just threw up on someone's golf clubs in the living room. I thought you should know."

Naturally it had to be the paranoiac's!

Before we were married I never even knew the Baron could play golf. He never mentioned it. The only time we ever went near a gold course it was long after dark.

A perfectly sensible man who makes no fuss whatsoever about never having clean socks, he has been known to do a little raving and

314

ranting when his golf shoes disappeared from the closet and showed up in the Goodwill bag.

It never fails to amaze someone like me that a grown man who forgets the refrigerator is located in his own house can spot a tiny little white ball 250 years down the fairway. Most times he can't concentrate that long!

Football season ended, and I ran to the attic to bring down the screens, and busily set about pulling down cans of paint.

"What are you doing?" he said.

"It's time to re-paint, re-furbish, re-decorate."

"It's time to work on my chip shot. The screens can wait."

And so he arises at dawn, drives through fog and mist to wait in line to be told, maybe, yes, there might be a time for him to tee off.

He, who chafes if the mashed potatoes are the least bit slow in being passed around the dining room table, obediently stands in line for 45 minutes, his clubs at his feet, his vacuum bottle clutched in one hand.

("How come I never see Arnie Palmer walking around with a vacuum bottle in his hand?" I ask. When I'm that good," he tells me, "you can carry my vacuum bottle!" Thanks a lot, I tell him.)

For the privilege of standing in line, getting blisters on his ankles, and coming within an inch of a coronary, he pays outstanding amounts (Remember the time he argued about the 35-cent candy bar when he went to see "The Godfather?")

He comes home, sunburned and bleary-eyed, crawls up the steps, and lands panting in front of the television set where he manages to switch it on just in time to see the 16th hole of the Montezuma Farewell Golf Tournament outside the pyramids of Central Mexico.

"Almost missed it," he pants. His golf shoes are placed carefully beneath the coffee table. His clubs are laid lovingly before the fireplace. The dog appears interested. "No, no!" he shouts at her. She skulks away, to hunt for other forbidden treasures.

"The children are giving an arts and crafts show at the playground this afternoon."

He winces with pain. "It's so far to walk!"

"The school is next door."

"I know. You go!" He smiles.

"This afternoon the garden hose broke and flooded the car, and I overdrew the checking account." I tell him this as the playoff advances to the 18th green.

"Yeah, yeah, you're kidding?" He smiles some more.

The children trek through the living room bearing posters and pots of paint. "Who's that?"

"That's Daddy. Remember. The nice man who takes you piggy back to the parades."

"Mother, I'm 19 years old. It embarrasses me when you talk like that."

"I'm sorry, darling, but it isn't easy trying to schedule dinner between greens. At least there is an intermission at football games!"

She Survives Cubs, Little League, Yoga ... Only to Face Camping out

July 2, 1972

To think that I've survived Cub Scouts, Little League and beginner's yoga, only to have to face camping out.

There simply is no one to turn to. No branch of middle-aged Campers Anonymous. No understanding ear to listen and give supportive therapy while I apply Caladryl to my poison ivy.

Three nights in a mildewed tent with dirt under my fingernails and all my children can do is pound me on the back and tell me to build up the fire while they go out in the canoe.

Three mornings with fur on my teeth and bones that would not bend and all my husband of 20 years could do was pound me on the back and tell me to build up the fire while he went out in the rowboat.

What could I do but enter the forest primeval and gather the wood? They sure weren't going to get me into a canoe or a rowboat. The only boats I go on are the ones with elevators and shuffleboard.

"Try it, you'll like it," grinned my camper-mate, loading my arms with sleeping bags. "Commune with the elements!"

I communed. Twenty-three mosquito bites. Poison ivy around the ankles. Incipient pneumonia. Bursitis. Possible advanced case of paranoia.

Other women go to the beauty parlor Friday afternoon. I have to go to three drugstores to find a snakebite kit. With tears in my eyes.

"Try it, you'll like it," grinned my overgrown Cub Scout of 19 summers as he piled tent poles on my shoulders. "The quiet is something else."

Quiet? A massed chorale of 375 birds began their rehearsal at 4:30 a.m. and some hardy camper sang Italian arias until midnight by the campfire next to us.

The only reason the Baron and I still are married is that we long ago agreed never to speak to one another before noon. I am programmed to spend the first half-hour of each morning in sleepwalking with as few disturbances as possible. I am not accustomed to walking in my pajamas three blocks through the underbrush to use the facilities and there to meet a bright-eyed camper freshly shaved and whistling while he brushed his teeth.

"Good morning, m'am," he gargled.

"Uhn," I replied, leaning against an oak tree and scratching.

"Gorgeous morning. I've seen seven warblers already this morning, m'am," he persisted.

"Could I get a disability discharge?" I asked. "A hardship discharge?"

"Beg your pardon, m'am?"

"I wanna be a civilian again."

"If you hurry, you'll be just in time for the 17-mile hike up Suicide Trail," he gargled.

"My hiking boots were lost when the Apaches cut us off back at the BP Station," I told him slowly, trying not to chatter and shake in the 30-degree temperatures.

I heard him howling as he walked up the path, a towel slung over his shoulder. A tiny chipmunk came out and glinted at me. "Go away. I am from the city, Alien. You understand, Alien?" I told him.

The marshmallows melted and the ice melted. I forgot to pack silverware and the sugar. Every time I wanted to light the stove I had to read the book of directions because I kept forgetting the sequence.

We were just sitting down to eat our meals when everyone else was heading for the lake to swim and fish.

Sleeping, snugly, five in a row, I discovered one child still snuffles in her sleep, one talks in her sleep and the other sighs. One can become permanently impaired trying to turn over on an air mattress in a tent full of people. One can dress completely in a sleeping bag, but it is senseless after awhile to bother getting undressed because one can freeze to death in the process, and remember, it is three blocks to the facilities.

"What are you thinking of?" asked the Baron softly, taking my hand in the fading twilight as we watched our fire go out and heard the neighbors begin their Italian arias.

"I am thinking of a Holiday Inn with furry wall-to-wall rugs and hot water and room service. I am thinking of a hot meal that I don't have to gather wood for."

"You sure know how to hurt a person," he said handing me the bottle of Caladryl.

It's a Thanksgiving Miracle: Cocker Survives Surgery

1972

It is the season for miracles.

It is the season for the unexplained, the unexpected. Some call it Thanksgiving. Call it what you will.

The veterinarian was blunt, his eyes arranged to show no emotion. "You will have to have the tumor removed immediately. I suggest you leave her here tonight and we'll operate tomorrow."

I held the shivery black furry cocker spaniel in my arms over the antiseptic white table in the examining room and tried to remember how to be an adult.

"What are her chances?"

"Fifty-fifty."

"Let me take her home for the night."

He knew it was a mistake. "All right," he said.

She huddled on her side of the car, cold on the vinyl upholstery, smelling out fear, her eyes dimmed with cataracts, no longer straining to see the trees whipping past.

She has been, after all, a part of 14 years of our lives: birthdays, Christmases, arguments, vacations, daily walks.

My husband had brought her home in a box meant for a layer cake. We couldn't afford the layer cake let alone a dog. "You must be crazy," I remember snapping at him. Then I looked at her, and there was no turning back.

She got up at night when the children were ill with fever, and I was ill with worry.

She was waiting every morning of our lives, barking furiously, running around in circles like a silly clown, proclaiming the delicious excitement of another morning.

She barked at strangers until the day she could no longer hear. Embarrassed by her new difficulty, she soon learned to rely on light and hand signals. I wondered what it must be like in that strange quiet deafness where neither the sound of a leaf falling nor the squeal of a car braking could be heard.

But the other senses took over and refined themselves to meet her needs. She could sense a presence. She could sense an absence. She hung around a lonely child, a child needing comfort, and soon the two of them would be on the floor romping and snuggling together.

She was a blatant beggar, standing by the side of the kitchen cupboard until someone noticed her and fed her the tidbit of a cookie or a cracker or the dog biscuit. Fond of spaghetti, she nevertheless would wait patiently until all were finished with dinner before she would go into her frantic dance signaling her delight in the culinary world.

She was very much a large part of all our lives.

Leaving the animal hospital, I drove to the church where we were to pick up one of the teen-agers. She got out of the car, long ears flapping in the sharp cold wind and began to run among the trees.

Rolling in the piles of dry leaves, she would shiver with excitement, then bound up all on all fours and race toward me, the light of the moon reflecting in those tired old eyes.

There were a thousand smells, a thousand different delights: a leaf here, a bent twig there, the spoof of a shadow. After 14 years, she was in her heart only a pup. She played hide-and-seek with me, peering out from behind a building.

The sky was crystal clear, the moon a beacon. There was only the sound of our breathing and the leaves moving in the occasional gusts of wind.

But, she, after all, didn't know this might be her last romp. It was just another series of wonderful days to be enjoyed, despite difficulties, infirmities, small defeats.

On the drive home the window was wet with her panting and the steering wheel was wet with my tears.

The following morning I delivered her in a subdued, frightened quiet bundle to the young boy sweeping out the reception room of the animal hospital. Our own house was terribly quiet; everyone was too polite, too restrained.

That night the veterinarian called, and in an effort to control the tinge of joy in his voice, he told us to come and pick up our dog who was awake and eager to be with the ones she knows best.

There was a recuperation ahead. There were stitches to be removed. Weak and still giddy from the after effects of surgery, she nevertheless took care to greet each one of us with a warm swipe of her tongue. Then she leaned gratefully into her old blanket and fell asleep.

I went outside and scuffed the dry leaves and tried to remember the particular cool pale brilliance of this particular night when a small dog had taught us the miracle of Thanksgiving.

Class Awed by Moon Rocks
During Trip to Washington

1972

A remarkably orderly line of several hundred people waited in the chill morning air to tour the White House recently during spring vacation. Good natured and relaxed, they chatted with one another and compared cameras and maps.

Across the street cherry trees and forsythia bushes kept tightly-furled leaves in check, denying for a few more days the insistence of spring. Only the high school girls in flowery prints created the spring colors one comes to expect in the nation's capital during that annual trek of several thousand seniors, noisy, enthusiastic, awed and immersed in the intricate workings of civics class "for real."

We chose the lunar rocks, saving the White House for less crowded times.

There in the rotunda of the Smithsonian, nestled under plexiglass, surrounded by impressive velvet ropes and guarded by a burly gentleman in uniform, was the lunar sample. A surprisingly smooth rock, about the size of a fist, it looked ordinary, something from the creek down by the woods, something from your aunt's rock garden, something from one of the kid's forts. But the mystique generated by the astronauts' tense initial exploration on the surface of the moon transfers itself automatically to people's imaginations, and their faces glow with reflected lights of fascination and speculations as they view the sample.

One can view the massive booster engine, one of five that lifts the tiny capsules into the sky, or one can tour the simulated cockpit of a passenger airplane (no one thought the hijacking horseplay amusing even in a simulated cockpit!) Meantime, overhead the fragile, amazingly small aircraft of Lindberg moves ever-so-slightly in a small breeze, and people race beneath it never noticing, while occasionally an old-timer with a shock of white hair leans against the wall and muses quietly, remembering that first transatlantic flight.

We ask the burly guard how to find the Hall of Explorers in the National Geographic Building. He laughs apologetically, honestly admitting his lack of knowledge of the city. "I'm from Providence, R.I., and ran out of work there."

We leave the hippies in Indian headbands discussing the lunar sample, the guard from Providence and the ghost of Lindbergh, and decide to have lunch in historic Georgetown.

The damp, somewhat gray weather only enhances the narrow brick sidewalks of Georgetown with its rows of extraordinarily well-kept townhouses, low-slung sports cars and ivy walls with tiny beads of moisture shining green.

The girls are mesmerized with a feast of contrasts: girls in maxis, matrons in expensive leather gloves, women in saris shopping for tea, women in high, white boots shopping for plastic furniture, Afro haircuts with delicate dangling earrings, barefeet in handmade sandals of a thousand designs, a gentleman in a cutaway wearing a turban. To stand and watch is enough for the moment.

Then begins the methodical path through shops where old chess sets and Chagall prints and tiny Zodiac puzzles draw them as surely as the antique cuff links and the Greek pendants on leather bands.

There are marble ornaments for glass-topped tables and crystal chandeliers along with incense and silk-screened fabrics. We buy bread flown from Paris the previous afternoon, and a young Middle Eastern gentleman explains patiently to the wide-eyed girls how goat's cheese is used and they touch the intricate spiral folds of the very product.

Leaving the dim interior and romantic stories of the cheese-seller's shop, we proceed in unremitting fashion, like American lemmings, to the nearest hamburger shop, where the girls devour double burgers and milk shakes and French fries. It is, somehow, a letdown. We should have a grassy hillside nearby with goats grazing and the sharp scent of the sea. Instead an immaculate gentleman in starched white shirt, laundry creases bending with him, reminds everyone to clear their table and make way for the next group of purists and trades people.

In the late afternoon sun, a pale orb in a pewter sky, the capitol graces the horizon with infinite dignity, protestors walk before the White House. A block and a half down the street there is a shop specializing in electronic listening devices. Taxis stop respectfully for pedestrians. Everyone is wearing mod sunglasses and we pause to look at the sedate curtained windows of Blair House where so much history has been woven.

There is no time for the Washington Monument, except for a glance to see the ring of brightly-hued flags whipped by the wind. Too early for the cherry blossoms, we end the day contemplating the results of an archaeological "dig" in Central America and buy a book on the Middle Ages.

We muse quietly on the way home, giant jets soaring overhead in rhythmic patterns. Perhaps there are people leaving for Paris, Rome, Cleveland or Houston? Behind us the first lamplight of the evening sends a complimentary glow over the city's outline. A day of contrasts, a day of ironies. Tomorrow there will be another line turning patiently around the White House, cameras slung on sturdy shoulders, while another group of protestors yawn and watch the sky waiting for some omen of spring.

Endnotes

1. "Omnibus" was a cultural and educational TV show which broadcasted from 1952 to 1961.

2. Arlene Francis was a TV actress best known for her long-standing role as a panelist on the game show "What's My Line," which ran from 1950 through the mid-1970s.

3. Johnny Mathis is a singer and songwriter of jazz and pop standards, who began his career in the fifties. He is regarded as the last in a long line of traditional male vocalists who emerged before rock emerged in the sixties.

4. Frankie Avalon was an American actor, singer and teen idol in the fifties and early sixties, when he starred in TV's beack party films.

5. Tuesday Weld was a film and TV actress.

6. Bette Davis was an Academy Award-winning actress in film, TV and theatre.

7. Mickey Spillane was a popular author of crime novels.

8. Mickey Mantle was a star baseball player who was inducted into the National Baseball Hall of Fame. He played for the New York Yankees.

9. "Captain Kangaroo" was a children's TV series which broadcasted from 1955–1984.

10. Eliot Ness was a government agent who enforced the Prohibition in Chicago and leader of the team nicknamed "The Untouchables."

11. Mata Hari was the stage name of a Dutch exotic dancer who was executed for alleged espionage during World War I.

12. Wilma Flintstone was a character in "The Flintstones," an animated television series.

13. Helen Hayes was an Academy Award-winning actress whose career spanned nearly seventy years.

14. Dr. Benjamin Spock was a pediatrician and the author of *Baby and Child Care*, published in 1946. It was one of the biggest selling books of all time. His parenting information and advice have influenced generations of parents.

15. Rock Hudson was a popular film actor frequently cast as a handsome and romantic leading man.

16. Dr. Arnold Gessell was a renowned authority on child rearing and development in the forties and fifties.

17. Suzy Parker was a supermodel and signature face of designer Coco Chanel

18. Joe DiMaggio was a baseball star who played for the New York Yankees.

19. Barry Goldwater was a five-term U.S. Senator and the Republican candidate for president in 1964. He was an extreme conservative who upset many of his potential supporters by voting against Johnson's Anti-Poverty Act (1964).

20. Theda Bara was a popular silent film actress.

21. Ed Sullivan hosted TV's longest-running variety show in the fifties and sixties. Topo Gigio was a puppet who played an Italian mouse and was a regular novelty act on the show.

22. Actress Elizabeth Taylor co-starred with Richard Burton, her fifth of eight husbands, in "Cleopatra" in 1963.

23. In 1939 writer James Thurber published a short story, "The Secret Life of Walter Mitty." The story was made into a movie in 1947. Because a timid Mitty imagines himself as a wartime pilot, surgeon and naval commander, his name became short-hand for anyone wishing for a more adventurous life.

24. Miss Nancy was the host of "Romper Room," a children's show that originated in Baltimore and later became syndicated. Miss Nancy hosted the show from 1953–63.

25. The Mamas and the Papas were a leading vocal group of the sixties after the British invasion of the Beatles and The Rolling Stones.

26. The Watusi was a popular dance during the early sixties.

27. Academy Award-winning actor Spencer Tracy appeared in 70 films from 1930–1967.

28. Sandy Koufax was a pitcher for the Brooklyn/Los Angeles Dodgers.

29. Brooks Robinson played third base for the Baltimore Orioles from 1955–77.

30. Singer and actress Doris Day was known for the wholesome roles she played in films of the fifties and sixties.

31. The Monkees were a pop-rock quartet created for a television series of the same name.

32. Ray Milland and Betty Hutton were both film actors.

33. Communications theorist Marshall McLuhan coined the expressions "the medium is the message" and the "global village."

34. Leonard Bernstein was an American conductor, composer and pianist.

35. Glenn Miller was a jazz musician and band leader in the swing era of the late thirties and early forties.

36. Peter Sellers was an English comedian and actor who played Inspector Clouseau in the Pink Panther movies of the sixties.

37. Greer Garson was a movie star in the late 1930s and 1940s.

38. Martha Ray was a comic actress and singer known as "The Big Mouth" because of her oversized mouth.

39. Actress Ginger Rogers is principally remembered for her role as Fred Astaire's dancing partner in a series of ten Hollywood musicals.

40. Ethel Kennedy is the widow of Robert F. Kennedy.

41. Agnes Moorehead was an Oscar nominated actress who starred in the popular suspense radio play and movie, "Sorry Wrong Number," in which she overhears plans for a murder. She is best-remembered for role on the TV series "Bewitched" as Samantha's mother.

42. The first moon walk was July 21, 1969, during the Apollo 11 mission.

43. Sir Stirling Moss is a British race car driver.

44. "Jack Armstrong, the All-American Boy" was a radio adventure series which maintained its popularity from 1933 to 1951. It was sponsored by Wheaties, the cereal brand.

45. George Bernard Shaw (1856–1950) won a Nobel Prize in Literature.

46. Benny Goodman was a jazz musician in the Big Band Era of the twenties and thirties.

47. Burt Bacharach is a popular composer, songwriter and pianist.

48. Robert Graves was a prolific film actor in the twenties and thirties.

49. Ann Landers and Abby van Buren were syndicated newspaper advice columnists. David Reuben published the bestseller, *Everything You Always Wanted to Know About Sex*, in 1969.

50. James Dickey was a writer whose novel *Deliverance* was made into a film in 1972.

51. Erich Remarque, author of *All Quiet on the Western Front*, worked for a time as a racecar drive.

52. Johnny Carson was a late night TV comedian who hosted "The Tonight Show" from 1962–1992.

53. "And Then Came Bronson" was a TV series from 1969–79, starring Michael Parks as a nomadic traveler on a Harley-Davidson motorcycle.

54. Dennis Hopper starred in "Easy Rider" with Peter Fonda and Jack Nicholson in the 1969 road movie.

55. The Bee Gees were foremost stars of the disco era in the 1970s

56. Peggy Lee was an acclaimed jazz singer and songwriter.

57. William F. Buckley is a longtime conservative American political commentator and columnist, and editor-in-chief of the National Review

58. Jackie Onassis was the widow of President John F. Kennedy. In 1968, she married Greek shipping magnate Ari Onassis, who was in the early stages of filing for divorce when he died in 1975.

59. Ali McGraw starred in "Love Story," a movie that was a hit in 1970

60. Clara Bow was a silent film actress of the twenties.

61. Carole Lombard was an Oscar-nominated actress.

An Interview with Dottie

In 2006 Dottie talked with her youngest daughter, Diane, who edited this collection, about writing "Home at Heart." Here Dottie answers Diane's questions, frequently turning to shared memories of their family.

When did you begin working for the *Patriot News* in Harrisburg?

I started at 18 as a female writer in the social department doing women's news. Later they sent me out with a photographer to do general feature stories. I also had a stint with the all-male sports desk. I worked full time until David [her oldest child] was born and then went back to work almost full-time. I worked in the composing room and learned how to put the paper together. That's when Newhouse [the newspaper publishing company] bought the *Patriot News*. I was offered a job to go the *Newark Star Ledger* in New Jersey, and I turned it down. I was free-lancing feature articles for the Harrisburg Patriot News.

How did you begin writing your weekly column?

I was pregnant with Donna [her middle child], and I wanted to just work part time. I would go in three mornings a week and do a feature or two. Then I realized that by writing a column I could write at home. I wrote a couple samples and they liked them. That's how it all started. They just told me to write what I wanted. They didn't edit me a whole lot. Never guided what I wrote.

How much did the newspaper pay you?

I made $60 a month. It was a lot to me then, in the fifties. The amount never changed.

And at one point they gave me a proposal to syndicate it. That was early on. But you all [her children] were little then, and it was a lot of work to collect samples and submit the proposal, so nothing ever came of it.

What was it like to write at home while you were rearing three very young children with their moment-to-moment needs?

I still carry around in my wallet a little note that you slid under my bedroom door. The typewriter was in my bedroom, and I used to go up Tuesday afternoon and close the door and think, "I have until 5 o'clock, and I have got to kick this out." One day you slid that note under the door saying, "I am huggy [sic] please come out." And I've been guilty ever since. I still dream you don't have a warm sweater.

When was your weekly deadline?

I think I had to have it in the mail by Tuesday, and sometimes I would drive up to York Road and put it on a Greyhound bus to get it there in time.

Did you really feel like the miscast housekeeper you portrayed yourself as, or was that character a persona you adopted?

Oh, no, I definitely was. No one ever taught me how to keep house. I grew up as an only child and didn't know what it was like with other kids around. I grew up in the public library all by myself. I was definitely a misfit as a housekeeper.

How much liberty did you take in changing the truth?

I gave Dad a whole different persona. I made him looser, funnier and more talkative. He didn't mind. I'd ask, "Do you mind if I say this?" He couldn't care less. He never really commented on them. People would mention something in my columns at work, and he'd just smile and say, "Oh yeah that's what my wife does."

Tell me about selling jokes to comedian Phyllis Diller.

In the sixties I was selling jokes to Phyllis Diller because I knew how she felt. She made a lot of jokes about her husband, which I also did, and lots of jokes about housekeeping. I sent her some jokes and she bought them. Once she called me from the back room of some club in St. Louis and told me to read this book about magic. I might have sold her $20, or $30 or $40 worth of jokes and that was about it.

Among all of the pieces you wrote, do you have a favorite?

The best column is the one that I wrote after our dog, Angel, survived surgery. The vet framed it and it was still on the wall of his office the last time I was there.

Your columns throughout the sixties show how well read you were and follow popular and political culture.

A lot of that had to do with the times. You and I were both fascinated by Alan Watts who was living in Sausalito on a boat. We would go down to the bookstore downtown on 31st Street in Baltimore, and buy pastries and read all these philosophers. A lot of that had to do with your growing up years. We had some good times together. I was learning the cultural references through you, and it was an interesting and a great time. It was a fascinating time in America.

But you were listening to the music and reading the books of that era. I didn't see parents of my friends doing that.

Part of it might have been the whole experience of having three energetic and involved teen-agers at home and working with dozens of terrific undergraduates at Hopkins.

What is your impression today when you look back at the sixties and the early seventies?

It really irritates me that people dramatize those times so much differently than what they were. It was a wonderfully exciting period, a time when there was hope and promise and growth, even though there was a lot of confrontation and worries about a third world war. It was a time of tremendous growth and tremendous change for the whole country and for our culture.

The forward progress of science and technology, and a greater global awareness, are two drivers of great change over the last 50 years. How do you view these changes as related to your columns?

Looking back to the era when the columns appeared, it is clear our culture and family life norms have changed in many small, and some spectacular, large ways. There are wry nostalgic bits on the Internet about the days when kids piled in the car with no seat belts, when penny loafers had places for a dime to call home, because there were no cell phones then. This was before DVDs, blogs, laptops, play stations, microwave dinners, and color-coded terror alerts. Nevertheless, at the core of today's family life and that of yesteryear, the tenacious threads of love and play and hard work persist—and, I hope, some islands of quiet repose.

In 1972 you stopped writing. Why?

I guess it became a burden, and I was making enough money without it. I guess I was finished. There definitely wasn't as much material and my job was more consuming.

Did writing about the humorous side of life change your attitudes in the long run? Did it make you more upbeat?

Yes, but I think that runs in our family. More-ma, my mother, was always very ready to laugh at things, and your Dad, too. I can remember when More-ma and I bought a Christmas tree in downtown Harrisburg square and dragged it home. We didn't have a car, and you couldn't take it on a bus. So we dragged this tree up Second Street about ten blocks to the apartment we had then, and we laughed like maniacs the whole way.

I think that's been a strong strain in our family: when it all gets too much you might as well laugh. I think that as a family it was a way to relieve tension. There was always so much going on.

978-0-595-44552-3
0-595-44552-7

Printed in the United States
84946LV00001B/40-66/A